SPECIAL OPERATIONS FORCES

Special Operations Forces:

A National Capability

EDITED BY:

Dr. Emily Spencer

CANADIAN DEFENCE ACADEMY PRESS

Canadian Defence Academy Press
PO Box 17000 Stn Forces
Kingston, Ontario   K7K 7B4

Produced for the Canadian Defence Academy Press
by 17 Wing Winnipeg Publishing Office.
WPO30698

Library and Archives Canada Cataloguing in Publication

Special operations forces : a national capability / edited by Emily Spencer.

Produced for the Canadian Defence Academy Press by 17 Wing Winnipeg Publishing Office.
Includes bibliographical references and index.
Available also on the Internet.
Issued by: Canadian Defence Academy.
ISBN 978-1-100-18933-8 (bound).--ISBN 978-1-100-18934-5 (pbk.)
Cat. no.: D2-278/1-2011E (bound)
Cat. no.: D2-278/2-2011E (pbk.)

1. Special forces (Military science)--Canada.   2. Special forces (Military science)--Canada--Congresses.   3. Special operations (Military science)--Canada.   4. Canada. Canadian Special Operations Forces Command.   I. Spencer, Emily   II. Canadian Defence Academy   III. Canada. Canadian Armed Forces. Wing, 17

U262 S63 2011   356'.16   C2011-980103-5

Printed in Canada.

1 3 5 7 9 10 8 6 4 2

TABLE OF CONTENTS

TABLE OF CONTENTS

FOREWORD

Many would argue that the 21st century brought with it the "perfect storm" of conditions that has now created substantial global instability. Characterized by complexity, ambiguity and volatility, and underscored by the proliferation of the mass media, success in the contemporary operating environment (COE) will require agile, adaptable and rapid response forces that are capable of helping to project national interests.

The Canadian Special Operations Forces Command (CANSOFCOM) was created in February 2006 to provide the Government of Canada (GoC) with a range of unique capabilities to address most of the mission sets in the *Canada First* Defence Strategy (CFDS). With personnel drawn from all Canadian Forces (CF) components and occupations, CANSOFCOM provides the correct balance of skill sets and knowledge required to operate effectively alongside conventional forces in the COE.

In light of the requirement to work closely together with all defence and governmental partners, while adhering to the necessity of operational security, it is now time to encourage a dialogue with our partners from within the defence community, the media, and the Canadian public in order to gain a variety of perspectives on defence issues and avoid being inward looking and myopic regarding our present and future capabilities. Certainly Canadian Special Operations Forces (CANSOF) are a unique and vital national enabler and it is important to explore this capability through a variety of lenses in order to best prepare for the future operating environment (FOE).

As such, the Special Operations Forces Symposium held at the Royal Military College of Canada, 6-8 December 2010, was an important step in expanding this dialogue. This volume represents an amalgam of the presentations and ideas that were put forward by scholars and military practitioners in order to both educate, as well as create, discourse on the subject of SOF.

Therefore, it is with great pleasure that I introduce this collection of essays that explain, analyze and discuss how Special Operations Forces in general, and CANSOF in particular, provide the GoC with a unique national capability that has proven to be effective in the COE and will certainly prove to be equally as valuable in the FOE. As our Command motto, *Viam Inveniemus* (we will find a way), suggests, despite the volatile, uncertain and unconventional nature of the COE – and perhaps even because of it – we will continue to provide a vital national capability to the GoC.

D.W. Thompson
Brigadier-General
Commander
Canadian Special Operations Forces Command

INTRODUCTION

Very few Canadians understand the concept of special operations forces (SOF), much less the idea that the nation currently has a well-respected, world class SOF capability. This capability had its genesis in a much earlier period, however. Canada's SOF legacy reaches back to the founding of the country. In fact, the "Ranger Tradition," which is considered by many to be the foundation of a number of American SOF units such as the US Special Forces and the US Rangers, quite arguably began in Canada. Indeed, Canada's SOF and "SOF-like" forces from the daring raids of French-Canadian partisans in the struggle for North America, to Loyalist raiders during the American Revolution, to various units in the Second World War and the postwar era, have always provided an important contribution to Canada's national security and interests. Quite simply, history demonstrates that SOF is an important national capability and one which our nation has relied on for centuries.

While the original emphasis on special men/women, special training and special missions has remained true, SOF have nonetheless evolved. The traditional mission sets have changed and our current understanding of SOF reflects the more nuanced and complex security environment in which SOF operates today and its pivotal responsibilities therein. SOF are now doctrinally defined as:

> ...organizations containing specially selected personnel that are organized, equipped and trained to conduct high-risk, high value special operations to achieve military, political, economic or informational objectives by using special and unique operational methodologies in hostile, denied or politically sensitive areas to achieve desired tactical, operational and/or strategic effects in times of peace, conflict or war.

INTRODUCTION

This book captures some of the complexities that define Canadian special operations forces, as well as the contemporary operating environment. Based on presentations and papers delivered at the Royal Military College of Canada/Canadian Special Operations Forces Command (RMCC/CANSOFCOM) Symposium "SOF: A National Capability" held at RMCC on 6-8 December 2010, this volume provides insights and perspectives of both SOF practitioners and scholars. It also marks a growing effort to develop a distinct Canadian body of SOF knowledge to both assist the professional development of the SOF community and, importantly, to assist with raising awareness of the pivotal role SOF plays in contributing to advancing Canadian national interests and security.

As such, the book begins by describing the Canadian SOF legacy, which clearly articulates the country's longstanding experience with SOF and SOF-like organizations and how SOF has evolved through the decades to meet the nation's needs. Under the broad theme of SOF as a national capability and enabler, the volume then moves on to look at crucial components of force development and ways in which SOF help to shape the area of operations. Subsequently, *SOF: A National Capability* explores important issues such as the role of SOF as an economy of effort/economy of force option in the contemporary operating environment and it also examines the budding media-SOF relationship.

In sum, *SOF: A National Capability* provides important insights into the contributions of SOF in general and within the Canadian case in particular. This volume is meant to increase understanding and encourage discussion on this very important national capability.

CHAPTER 1

THE CANADIAN
SPECIAL OPERATIONS FORCES' LEGACY

COLONEL BERND HORN, PhD

In October 2001, the Canadian minister of national defence (MND) was repeatedly criticized by the media for the perceived failure of not doing enough to assist our American brethren in Afghanistan in the aftermath of the tragic terrorist attack on the twin towers of the World Trade Center in New York City, in the early morning hours of 11 September 2001 (9/11). During one such scrum, the MND finally revealed that Canada was indeed helping. In fact, he made mention that Canadian "commandos" were supporting the American effort in theatre.

The revelation came as a shock to most Canadians. Few actually knew that Canada possessed "commandos" or more accurately special operations forces. But, the knowledge that such special troops were in action was enough to quiet the outcry. Nonetheless, the larger issue still remained, who were these shadow warriors? Their existence was a well guarded secret. Neither Canadians, nor anyone else for that matter, knew much about Joint Task Force Two (JTF 2), much less any other of the SOF-like organizations that had existed in the country's history that made up the Canadian SOF legacy.

Significantly, Canada's SOF traditions can be traced back to the Ranger tradition of colonial North America where raiding, or "direct action," as well as special reconnaissance allowed the embryonic Canadian nation to punch above its weight and achieve strategic impact through tactical action. The national SOF legacy continued in the Second World War with a number of specialized units and into the Cold War period in the form of the Canadian Airborne Regiment.

Canadian SOF's more modernized form was created in 1986, with the creation of the Royal Canadian Mounted Police (RCMP) Special Emergency Response Team (SERT), which was established as a hostage rescue unit. In 1992, the role was taken over by the military and was recreated as JTF 2. The military evolved the unit into a Tier One SOF organization. In 2005, the Chief of the Defence Staff, General Rick Hillier, decided that as part of the continuing transformation of the Canadian Forces he would create a fourth service, a Canadian Special Operations Forces Command. "We intend," he declared on 19 April 2005, "on bringing JTF 2, along with all the enablers that it would need to conduct operations successfully, into one organization – one commander, one organization."[1]

As such, on 1 February 2006, CANSOFCOM officially stood up, completing the Canadian SOF evolution with the creation of an independent SOF command, the fourth service within the CF. This chapter provides a window into the Canadian SOF experience.

THE RANGER TRADITION

The general public has become more attuned to SOF as a result of 9/11 and the war in Afghanistan. In fact, the revelation of an elite Canadian counter-terrorist unit only became widespread knowledge as a result of a media disclosure that they were deploying to Afghanistan in support of the American effort. However, the nation's SOF legacy runs deep. After all, nothing embodies the idea of daring special operations more than the practice of *la petite guerre* by the French-Canadian raiders during the struggle for colonial North America. Facing a harsh climate, unforgiving terrain and intractable and savage enemies, the intrepid Canadian warriors personified boldness, courage and tenacity. Their fearless forays and daring raids behind enemy lines struck terror in the hearts of their Native antagonists, as well as the British and American colonists and soldiers. In fact, for an extended period of time, these tactical actions had a strategic effect on the vicious struggle for North America in the 17th and 18th centuries.

Schooled in the bitter war of annihilation with the Iroquois in the 17th century, the French-Canadians developed a class of fighters who were able to adapt to the new style of warfare required in the New World.[2] Moreover, they demonstrated an intellectual and tactical agility that made them unsurpassed in "raiding" and what would later be dubbed commando operations. Their emphasis on stealth, speed, violence of action, physical fitness and courage, combined with operations with indigenous allies, created a force that successfully wreaked havoc on their enemy.

This capability, much to the misery of the English, was consistently displayed as the two competing European powers increasingly fought for control of North America. Quite simply, the French relied on the outnumbered Canadians to hold onto French territory through the proficient execution of their distinct Canadian way of war, specifically small parties of experienced *coureur de bois* and partisans that conducted dangerous scouts, ambushes and raids in English territory.[3] As such, raids against the English in Hudson's Bay in 1686, the Seneca in New York in 1687, the Iroquois in 1693 and 1696, and a number of devastating strikes against English settlements such as Casco, Deersfield, Haverhill, Salmon Falls and Schenectady during a succession of wars from 1688 to 1761 provided proof of the effectiveness of the French-Canadian raiders who specialized in the conduct of lightening strikes behind enemy lines.

Many French and Canadian leaders, particularly those with extended exposure to the North American manner of war, or those born and raised in Canada, came to reject the conventional European manner of making war. Rather, they believed that the optimum war fighting technique was achieved by a mixed force that included the military strengths of regulars (e.g. courage, discipline, tactical acumen) with those of the volunteers and Indians (e.g. endurance, familiarity with wilderness navigation and travel, marksmanship) who relied more on initiative, independent action and small unit tactics than on rigid military practices and drills. The effectiveness of the Canadians was evidenced in the fear they created in their enemies. British generals and numerous contemporary English accounts conceded that the Canadian raiders "are well known to be the most dangerous enemy of any ...reckoned equal, if not superior in that part of the world to veteran troops."[4]

The impact of the French-Canadian raiders was immense. One British colonel confided, "I am ashamed that they have succeeded in all their scouting parties and that we never have any success in ours."[5] This state of affairs continually blinded the British command and deprived them of intelligence of French preparations or plans. Understandably, this often led to poor and untimely decisions laden with unfortunate consequences, whether the ambush of a British column or the loss of a strategic fort.[6] Moreover, the constant depredations, ambushes and raids of the Canadians and their Indian allies caused a constant material and economic drain on the British. But equally important, they created an overwhelming psychological and moral blow against the Anglo-American colonies. The British forces seemed unable to strike back. It was a constant series of defeats, thwarted campaigns and offensives, and devastated colonies. Everywhere, the Canadians and Indians would appear as phantoms in hit and run attacks leaving in their wake smouldering ruins and the mutilated bodies of the dead and dying. Despite their small numbers, they consistently inflicted a disproportionately high number of casualties on the enemy. The end result was an utterly paralyzing effect on the English combatants and colonists alike.[7]

The unmitigated success of the French-Canadian raiders forced the British to develop a similar capability of their own. One of the first efforts was in 1744, in the North American theatre of operations, as part of the larger War of the Austrian Succession (1740-1748). During this conflict the British presence in the Maritimes was once again prey to the marauding Abenakis and Micmac Indian war parties that were aligned with the French. As a result, an "independent corps of rangers" also known as the corps of Nova Scotia Rangers, was raised in New England. Two companies were recruited and deployed to Annapolis, Nova Scotia in July 1744 to reinforce the garrison. In September, a third company arrived led by Captain John Goreham.

Goreham's command was composed of 60 Mohawks and Métis warriors. Familiar with the Indian way of war, they swiftly engaged the French and their Indian allies. Massachusetts Governor William Shirley commended Goreham and his Rangers for their success, stating that "the garrison is now entirely free from alarms."[8] The majority of the companies later returned to Massachusetts where they originated, leaving John Goreham and his company to patrol Nova Scotia alone from 1746-1748. Their success was such that Shirley wrote, "the great service which Lieut. Colonel Gorham's Company of Rangers has been of to the Garrison at Annapolis Royal is a demonstration of the Usefulness of such a Corps."[9]

Goreham's Rangers continued to serve on the volatile frontier. Prior to the onset of the French and Indian War, also known in its global context as the Seven Years War (1756-1763), Goreham's Rangers were used to protect the British settlements in Nova Scotia against Indian raids. However, with the official outbreak of the war, they became increasingly involved in military operations specifically because of their expertise at irregular warfare.[10]

Despite their success, in the most current conflict Goreham's Rangers were eclipsed by another British effort aimed at matching the effectiveness of the French-Canadian raiders in the strategically important Lake Champlain theatre of operations. What the British eventually created was the legendary Rogers' Rangers. In the early stages of the war, when fortunes seemed to be against the British, Robert Rogers' knowledge and experience with the "haunts and passes of the enemy and the Indian method of fighting" soon brought him to the attention of his superior, Major-General William Johnson.[11] By the fall of 1755, Rogers was conducting dangerous scouts deep behind enemy lines. Rogers' efforts soon earned him an overwhelming reputation. These efforts also led Major-General William Shirley, then the Commander-in-Chief of the British Army in North America, to argue:

> It is absolutely necessary for his Majesty's Service, that one Company at least of Rangers should be constantly employ'd in different Parties upon Lake George and Lake Iroquois [Lake Champlain], and the Wood Creek and Lands adjacent...to make Discoveries of the proper Routes for our own Troops, procure Intelligence of the Enemy's Strength and Motions, destroy their out Magazines and Settlements, pick up small Parties of their Battoes upon the Lakes, and keep them under continual Alarm.[12]

By the winter of 1756, Rogers' bold forays with his small band of unofficial rangers behind enemy French lines were regularly reported in newspapers throughout the colonies. They provided a tonic to a beleaguered English frontier. In March 1756, Major-General Shirley ordered Rogers to raise a 60 man independent ranger company that was separate from both the provincial and regular units. As such, it was titled His Majesty's Independent Company (later Companies) of American Rangers. His unit was directed to scout and gain intelligence in the Lake Champlain theatre, as well as "distress the French and their allies by sacking, burning and destroying their houses, barns, barracks, canoes, battoes...to way-lay, attack, and destroying their convoys of provisions by land and water."[13]

The reputation and accomplishments of the rangers soon had an impact on British officers. All wanted rangers to accompany their expeditions as a foil against the enemy's Canadians and Indians, as well as to use the rangers' ability to navigate and survive in the merciless wilderness. Without doubt, "Rogers' Rangers," as they became universally known, brought to life the ranger tradition in North America and ensured it would forever endure. Their deeds and prowess have with time become legendary, even if this legacy is not fully deserved. Nonetheless, the Rangers, led by the very adventurous, courageous, and exceptionally tough Robert Rogers, created a very romantic image that seemed to both symbolize, as well as define, the strength of the American Ranger.

Ironically, Rogers was repeatedly bested by his Canadian counterparts and normally suffered horrendous casualties. Generals Jeffrey Amherst and Thomas Gage considered the Canadians, owing to their skill and discipline, superior to the American Rangers.[14] In addition, throughout this period, Goreham's Rangers were also active. In 1758, they played an important part in the capture of the strategic Fortress of Louisbourg and a year later assisted in the expedition against Quebec. In fact, at the end of the conflict the British high command rated Goreham's Rangers, although rarely mentioned, as the most highly rated ranger organization employed during the war.[15]

Nonetheless, the Canadian and American rangers, in essence, established a tradition that depicted an adventurous, if not daring, attitude that was overly aggressive and always offensively minded. The ranger tradition that was created also embodied the concept of individuals who were seen as mavericks to the conventional military institution and mentality: men who were adaptable, robust and unconventional in their thinking and war fighting; men who could persevere the greatest hardships and, despite an inhospitable environment and merciless enemy, achieve mission success.[16]

THE SECOND WORLD WAR EXPERIENCE

This tenacious spirit would remain with Canada's warriors and be resurrected in future generations. The more contemporary component of Canada's SOF legacy coincided with the explosion of special operations forces at the commencement of the Second World War. In essence, modern day SOF are largely a phenomena of this era. As such, they were often born in crisis from a position of weakness. They were created to fill a specific gap. In the immediate aftermath of the early German victories the Allies found themselves devoid of major equipment, of questionable military strength and on the defensive throughout the world.[17]

Despite the still smouldering British equipment on the beaches of Dunkirk, the combative new Prime Minister, Winston Churchill, declared in the British House of Commons on 4 June 1940, "we shall not be content with a defensive war."[18] He was well aware that to win a war meant ultimately offensive action. Moreover, only through offensive action could an army provide the needed confidence and battle experience to its soldiers and leaders. Furthermore, only offensive action could sustain public and military morale. And finally, offensive action represented a shift in initiative. By striking at the enemy, inherently that opponent is forced to take defensive measures that represent a diversion of scarce resources.

That afternoon, Churchill penned a note to his Chief of Staff of the War Cabinet Secretariat, General Hastings Ismay. "We are greatly concerned ...with the dangers of the German landing in England," he wrote, "... why should it be thought impossible for us to do anything of the same kind to them?" He then added, "We should immediately set to work to organize self-contained, thoroughly-equipped raiding units."[19] After all, Churchill pondered, "how wonderful it would be if the Germans could be made to wonder where they were going to be struck next, instead of forcing us to try to wall in the island and roof it over!"[20]

On 6 June, Churchill sent yet another missive to Ismay. "Enterprises must be prepared," he wrote, "with specially trained troops of the hunter class who can develop a reign of terror down these coasts, first of all on the butcher and bolt policy." He vividly described, "There comes from the sea a hand of steel that plucks the German sentries from their posts."[21] He then curtly directed the "Joint Chiefs of the Staff to propose measures for a vigorous, enterprising, and ceaseless offensive against the whole German-occupied coastline." He added the requirement for deep inland raids that left "a trail of German corpses behind."[22]

SPECIAL OPERATIONS EXECUTIVE

As such, during the early years of the war a plethora of SOF organizations and units such as the Special Operations Executive (SOE), the Commandos, the Long Range Desert Group (LRDG), the Special Air Service (SAS) and the American Rangers, to name a few, emerged creating a means to strike back at the seemingly invincible German military machine.

One of the first unconventional efforts was the creation of the SOE, which was a British secret service intended to promote subversive warfare in enemy occupied territory. It was formed in July 1940 in the aftermath of the disastrous retreat from Dunkirk as England braced itself for the inevitable invasion. It was designed as a "full scale secret service, the mere existence of which could not be admitted either to Parliament or to the press."[23] The SOE became responsible for "all operations of sabotage, secret subversive propaganda, the encouragement of civil resistance in occupied areas, the stirring up of insurrection, strikes, etc., in Germany or areas occupied by her."[24]

The Canadian connection was not long in coming. Shortly after its creation, the SOE queried the senior Canadian commander overseas, Major-General A.G.L. McNaughton, for Canadian volunteers. Specifically they were looking for French-Canadians for service in France, Canadians of Eastern European descent for the Balkans and Chinese Canadians for Far East operations. Clearly, the racial, linguistic and cultural attributes and knowledge of these volunteers would provide the SOE with, in many aspects, ready-made operatives. Inculcating the specific technical skills would just be a matter of training.

The Canadian volunteers, like the remainder of the men and women trained to serve in the SOE during the Second World War "were quickly made to forget all thoughts about Queensbury rules and so-called 'gentlemanly' warfare....[and they] were taught a vast range of sabotage techniques and bizarre methods of killing."[25] Moreover, they were thoroughly trained in advising, arming and assisting members of the various resistance movements in the enemy-occupied countries.

As much of the art and science of SOF was in its infancy, it is not surprising that SOE selection was inefficient. Initially it consisted of a three- to four-week selection/training course that was deemed too leisurely and ineffective. Many of those on course failed at the end of the process, which proved a waste of time and resources. Therefore, by July 1943, a selection course (student assessment board (SAB)) was developed that applied a variety of psychological and practical tests to candidates over a four-day period. In this manner, they screened out questionable volunteers early in the process. The SAB took less time and provided better results.

Successful volunteers went through several phases of training. The first phase focused on ensuring all operatives were in top physical condition. In addition, the course provided students with an in-depth proficiency with Allied and German small arms, as well as expertise in explosives and demolition work. The first phase also provided instruction in the recognition of German uniforms and equipment. The next stage of training was conducted at the commando training centre in Arisaig, in the Western highlands of Scotland, near the Isle of Skye. This phase provided rigorous field training and live fire exercises. Following the commando training came parachute qualification in Manchester. At the termination of qualification training, operatives were then separated according to their respective skills and sent to specialized training centres.

The Canadian connection to the SOE went beyond the volunteers who served in the organization. It also extended to the establishment of Special Training School (STS) 103 or Camp X, which was located on secluded farmland outside of Whitby, Ontario. The camp served two functions. The first was to train men recruited in Canada, such as French-Canadians and refugees from Eastern Europe, for service with the SOE in Europe. The second function was to give top secret assistance to the American's foreign intelligence service, an activity that could not be done in the US as long as the US remained neutral in the war.[26]

Camp X was the first secret-agent training establishment in North America. It opened on 9 December 1941 and trained individuals according to their cultural groups. The officers, less the camp adjutant, were all British, however, the senior non-commissioned officers were all Canadian. Camp X closed on 20 April 1944.

Throughout the war approximately 227 Canadians served in the SOE in the various theatres of the conflict. In addition, some Canadian Royal Canadian Air Force personnel and those posted to Royal Air Force units also served in the Special Duty Squadrons used to drop weapons and insert and extract SOE personnel.[27] In the end, the value of the SOE was immense. In a Supreme Headquarters Allied Expeditionary Force (SHAEF) report to the Combined Chiefs of Staff on 18 July 1945, General Dwight "Ike" Eisenhower's staff noted, "without the organization, communications, training and leadership which SOE supplied...resistance [movements] would have been of no military value."[28]

VIKING FORCE

The SOE, however, was not the only innovative, unconventional effort. In a remarkable display of military efficiency, by 8 June 1940, two days after Churchill's directive, General Sir John Dill, the Chief of the Imperial General Staff, received approval for the creation of the Commandos and that same afternoon, Section MO9 of the War Office was established. Four days later, Churchill appointed Lieutenant-General Sir Alan Bourne, the Adjutant-General of the Royal Marines as "Commander of Raiding Operations on Coasts in Enemy Occupation and Advisor to the Chiefs of Staff on Combined Operations."[29]

The men drawn to the Commando idea very quickly coalesced the concept that was expected. Raiding was their primary role. In essence, they were to be trained to be "hard hitting assault troops" who were capable of working in cooperation with the Navy and Air Force. As such they were expected to capture strong points, destroy enemy services, neutralize coastal batteries and wipe out any designated enemy force by surprise as detailed by higher headquarters.[30] They were also told that they would have to become accustomed to longer hours, more work and less rest than the other members of the armed forces.

Predictably, the concept of commandos attracted a like-minded group of aggressive, action-orientated individuals who quickly shaped the essence of the commando idea. "There was a sense of urgency, a striving to achieve an ideal, an individual determination to drive the physical body to the limit of endurance to support a moral resolve," one veteran officer explained. "The individual determination," he added, "was shared by every member of the force, and such heights of collective idealism are not often reached in the mundane business of soldiering."[31] Together they forged a "commando spirit" that was comprised of: determination; enthusiasm and cheerfulness, particularly under adverse conditions; individual initiative and self-reliance; and finally, comradeship.[32]

Canada was initially slow to react to the commando concept. Moreover, its commitment to creating an elite commando unit in the Second World War did not last very long, betraying the nation's underlining sentiment towards SOF type units. In fact, the creation of the Canadian "Viking Force" was actually a response to public criticism at home and the opportunity the British raiding program provided. Major-General Harry D.G. Crerar, reacting to public criticism and government pressure to get Canadian troops into the fray since they had been in England for almost two years and had still not engaged in battle with the enemy, took the initiative as the acting commander of the Canadian Corps and spoke to his immediate superior, Lieutenant-General Bernard Law Montgomery, Commander Southeastern Army in England, about utilizing Canadian troops in a commando role.

Montgomery was not a proponent of SOF forces, but he did see raiding as a means to instil offensive spirit and combat experience within his command. As such, Crerar did not have a hard sell. "I believe that occasions will increasingly present themselves for small raids across the Channel opposite the Army front," Crerar argued, "in default of a reputation built-up in battle the [Canadian] Corps undoubtedly would receive great stimulus if, in the near future it succeeded in making a name for itself for its raiding activities — a reputation which, incidentally, it very definitely earned for itself in the last war." Montgomery replied, "your men should be quite first class at raiding" and he gave Crerar the green light to run Canadian raiding activities from the port of Newhaven.[33]

Crerar lost no time and on 6 March 1942 discussed raiding operations with the Director Combined Operations, Lord Louis Mountbatten. Mountbatten was initially reluctant to accept

Canadian participation in raiding because he felt that it would dilute the role of the British Commandos who had a monopoly on the activity. However, Mountbattten was well attuned to political realities and made an exception. He laid out two conditions for the Canadians:

a. that ample time should be allowed for proper organization and training – this was stated to be six to eight weeks; and

b. that the enterprise should be known only to the Corps Commander and BGS [Brigadier-General (Staff)] and a limited number of his own (Mountbatten's) staff.[34]

That afternoon a second meeting between Crerar, BGS Guy Simonds and Brigadier J.C. Haydon, commander Special Service Force (SSF), transpired.[35] In this forum the senior officers present reached a decision to create a Canadian commando unit of 200 men, who were to start training by mid-March.

The Canadian commando unit, named Viking Force, was based on 2nd Division. Within a fortnight 267 volunteers from the division were training at Seaford in the muddy estuary of the Cuckmere River in Sussex. The Viking Force organization was based on a British Commando unit but existed on a smaller scale. The headquarters section was led by a major and comprised 24 all ranks. A further 36 officers and men staffed the support squadron (i.e. intelligence, signals and medical sections). The remaining 130 personnel were divided into two troops, each consisting of five officers and 60 men. The Viking Force placed heavy emphasis on firepower. In addition to the standard .303 Lee Enfield rifle, each troop carried four Bren light machine guns and eight Thompson sub-machine guns, as well as two anti-tank rifles and a two-inch mortar.

Within days of the commencement of training, instructors whittled the large group of volunteers down to its official strength of

190 all ranks. From 4 April 1942, personnel from the SSF joined the men of Viking Force to increase the intensity of the training and begin to turn them into hardened commandos. The commanding officer (CO) responsible for whipping the Canadian neophyte commandos into shape was Major Brian McCool of the Royal Regiment of Canada.

During the last half of April 1942, training intensified. It now included speed marches with weapons and 60 pound rucksacks, river crossings, leaping from crags into sand pits 15 feet below, cliff climbing and night manoeuvres. During these training exercises, if the men did not get back to the beaches in time to be ferried to the mother ship, they had to swim back with their full equipment.

On 30 April, Montgomery visited Major-General Andrew McNaughton, the Canadian Corps commander, and they agreed that the Canadians should form the main striking force for a planned raid on the French port of Dieppe. That same day McNaughton's headquarters issued a training instruction to enlarge the scale of combined operations training. This new direction was designed to cover the training of 4 and 6 Brigades for the large conventional raid planned on Dieppe. Therefore, before Viking Force was even fully established, BGS Simonds had already laid the blueprint for their demise. "Personnel of detachments which have completed [combined operations / commando] training in accordance with Instruction No. 7," he ordered, "will be returned to parent units and employed as a cadre to develop combined operations techniques within the latter."[36]

As a result, Viking Force became swept up in the preparations for Operation RUTTER (i.e. the Dieppe Raid) and the intensive training that had been reserved for the elite of Viking Force was now extended to the entirety of 4 and 6 Brigades. Quite simply, Major McCool and his cadre became instructors for the others. In this regard, from the end of May to the beginning of July the Viking Force cadre became key to the efforts to help 4 and 6 Brigades master the rigours of amphibious warfare.

However, with the emphasis on conventional forces to take over the raiding role it was not surprising that Crerar wrote on 4 June 1942, "The opportunity to land on enemy shores may not long be denied us." He added, "The training of detachments, units and formations of the Canadian Corps, with this end in view has already proceeded some distance...It is the intention that it shall be carried through to the stage when every formation of the Corps is thoroughly capable of taking full part in operations involving the landing on beaches in enemy occupation, and the rapid seizure and development of 'bridgeheads.'" He ended his missive with a revealing comment: "There must be no need for the Canadian Corps to call upon outside, and special 'Commando' units for assistance in initial beach-landing operation."[37]

The new Canadian approach was the polar opposite to the original intent. Viking Force had been intended as a hard-hitting group of specially trained raiders whose job was to inflict damage on the enemy in limited operations using surprise as a major element and then employing their skills to withdraw before the enemy had time to recover. Diluted among the battalions in 4 and 6 Brigades during the ill-fated Dieppe Raid on 19 August 1942, the original Viking Force commandos were never given the opportunity to do the job they had been trained for. In the aftermath of the disastrous raid, no effort was made to resurrect Viking Force.[38]

ROYAL CANADIAN NAVY BEACH COMMANDOS

However, the Dieppe Raid did lead to the establishment of another SOF-like Canadian organization, namely the Royal Canadian Navy (RCN) Beach Commandos. Their genesis stemmed from the Dieppe Raid where Royal Naval (RN) Beach Parties ("C', "D", and "H") were responsible for disembarking troops and vehicles from assault landing craft, organizing and supervising suitable "beach" areas and loading serviceable vessels at the time of withdrawal. Of the 200 Navy personnel assigned to the Beach Parties during the Dieppe Raid 63 became casualties. As a result, all three RN Beach Parties had to be totally reconstituted. Not surprisingly, soon after Dieppe the Admiralty decided to change the Combined Operations Beach Party Branch name to "Naval Commandos." Accordingly, the Admiralty directed that 20 Beach Commandos would be required for the invasion of Occupied Europe (i.e. two each for three assault divisions, one per assault brigade with 100 percent spare in reserve).[39]

The RCN soon created its own capability and in late 1943 established RCN Beach Commando "W." This unit was modeled upon its Royal Navy counterpart and comprised of 84 RCN Volunteer Reserve men (i.e. 12 officers and 72 ratings). The naval beach commando was described as "a unit especially trained in the control and handling of landing craft on the beaches …[and] is designed to handle landing ships, craft and barges of an assault brigade group and the further ships, craft and barges landed on the same beaches."[40] Beach commandos were also responsible for neutralizing beach obstacles, mines and booby traps.

RCN Beach Commando "W" was assigned to Force "J" on Juno Beach during the Normandy invasion on 6 June 1944 and served with valour and distinction. Canadian newspapers quickly trumpeted the role of the Beach Commandos and described them as the "leather-tough Canadians" and "tough, scrappy and self-reliant."[41] Beach Commando "W" was disbanded at the end of August 1944.

1ST CANADIAN PARACHUTE BATTALION

Canada's SOF legacy in the Second World War did not end with the Dieppe Raid. One month prior to the disastrous assault, another "SOF-like" organization that fits into the legacy of Canada's

SOF community was created, namely the 1st Canadian Parachute Battalion (1 Cdn Para Bn). Although contemporary airborne units are not considered SOF, 1 Cdn Para Bn, like many of the neophyte airborne organizations that sprang up early in the Second World War, meets many of the SOF criteria. The paratroopers were specially selected, specially trained and given special missions behind enemy lines. They possessed an indomitable spirit that defied any challenge. In fact, the selection rate for 1 Cdn Para Bn in its infancy was only 30 percent.[42]

At its creation, both the Army's generals, as well as the media at large, were clear on the type of individual and organization they were creating. Robert Taylor, a reporter for the *Toronto Daily Star* described the volunteers as "action-hungry and impatient to fill their role as the sharp, hardened tip of the Canadian army's 'dagger pointed at the heart of Berlin.'"[43] Senior military officers described the new Canadian paratroopers as "super-soldiers" and newspapers, with unanimity, invariably described the parachute volunteers as "hard as nails" representing the toughest and smartest soldiers in the Canadian Army.[44] One journalist wrote, "They are good, possibly great soldiers, hard, keen, fast-thinking and eager for battle," while another asserted that they were "Canada's most daring and rugged soldiers...daring because they'll be training as paratroops: rugged because paratroops do the toughest jobs in hornet nests behind enemy lines."[45] Others painted a picture of virtual super-men. "Picture men with muscles of iron," depicted one writer, "dropping in parachutes, hanging precariously from slender ropes, braced for any kind of action... these toughest men who ever wore khaki."[46] Another simply explained that "your Canadian paratrooper is an utterly fearless, level-thinking, calculating killer possessive of all the qualities of a delayed-action time bomb."[47]

But it had not always been that way. Initially, the senior generals had rejected the need for Canadian paratroops citing a lack of role and purpose for such specialized troops in the Canadian context. However, by the spring of 1942, both the British and Americans fully embraced the concept of airborne forces. And, as the tide of the war began to swing in favour of the Allies, the focus quickly swung from one of defence to that of offence. And nothing embodied raw offensive, aggressive action more than paratroopers. Very quickly, airborne troops became a defining component of a modern army. Not to be left out, senior Canadian military commanders quickly reversed their earlier reservations and recommended the establishment of a parachute battalion to J.L. Ralston, the MND. The Minister readily agreed and on 1 July 1942, the Canadian War Cabinet Committee approved the formation of a parachute unit, namely 1 Cdn Para Bn.

The unit's training was in many ways innovative for the time and exceeded the challenges faced by other combat troops. Greater emphasis was placed on the individual soldier for leadership, weapon handling and navigation. Orders for exercises and later operations were always given to all ranks so that regardless of circumstances of a parachute drop everyone had an understanding of the mission so that they could execute the necessary tasks whether or not officers or senior non-commissioned officers (NCOs) were present. As such, the unit placed an exorbitant emphasis on courage, physical fitness, tenacity and particularly on individual initiative.

With no domestic defence role in Canada, the unit was offered up to the Commander of Home Forces in England. The British quickly accepted the offer and the government announced in March 1943 that 1 Cdn Para Bn would be attached to the 3rd Parachute Brigade, as part of the 6th Airborne Division. For the remainder of the war the Battalion fought as part of a British formation. It established a remarkable record. The Battalion never failed to complete an assigned mission, nor did it ever lose or surrender an objective once taken. The Canadian paratroopers were among the first Allied soldiers to have landed in occupied Europe, the only Canadians who participated in the "Battle of the Bulge" in the Ardennes, and by the end of the war they had advanced deeper into Germany than any other Canadian unit. Unquestionably, the paratroopers of the 1st Canadian Parachute Battalion, at great cost and personal sacrifice, pioneered a new innovative form of warfare and demonstrated agility of thought and action, as well as an unrivalled warfare spirit in their daring assaults behind enemy lines. They were disbanded on 30 September 1945 at Niagara-on-the-Lake.

THE FIRST SPECIAL SERVICE FORCE

Interestingly, in July 1942, at the same time as 1 Cdn Para Bn was established the Canadian War Cabinet authorized a second "parachute" unit, designated the 2nd Canadian Parachute Battalion (2 Cdn Para Bn). The name of this unit, however, was misleading. It was not a parachute battalion at all, but rather a commando unit. The designation was assigned for security reasons to cover the true nature of its operational mandate.[48] On 25 May 1943, the name was changed to reflect this role. It was re-designated the 1st Canadian Special Service Battalion and it represented the Canadian element of the joint US/Canadian First Special Service Force (FSSF).[49]

Nonetheless, its genesis originated in England with Lord Mountbatten's Combined Operations Headquarters (COHQ) and Prime Minister Churchill's personal support. The original concept, code named Operation PLOUGH, entailed a guerrilla force capable of operations in Norway to attack the hydro-electric and heavy water plants in that country to disrupt the German war industry and the Nazi atomic weapons program.[50] Some thought was also put to using the force to destroy the Ploesti oil fields in Romania or to destroy hydro-electric facilities in Italy. In all, the planners reasoned that in any of these targets a hard-hitting raiding force would not only damage Germany's vital war industry but it would also tie up

German forces required to protect facilities and chase down the guerrilla force.[51]

The Americans accepted the project and Prime Minister Churchill and Lord Mountbatten very quickly convinced the Canadians to participate as well. As a result, a US/Canadian brigade-sized formation was created with Americans and Canadians serving side-by-side, wearing the same American uniform, in a military command that was completely integrated. At any given moment it was impossible to differentiate Canadian from American and *vice versa*. Each had officers commanding troops of the other nation. At inception, the Canadians contributed 697 all ranks to the formation, representing approximately a quarter of the total number of troops.[52]

As was the case with 1 Cdn Para Bn, the Canadian Army took the commitment seriously and attempted to pick the best soldiers possible for this unique endeavour. Colonel Robert T. Frederick, the American commander of the FSSF, made it clear that he preferred that Canadian volunteers be chosen in the "lower ranks between 18 and 45 [years old], physically rugged and mentally agile, physically able and willing to take parachute training."[53] It became obvious to everyone concerned that superior physical fitness, experience, maturity, and youth were the cornerstones on which the FSSF would be forged.[54] In addition, Frederick stressed that it was imperative that each man be able to work efficiently independently or in small groups, regardless of the tactical situation or operational theatre. Ross Munro, the renowned Canadian war reporter noted that the First Special Service Force "will be a continental edition of commandos of the British Army." He added, "In selecting the men to make it up, emphasis will be placed on 'youth, hardiness and fitness.'"[55]

As the initial focus of the FSSF was to be sabotage, raiding and guerrilla type warfare, the Forcemen were trained in a wide spectrum of skills including parachuting, demolitions, unarmed combat, extensive weapons handling, mountaineering and arctic warfare. Physical fitness very quickly became the decisive selection tool. Only the hardiest of men could persevere the training. For instance, members of the FSSF were "capable of marching 35 miles a day across rough country or 90 miles without rest."[56]

Indeed, the Force was to be ready to deploy to Norway on 15 December 1942 for an arduous and very dangerous mission. As such, even as the FSSF was in the process of establishing itself, its training regime and tempo were in over-drive. Upon arrival, members undertook their jump training, which in some cases, was all of 48 hours as opposed to the more standard three week course. In August 1942, journalist Don Mason captured the contemporary image of the force that was being created in Helena, Montana, where they were based. "The cream of Canada's hard-fighting army youth," he described, "is training in the United States to-day for 'aerial commando' raiding which one day soon will make the German and the Jap think cyclones have struck where they thought they were safe and secure."[57]

However, by late 1942 it became clear that Operation PLOUGH was not going to happen. There were three major impediments. First, Frederick's request for the temporary diversion of 750 Lancaster bombers forecast for the middle of January 1943 to insert his formation hit an immediate wall. The intractable architect of Britain's strategic bombing campaign, Air Chief Marshal Charles Portal of the Royal Air Force (RAF) responded, "That is our best bomber." He continued, "if you can show us where Plough can accomplish more in its operation than one thousand Lancasters could do on the bombing runs we shall consider the plane for your uses."[58]

Frederick's next dose of reality occurred when the Combined Operations Command planners briefed him on the Commando raiding program and, more importantly, the work of Brigadier Colin Gubbins' SOE and their Norwegian sabotage campaign. Although the SOE had never even heard of the PLOUGH Project, or the FSSF for that matter, they too had plans for sabotaging most of the targets that the FSSF was theoretically earmarked to destroy. Significantly, Gubbins' plan required very few aircraft and only two or three Norwegian soldiers for each target.[59]

The final nail in the coffin resulted from Colonel Frederick's discussion with Major-General Wilhelm von Tangen Hansteen, the Commander-in-Chief of the Norwegian Armed Forces. Hansteen bluntly informed Frederick that the King and Prime Minister of Norway opposed the concept of the PLOUGH Project. They were concerned that the large-scale destruction of power would create a greater hardship on the Norwegian people than it would on the Germans. Moreover, although they welcomed any assistance in ousting the occupying German forces, they did not wish to do so by destroying the vital industrial infrastructure that was key to Norway's economic well-being.[60]

And so, with no apparent aircraft, no host country support, and a competing organization that appeared to have a more efficient, more precise and less resource intensive means of achieving the same goal, Colonel Frederick quickly realized that the PLOUGH Project was doomed. Any doubt he may have harboured was quickly dashed when he returned to London to meet with Lord Mountbatten prior to his flight to Washington D.C.. The Chief of Combined Operations candidly explained to Frederick that the PLOUGH Project was no longer a pressing issue. By this time, Combined Operations and the whole raiding concept were under siege by the War Office. The Allied effort, particularly as a result of American might and industrial capacity, was slowly beginning to turn the tide of the war. Raiding and subversive activities, never fully supported by the mainstream military, were further marginalized as large-scale conventional operations, such as the invasion of Northern Africa, took shape.

Moreover, Mountbatten had no means of influencing the release of aircraft and he conceded that SOE provided a more economical means of achieving the desired result, not to mention at a more politically acceptable price for the Norwegian government in exile in London. As such, both men agreed to let PLOUGH die. Frederick quickly sent a message to his formation in Helena, Montana. True to Frederick's character, it was short and to the point:

> Suspend effort on present line...New plan may be radically different and not concerned with hydroelectric or other industrial installations....Cease training on hydroelectric installations and...stress general tactical training, to include attack of fortifications, pill boxes, barracks and troop concentrations. Change in weapons may be necessary to provide greater firepower, so suspend further small arms training pending a decision.[61]

On his return to North America, Colonel Frederick briefed General George Marshall, the American Army Chief of Staff. He then left for Montana unsure whether the FSSF would be continued or scrapped. It was now left with the General Staff to get a political decision. By 8 October 1942, the Canadian Chief of the General Staff forwarded a telegram to Lieutenant-General McNaughton, Canada's overseas commander, informing him of the latest turn of events. The Canadians were now waiting for the Americans to make known their intentions prior to articulating their continuing support.

However, Major-General Murchie's missive provided some telling clues. The alternatives considered were:

A. Continue with Special Service Force if Americans so desire.

B. Amalgamate with 1st Parachute Battalion.

C. Disband and Disperse Personnel.

D. Retain as an Ordinary Parachute Battalion For Home Service and Abroad.[62]

Importantly, Murchie highlighted the negative effects of options B, C and D. He stated each has the "disadvantage of unwelcome publicity over cancellation of highly publicized Special Service Forces as have B and C over apparent curtailment of our plans for Cdn [Canadian] Parachute Troops."[63]

In due course, the Americans decided to proceed with the FSSF. On 17 October, General Marshall informed Major-General Maurice Pope, the Chairman of the Canadian Joint Staff in Washington D.C. that a decision had been reached to retain the FSSF as a special unit.[64] It was now up to the Canadians to confirm their continued participation. Although militarily a will to continue seemed to be present, the ultimate decision was the purview of the politicians.[65] As such, the War Cabinet Committee discussed the issue on 28 October 1942. From a Canadian perspective, the existence of the "elite" First Special Service Force was considered by the government to be of marginal operational value after its original mission was cancelled. The *Minutes of the War Cabinet Committee* noted, "Though the future employment of the unit was doubtful, beyond its existence as a 'stand-by' force, acceptance of the US proposal [continue unit's existence for special operations] was recommended as a token of intimate co-operation between the two countries."[66]

As such, the FSSF became in many ways highly specialized infantry capable of a wide range of operations in virtually any terrain. In August 1943, the FSSF participated in the assault on Kiska Island. As the Japanese had already withdrawn from the Aleutians, the FSSF was quickly returned to the mainland and prepared for operations in Italy. Here the Force made a name for itself because of its successful assault on Monte La Difensa, a seemingly impregnable German defensive position on the top of a 945-metre high (3,100 feet) mountain. To date the Germans had repelled numerous Allied attacks and thus delayed the advance towards the main German Gustav defensive Line and Rome, which lay beyond. On 3 December 1943, by a daring night assault that entailed climbing up the rear cliffs of the mountain, which the Germans considered impassable, the FSSF successfully captured the summit. However, the assault and subsequent struggle to maintain their hold over the saucer shaped mountain top and extend their grip to the adjacent Monte La Remetanea inflicted a terrible toll on the formation. In the aftermath of the battle, the FSSF would never reach its former level of specialized capability or personnel. Reinforcements were simply pulled directly from normal reinforcement pools and given basic training on weapons and tactics.

Nonetheless, the FSSF reinforced its reputation at Anzio in February 1944 where, despite their light armament and only approximately 1,200 all ranks, they held an extended portion (13 kilometres) of the vital Mussolini Canal sector. Through aggressive night raiding they struck fear into the enemy, who believed they were facing up to a small division. The German soldiers were so terrified by the FSSF raids that they nicknamed them the "Black Devils." In the subsequent break-out phase, the FSSF advanced on Rome. Upon its capture and a brief period of rest and recuperation, the Force seized two of the Hyères Islands in the Mediterranean Sea to protect the left flank of the landings on the French Riviera in August 1944. The FSSF then joined the 6th Army Group in the advance through Southern France.

The Canadian component of the FSSF, however, proved to be problematic for the Canadian government. Facing a manning shortage and as a result, a conscription crisis, the continuing demands to provide reinforcements for the FSSF, which was difficult to administer and in the context of the dying days of the war was also arguably redundant, prompted the Canadian government to make a simple decision. The time had come to pull the Canadians from the Force. As such, the FSSF was disbanded at Menton on 5 December 1944.

The disbandment of the FSSF was not surprising. As the tide of the war shifted in favour of the Allies, who by late 1942 had begun to field large modern armies, SOF evolved to provide specific capabilities not resident with the larger conventional military and perform distinct tasks such as raiding, sabotage and economy of effort missions to tie down enemy forces. These activities were soon eclipsed by tasks such as strategic reconnaissance and unconventional warfare. But even at that, the Allied strategy had become a very attritional conventional approach, much akin to a large steam roller simply flattening the opposition before it. As such, the precision and special capabilities provided by SOF were neither required, nor appreciated by most senior military commanders.

In the end, despite the overall success and value of special operations, SOF never fully received acceptance by the larger military community.[67] The irregular nature of the tactics, the unconventional, if not rakish nature of the operators, who were often seen as lacking discipline and military decorum, as well as the almost independent status of the SOF organizations were alien and distasteful to the more traditional and conservative minded military leadership. Not surprisingly, at the end of the war, as already noted, most SOF organizations were disbanded.

Canada was no different. In fact, Lieutenant-General McNaughton provided a clear picture of his perception of SOF. "I have watched with interest the organization here [England] of such special units as Commandos, Ski Battalions and Paratroops," he noted.

27

He concluded, "The cycle is always the same – initial enthusiasm which is very high, drawing good officers and men from regular units, distracting and unsettling others, and upsetting the units' organization." As a result, he clearly stated his opposition to the formation of such units.[68]

THE CANADIAN SPECIAL AIR SERVICE COMPANY

Not surprisingly then, as noted, all Canadian SOF units were disbanded by September 1945. However, in 1947, a brief breath of air seemed to rekindle the flames of a national SOF capability. Former members of the SOE, FSSF and 1ˢᵗ Cdn Para Bn developed a plan to resurrect a distinct Canadian SOF entity. Their methodology was as shadowy as the unit they intended to build.

The long, costly global struggle had taken its toll and a debt-ridden and war weary government was intent on a postwar army that was anything but extravagant. Notwithstanding the military's achievements during the war, the Canadian Government articulated two clear requirements for its peacetime army. Firstly, it was to consist of a representative group of all arms of the service. Secondly, its primary purpose was to provide a small but highly trained and skilled professional force that in time of conflict could expand and train the citizen soldiers who would fight that war. Within this framework SOF had no relevance.

As the Army worked feverishly at demobilizing and at the same time creating the structure for the postwar Canadian Forces, the CO of the small Canadian Parachute Training Centre in Shilo, Manitoba became instrumental in the next phase of Canadian SOF.[69] He selectively culled the ranks of the disbanded 1 Cdn Para Bn, which also included those from the FSSF. Quite simply he chose the best from the pool of personnel who had decided to remain in the Active Force to act as instructors and staff for his training establishment.

Devoid of any direction from Army Headquarters, the CO and his staff focused on making contacts and keeping up to date with the latest airborne developments. These prescient efforts were soon to be rewarded. It was the perpetuation of links with Canada's closest allies, as well as the importance of staying abreast of the latest tactical developments in modern warfare, specifically air-transportability, that provided the breath of life that airborne and SOF advocates were searching for.

Not surprisingly, Canadian commanders were looking abroad for the way ahead in the post war environment. As such, in 1947, a National Defence Headquarters (NDHQ) study revealed that British peacetime policy was based on training and equipping all infantry formations to be air-transportable. Discussions with allies quickly ascertained that both the British and Americans would welcome an Airborne Establishment in Canada that would be capable of filling in the "gaps in their knowledge" – specifically in areas such as the problem of standardization of equipment between Britain and the United States, and the need for experimental research into cold weather conditions. To its allies, Canada was the ideal intermediary.

Canadian military leaders quickly realized that cooperation with their closest defence partners would allow the country to benefit from an exchange of information on the latest defence developments and doctrine. For the Airborne and SOF advocates, a test facility would allow the Canadian military to stay in the game. In the end, for the sake of efficiency of manpower and resources, NDHQ directed that the parachute training and research functions reside in a single Canadian Joint Army/Air Training Centre. As a result, on 15 August 1947, the Joint Air School (JAS), in Rivers, Manitoba was established.

The JAS became the "foot in the door." It was responsible for the retention of skills required for airborne and with some ingenuity special operations, for both the Army and the Royal Canadian Air Force (RCAF). More important, the JAS, which was renamed the Canadian Joint Air Training Centre (CJATC) on 1 April 1949, provided the seed from which a SOF organization would eventually grow.[70]

The hidden agenda of the airborne advocates quickly took root. Once the permanent structure of the Army was established in 1947, they quickly pushed to expand the airborne capability within the JAS by submitting a proposal in the spring for a Canadian SAS Company.[71] This new organization was to be an integral sub-unit of the Army component of the JAS with a mandate of: filling Army, inter-service, and public duties such as Army/Air tactical research and development; demonstrations to assist with Army/Air training; Airborne Firefighting; Search and Rescue; and Aid to the Civil Power.[72] Its development, however, proved to be quite different than its name implies.

The initial proposal for the special sub-unit prescribed a clearly defined role. The Army, which sponsored the establishment of the fledgling organization, portrayed the SAS Company's inherent mobility as a definite asset to the public at large for domestic operations. A military appreciation written by its proponents argued the need of the unit in terms of its potential benefit to the public. It explained that the specially trained company would provide an "efficient life and property saving organization capable of moving from its base to any point in Canada in ten to fifteen hours."[73] Furthermore, the Canadian SAS Company was framed as critical in working in support of the RCAF air search-rescue duties required by the International Civil Aviation Organization agreement.

The proposed training plan further supported the benevolent image. The training cycle consisted of four phases broken down as follows: 1. Tactical Research and Development (parachute related work and fieldcraft skills); 2. Airborne Firefighting; 3. Air Search and Rescue; and 4. Mobile Aid to the Civil Power (crowd control, first aid, military law).[74] Conspicuously absent was any evidence of commando or specialist training which the organization's name innately implied. After all, the Canadian SAS Company was actually titled after the British wartime SAS that had earned a reputation for daring commando operations behind enemy lines.

In September 1947, the request for approval for the sub-unit was forwarded to the Deputy Chief of the General Staff. Significantly, it now had two additional roles added to it: public service in the event of a national catastrophe; and provision of a nucleus for expansion into parachute battalions. However, the proposal also noted that the SAS Company was required to provide the manpower for the large program of test and development that was underway by the Tactical Research and Development Wing, as well as demonstration teams for all demonstrations within and outside the CJATC.[75]

As support for the sub-unit grew, so too did its real identity. An assessment of potential benefits to the Army included its ability to "keep the techniques employed by [British] SAS persons during the war alive in the peacetime army."[76] Although this item was last in the order of priority in the list, it soon moved to the forefront.

NDHQ authorized the sub-unit with an effective date of 9 January 1948. Once this was announced, a dramatic change in focus became evident. Not only did its function as a base for expansion for the development of airborne units take precedence, but also the previously subtle reference to a war-fighting, specifically special forces role, leapt to the foreground. The new Terms of Reference for the employment of the SAS Company, which was confirmed in April, outlined the following duties in a revised priority:

a. Provide a tactical parachute company for airborne training. This company is to form the nucleus for expansion for the training of the three infantry battalions as parachute battalions;

b. Provide a formed body of troops to participate in tactical exercises and demonstrations for courses at the CJATC and service units throughout the country;

c. Preserve and advance the techniques of SAS [commando] operations developed during WW II 1939-1945;

d. Provide when required parachutists to back-up the RCAF organizations as detailed in the Interim Plan for air Search and Rescue; and

e. Aid Civil Authorities in fighting forest fires and assisting in national catastrophes when authorized by Defence Headquarters.[77]

The shift was anything but subtle. The original emphasis on aid to the civil authority and public service type functions, duties that were attractive to a war weary and fiscally conscious government, were now re-prioritized if not totally marginalized. It did, however, also represent the Army's initial reaction to the Government's announcement in 1946, that airborne training for the Active Force Brigade Group (Regular Army) was contemplated and that an establishment to this end was being created.

The new organization was established at company strength – 125 personnel of all ranks. It was comprised of one platoon from each of the three regular infantry regiments, the Royal Canadian Regiment (RCR), the Royal 22nd Regiment (R22eR) and Princess Patricia's Canadian Light Infantry (PPCLI). All members were volunteers, most with wartime airborne experience, who were carefully selected. They were all bachelors, in superb physical condition, and possessed initiative, self-reliance, self-discipline, mental agility and an original approach.

If there was any doubt of the intention of the unit, it was quickly dispelled when Captain Guy D'Artois, a wartime member of the FSSF, and later the SOE, was posted to the sub-unit as its second-in-command. However, due to a difficulty in finding a qualified major, he became the acting officer commanding.[78] After all, his credentials were impeccable. D'Artois had dropped by parachute into Mont Cortevaix in France, then under German occupation, in April 1944. Prior to the sector being liberated, he had trained 600 partisans, established the Sylla underground, developed an 800-kilometre secure telephone line and attacked the occupying Germans troops on numerous occasions within his area of operation. Moreover, he instilled in his French allies a taste for victory. For his feats, D'Artois was awarded the Distinguished Service Order and the French La Croix de Guerre avec palme from General Charles de Gaulle. His service with the underground earned him the praise: "Major D'Artois is the embodiment of nobility in figure, strength and stature but more importantly, nobility in simplicity and kindness."[79]

D'Artois brought his experience to the Canadian Special Air Service Company (Cdn SAS Coy). He trained his sub-unit of carefully selected paratroopers as a specialized commando force. His intractable approach and trademark persistence quickly made him the "absolute despair of the Senior Officers at Rivers [CJATC]." Veterans of the SAS Company explained that "Captain D'Artois didn't understand 'no.' He carried on with his training regardless of what others said." Another veteran recalled that "Guy answered to no-one, he was his own man, who ran his own show."[80]

But the issue was soon moot. To date, the continued survival of the JAS and its limited airborne and SOF capability, as represented by the Canadian SAS Company, was largely due to a British and American preoccupation with airborne and air-transportable forces in the postwar period. This preoccupation was based on a concept of security established on smaller standing forces with greater tactical and strategic mobility. In essence, possession of paratroopers represented the nation's ready sword. This was critical in light of the looming 1946 Canada/US Basic Security Plan (BSP) which imposed on Canada the requirement to provide one airborne/air-transportable brigade, and its necessary airlift, as its share of the overall continental defence agreement. By the summer of 1948, the SAS Company represented the total sum of Canada's operational airborne and SOF capability. Clearly, some form of action was required.

As a result, the Chief of the General Staff (CGS) directed that training for one battalion of infantry for airborne/air-transported operations be completed by 1 April 1949. After all, the BSP dictated that by 1 May 1949, the Canadian government be capable of deploying a battalion combat team prepared to respond immediately to any actual Soviet lodgement in the Arctic, with a second battalion available within two months, and an entire brigade group within four months.[81] This was the death knell for the Cdn SAS Coy.

The Canadian Army was now finally moving towards its airborne/air-transportable Active Brigade Group, which was titled the Mobile Striking Force (MSF). Its effect on the Canadian SAS Company was devastating. The respective highly trained SAS platoons provided the training staff for each of the Regular Force infantry regiments (i.e. RCR, R22eR, PPCLI) that rotated through the JAS for parachute qualification and, upon completion, returned to their parent regiments to provide an experienced airborne cadre for each of these regular force infantry regiments. The slow dissolution of the Canadian SAS Company was formalized by the CGS when he announced that the sub-unit would not be reconstituted upon the completion of airborne conversion training by the R22eR, who represented the last unit of the three Active Force infantry regiments to undertake it. The actual disbandment was so low key that no official date exists. Its personnel just melted away.

Nonetheless, the SAS Company served a critical function in Canadian airborne and SOF history. It was the "bridge" that linked 1 Cdn Para Bn and the three infantry battalions that conceptually formed an airborne brigade (i.e. the MSF). In so doing, it perpetuated the airborne spirit and kept the requisite parachute skills alive. In also perpetuated, albeit briefly, the concept of a selected, highly trained commando force capable of special operations in keeping with the SOE and SAS traditions of the Second World War.

THE CANADIAN AIRBORNE REGIMENT

At this point, the nation's SOF lineage went into a hiatus. Neither the existence of the MSF or its successor the Defence of Canada Force represented any form of a SOF capability. For that matter, arguably, neither even provided a real airborne capability. As always, external factors influenced internal organizational shifts. By the early 1960s the notion of an Army rapid reaction and Special Forces capability gathered momentum, largely fuelled by the American involvement in Vietnam. In 1966, Lieutenant-General Jean Victor Allard, the new Commander of Force Mobile Command (FMC) (i.e. Canadian Army), decided that the Canadian Army would develop a similar capability. Specifically, he aimed to have a completely airportable unit, with all its equipment, deployed and in the designated operational theatre as quickly as forty-eight hours. Therefore, on 12 May 1966, the MND announced, "FMC would include the establishment of an airborne regiment whose personnel and equipment could be rapidly sent to danger zones."[82]

For the Army Commander, the new airborne regiment represented flexibility and a higher order of professionalism and soldiering. The Army Commander clearly believed that "this light unit is going to be very attractive to a fellow who likes to live dangerously, so all volunteers can go into it." His creation was to be open to all three services and manned exclusively by volunteers. "We intend," he asserted, "to look at the individual a little more rather than considering the unit as a large body of troops, some of whom might not be suited for the task."[83]

In the Spring of 1966, General Allard, then the Chief of the Defence Staff (CDS), took the next step and discussed the formation of what he fondly labelled the new "airborne commando regiment." Colonel Don H. Rochester was appointed as the commander-designate and he was given another year to refine the 'Concept of Operations,' organization, and structure. The prospects seemed unlimited. The "exciting thing about General Allard's concept," Rochester recalled, "was that this unit was to be radically different. Except for aircraft, it was to be self-contained with infantry, armour, artillery, engineers, signals and supporting administration." Furthermore, he explained, "all were to be volunteers and so well trained in their own arm or service that they could devote their time to specialist training."[84]

The Canadian Airborne Regiment (Cdn AB Regt) was officially established on 8 April 1968.[85] It consisted of an airborne headquarters and signal squadron (80 personnel), two infantry airborne commandos (278 personnel each), an airborne field battery (80 personnel capable of providing two, three gun troops of pack howitzers, or two groups of six medium (82mm) mortars), an airborne field squadron (81 personnel), and an airborne service commando (i.e. combat service support and administration – 89 personnel).

The Regiment's mandate was impressive if not overly optimistic. The Cdn AB Regt was required to be capable of performing a variety of tasks which included: the Defence of Canada; the United Nations (UN) 'stand-by' role; peacekeeping operations; missions in connection with national disaster; 'Special Air Service' type missions; *coup de main* tasks in a general war setting; and responsibility for parachute training in the CF. The respective Canadian Forces

Organizational Order (CFOO) stated, "the role of the Canadian Airborne Regiment is to provide a force capable of moving quickly to meet any unexpected enemy threat or other commitment of the Canadian Armed Forces."[86]   In addition, the Army Commander, Lieutenant-General W.A.B. Anderson, ordered the Cdn AB Regt planning team to visit both the US Special Forces Centre, as well as the British SAS Regiment to gather the "necessary stimulus and factual data upon which to develop your concept."[87] Moreover, he directed that an element of the Regiment must be proficient at: HALO [High Altitude Low Opening] team parachute descents; deep penetration patrols; underwater diving; obstacle clearance and laying of underwater demolitions; mountain climbing; and "Special Service Forces" type team missions.[88]

Although outwardly a conventional airborne regiment, by design it was clear that the Cdn AB Regt, both officially in accordance with its CFOO and through direction given by the CF chain of command, was intended to be capable of special operations as understood at the time.[89] The emphasis on "SOF"-like capability was also enshrined in the Operational Concept, as well as in the later doctrinal manual, *CFP 310 (1) Airborne - The Canadian Airborne Regiment*. Under the heading 'Special Operations' a long list of tasks were included that were clearly Special Forces in nature. Specifically, the document stated that the "Canadian Airborne Regiment is to be prepared to carry out the following operations for which it is specially trained: disruption of lines of communications, destruction of critical installations; psychological warfare operations; special intelligence tasks; recovery tasks; deception operations; internal security operations; counter-guerrilla operations; and support of indigenous paramilitary forces."[90]

The emphasis on special operations was not lost on the Cdn AB Regt's leadership, which focused at times almost exclusively on daring direct action commando-like raids. Moreover, as a number of former commanding officers noted, if something happened (e.g. terrorist incident), they knew they would get the call so they attempted to train individuals in the necessary skills required for special operations.

The quality of the original individuals was incontestable. Official recruiting themes stressed the superior attributes of the new genre of warrior. They emphasised the fact that the new paratrooper had to be an excellent athlete, an expert at small arms and a survival specialist. Furthermore, they underscored the necessity to be robust, courageous and capable of a high level of endurance. Not surprisingly, the Cdn AB Regt received a larger percentage of the more ambitious, determined and energized individuals. They skimmed the cream of the Army. Only experienced officers, non-commissioned officers, and soldiers were accepted. All riflemen within the commandos were required to be qualified to the rank of corporal. This requirement meant that the respective individual had previously served within a regular rifle battalion. As a result, they were already competent and experienced in the basic drills of soldiering. Equally important, they were on the whole older and normally, more mature. This requirement allowed the Regiment to direct its training effort towards specialized training such as mountain and pathfinder operations, patrolling courses, skiing, and unarmed combat.

The Cdn AB Regt quickly forged a reputation for undertaking tough, demanding and dynamic activities. It set new standards for physical fitness and training realism. In consonance with its status as a strategic force capable of global deployment, the Regiment travelled throughout Canada, the United States, as well as exotic locations such as Jamaica, to practise its lethal craft. It conducted training and exchanges with the British SAS, American Rangers and Special Forces, and the French Foreign Legion. By the early 1970s the Airborne Regiment was at its zenith of power. It had the status of a mini-formation, direct access to the Commander of the Army, and an increased peacetime establishment of 1,044 all ranks.

The Cdn AB Regt deployed to Montreal, Quebec during the Front de la Libération du Québec (FLQ) Crisis in October 1970 and four years later was dispatched to Cyprus during the Turkish invasion of that island. However, in all cases the Regiment functioned solely as conventional infantry. On 26 November 1976, the Cdn AB Regt was moved from Edmonton to Petawawa and its formation status was stripped.[91] It now became a simple unit within the newly re-roled SSF, which provided the Army with a relatively light, airborne/airportable quick reaction force in the demographic centre of the country which could be moved quickly to augment either of the flanking brigades for internal security tasks, to the Arctic, or to UN-type operations.[92]

The restructuring inflicted additional wounds. The Regiment was dramatically pared and it lost its preferred standing within the Army for both manning and exemptions from the mundane taskings that other units endured. Out of necessity it began to accept more inexperienced members across the board (at all rank levels) with the corollary degradation of capability. Moreover, it became increasingly under attack by senior CF leaders who were not favourable to "special soldiers," particularly during a period of constantly shrinking defence budgets.

Adding to the frustrations of the members of the Cdn AB Regt was the fact that, despite the Regiment's CFOO and international stand-by status, it was never deployed. Senior CF leadership argued that to deploy the Regiment would strip Canada of it strategic reserve. More realistically, the problem centred around the makeup of the airborne unit itself. It lacked the necessary mobility (i.e. armoured and wheeled vehicles) as well as support capability to deploy for extended periods of time. As a result, it was easier to send conventional units to do the operations, which were all conventional in nature anyways.

Continuing the downsizing of the Regiment to battalion status in
1992 further degraded both the status and capability of the Cdn
AB Regt. Nonetheless, in December of that year, the Cdn AB Regt
deployed to Somalia on a peace-making operation under Security
Council Resolution 794. Unfortunately, the Cdn AB Regt experienced disciplinary problems in theatre that detracted from their
actual performance.[93] The Regiment pacified its sector in less than
three months, earning the praise of Hugh Tremblay, the Director
of Humanitarian Relief and Rehabilitation in Somalia, who stated
to all who would listen, "If you want to know and to see what you
should do while you are here in Somalia go to Belet Huen, talk to
the Canadians and do what they have done, emulate the Canadians
and you will have success in your humanitarian relief sector."[94]

Nonetheless, the mission was ultimately redefined in the media
and the public consciousness as a failure due to the poor leadership and criminal acts of a few. The inexplicable and lamentable
torture killing of Shidane Arone, a Somali national caught stealing
within the Regiment lines, became the defining image of the Cdn
AB Regt's operation in Africa. The public outcry and criticism of
the Department of National Defence (DND) as a result of the attempted cover-up at NDHQ and later revelations of hazing videos
within the Cdn AB Regt created a crisis of epic proportions and
senior political and military decision-makers desperately sought
a quick and easy solution to their troubles. They swiftly found
one. During an official press release on the afternoon of 23 January 1995, David Collenette, the MND, announced, "although our
senior military officers believe the Regiment as constituted should
continue, the government believes it cannot. Therefore, today under the authority of the National Defence Act, I have ordered the
disbandment of the Canadian Airborne Regiment."[95]

In the end, the Cdn AB Regt represented Canada's only capability
to conduct special operations from 1968 to 1993. A widespread
feeling, by former members of the Cdn AB Regt was captured

by Brigadier-General Jim Cox. "In our hearts," he revealed, "we equated ourselves with the SAS and the SF [Special Forces] in the U.S."[96] In the end, although, especially towards the latter years of its existence, the Regiment did not share all the characteristics of a pure SOF organization, it did have both the official mandate and the implicit understanding of the senior CF leadership that it would be the entity that conducted special operations if required. Moreover, the Cdn AB Regt did practice Direct Action (DA) and Special Reconnaissance (SR) type tasks. In addition it exercised regularly and conducted small-unit exchanges with SOF organizations in the United States and Britain. As such, it fills an important position in Canada's SOF history.

SPECIAL EMERGENCY RESPONSE TEAM

Nonetheless, even before the Cdn AB Regt was disbanded, the genesis of Canada's true contemporary SOF capability began to germinate. A fundamental shift in the threat picture to Western industrialized nations erupted in the late 1960s. Political violence or, more accurately terrorism, became recognized as a significant "new" menace. Bombings, kidnapping, murders, and the hijacking of commercial aircraft seemingly exploded onto the world scene. Not only in the Middle East, but also in Europe, countries were thrust into a state of violence as both home-grown and international terrorists waged a relentless war that recognized no borders or limits. The murder of Israeli athletes at the 1972 Olympics in Munich, West Germany became one of the defining images of the crisis, as did the 1975 terrorist assault on the Organization of the Petroleum Exporting Countries (OPEC) headquarters in Vienna, Austria.[97]

But the problem went beyond a spill over of Mid-East conflict and politics. In Germany, groups such as the Baader-Meinhof gang (or Red Army Faction), created death and destruction. Holland was besieged by Moluccan terrorists and Britain struggled with the

Irish Republican Army (IRA) and the Northern Ireland question. Even in North America, terrorism reared its ugly head. The Americans saw the growth of radical groups such as the Weathermen, New World Liberation Front and Black Panther Party, to name but a few. In Canada, the FLQ began a reign of terror that culminated in the October Crisis of 1970. In addition, foreign terrorists imported their political struggles and launched attacks against targets in Canada. A few examples include: the storming of the Turkish Embassy in Ottawa by three Armenian men (Armenian Revolutionary Army) on 12 March 1985; the paralyzation of the Toronto public transit system on 1 April 1985, as a result of a *communiqué* sent by a group identifying itself as the Armenian Secret Army for the Liberation of our Homeland in which they threatened death to passengers of the transit system; and the downing of an Air India flight off the coast of Ireland on 23 June 1985, killing 329 people as a result of a bomb that was planted prior to its departure from Toronto's Pearson International Airport.

Not surprisingly, much like countries around the world, Canada decided it needed a counter-terrorist (CT) capability of its own.[98] Its first attempt was to create the Hostage Assault and Rescue Program (HARP) under the auspices of the RCMP in 1982. The small team was well-trained by foreign SOF personnel, but unfortunately a bureaucratic failure to reach a suitable administrative arrangement for the force scuttled the project. The RCMP wanted the operators to do tours of three months in Ottawa and then one and a half months back in their home precincts. The members wanted a permanent posting to Ottawa so they could move their families. In the end, no agreement could be reached and the program was shut down.

Three years later in 1985, with a number of high profile terrorist acts committed on Canadian soil, specifically the attack on the Turkish Embassy, the Government of Canada could delay no longer. It was time to establish a CT force of its own. The initial discussion of whether the new CT force should be military or police became a struggle between the CDS at the time and the RCMP commissioner. Neither wanted the responsibility of creating or owning the force. The Commissioner of the RCMP felt the proposed entity was more a military commando unit than a police organization. The CDS was of the mind that the type of individual created in such an organization could be problematic. He feared that once they were done their tour of service they would invariably become mercenaries of one sort or another and he did not want that type of fall-out and as a result did not want that type of unit within his Canadian Forces.[99]

In the end, the CDS had his way because the Solicitor General believed the CT task was a policing function. As a result, the following year, in 1986, the RCMP created the 75 member strong SERT as Canada's first Hostage Rescue (HR)/CT organization. The unit quickly established itself by drawing its personnel from existing trained police Emergency Response Teams (ERT) from across the country. They received comprehensive training much of it initially from a number of international CT experts. Although SERT was constantly busy, it was never deployed for an actual mission.

JOINT TASK FORCE TWO

By the early 1990s, the continuing efforts of the federal government to combat its enormous deficit led to continuing deep budget cuts to all government departments. The RCMP was not immune. Faced with financial constraints, the requirement to pay overtime to members of the SERT, a force that had been in existence for years but had not yet deployed, as well as the requirement to continually rely on military airlift and other support provided the impetus for change. Moreover, the military in the post-Cold War era was also amenable to taking on new roles.[100] The deputy minister at the time, Bob Fowler, was instrumental in pushing for DND to take on the role. As such, in February 1992, senior governmental, RCMP and DND decision-makers decided to transfer the HR/CT responsibilities from the RCMP SERT to a military organization. As such, JTF 2 was born.

The challenge for the unit was immense. It had to select and train its personnel, establish a new unit and be operational by 1 April 1993. The tight timelines meant that the first CO, Lieutenant-Colonel Ray Romses, had little choice but to utilize the RCMP SERT model for pre-selection, selection and qualification standards. The RCMP had two distinct entities. The Dwyer Hill Training Centre was run by an RCMP inspector responsible for the infrastructure and training. However, the command and control of the actual SERT was vested in another RCMP officer. Romses, however, would be responsible for both the operational and training functions.

The RCMP trained the first group of JTF 2 personnel. The newly trained military members now became the training cadre and from the second serial onwards, took control of instructing the remainder of the military personnel. Progressively, the RCMP SERT members took on less and less responsibility.

Timelines were tight, but JTF 2 was ready for the 1 April stand-up date. A formal hand-over parade and Mess Dinner were held at Dwyer Hill on 31 March 1992 to mark the handover of the HR/CT role from the RCMP SERT to the CF JTF 2. The following day, the unit was already undertaking operational tasks.

From the beginning, the CO realized that the unit would have to evolve. The RCMP SERT had been content to remain strictly a police HR type organization. Initial time constraints meant that JTF 2 had to take on that paradigm and the police culture that accompanied it. However, with the black role came the issue of utility. How often would it be used? Romses realized this could also create retention issues. Moreover, for JTF 2 to provide utility to the greater CF a green (SOF) role would need to be developed.*

As such, the unit began to evolve in the mid to late-1990s towards a more military SOF orientation and capability; however, HR/CT remained JTF 2's primary focus. In 1994, the CDS approved growth for JTF 2, as well as a transition from a pure black CT role to other special operations tasks. As a result, the unit undertook tasks around the globe that gave its members both experience in foreign locations, as well as exposure to senior military and civilian decision-makers.

Although the unit was expanding to include a green component, as already mentioned, its focus was still almost exclusively on black skills. A "green phase" during initial training was largely an introduction to fieldcraft for the non-combat arms volunteers. Within the unit there was also tension between those who favoured retaining the exclusive black role and "police culture" and those who wanted to push JTF 2 to be more akin to a military organization such as the British SAS and US Delta Force. External events provided the catalyst for change.

On the morning of 11 September 2001, millions watched their television screens mesmerized as events unfolded in New York City. In the early morning hours a passenger jet had ploughed into the top stories of the World Trade Center (WTC), in the financial core of the city. As most were trying to absorb what happened, a second large commercial airliner came into view and slammed into the twin tower of the WTC. It would only be a short time later that both towers collapsed onto themselves and crumpled to the ground, killing all those inside. A third aircraft slammed into

---

* The "black" role refers to counter-terrorist type tasks and the "green" role refers to Tier 1 SOF tasks such as Special Reconnaissance and Direct Action.

the Pentagon, killing and injuring hundreds more and a fourth hijacked jetliner heading for Washington D.C. slammed into the ground in Pennsylvania short of its objective due to the bravery of its passengers. In total, almost 3,000 people were killed in the attacks.

Within days it became clear that the Americans would take military action to strike at the terrorists who planned and conducted the attack, as well as those who supported and abetted them. Osama Bin Laden and his Al-Qaeda terrorist organization, sheltered in Afghanistan by Mullah Omar and his Taliban government, quickly became the centre of attention. Not surprisingly, the Americans, through Central Intelligence Agency (CIA) paramilitary forces and US SOF, in conjunction with the Northern Alliance, an anti-Taliban resistance movement, quickly launched an offensive to oust the Taliban and capture Bin Laden and his associates.

The Canadians quickly moved to support their American allies. The CF mobilized to send ships, aircraft and ground forces in support of the US mission titled Operation Enduring Freedom (OEF). Part of the CF force package was a special operations task force (SOTF) that deployed as part of OEF and was under operational control of the American commander of the Combined Joint Forces Special Operations Component Command. Their tasks included direct action, special reconnaissance and sensitive site exploitation.[101]

The JTF-2 based SOTF was deployed in theatre from December 2001 to November 2002.[102] At the time, JTF 2 was largely an unknown quantity and its role in theatre was initially marginalized. "They were curious because they [Americans] didn't really know us," one member of the Task Force conceded. He explained, "At the beginning, people said, 'Who the f--- is JTF 2?'"[103]

However, it took only one mission to demonstrate their skill sets and very quickly it became a force of choice. By the end of the tour, according to US military officials the JTF 2 SOTF had conducted "42 reconnaissance and surveillance missions as well as 23 direct action missions."[104] Tasks included "snatching senior Taliban officials," manning high altitude observation posts and combing mountain cave complexes.[105] Their performance earned them the trust and respect of the US commanders in theatre and the SOTF was given special tasks with American sub-units allocated to it under tactical control (normally Rangers or 82nd Airborne and aviation assets). In the end, the JTF 2 SOTF executed more missions than any other coalition SOF force assigned to the Combined Joint Special Operations Task Force – South (CJSOTF-S).

In fact, US Navy Commander Kerry Metz, director of operations for CJSOTF-S told Congress, "We were fortunate to have the finest special operations ...and we challenged our operators to conduct missions in some of the most hostile environments ever operated in." He explained, "we had special reconnaissance teams operating in the mountains of Afghanistan above 10,000 feet for extended periods without resupply."[106] The CJSOTF-S commander, Rear-Admiral Bob Harward, simply acknowledged "that his JTF 2 team was his first choice for any 'direct action' mission."[107]

Unquestionably, JTF 2 participation in OEF was a critical turning point in its evolution and CANSOF history. The value of the JTF 2 contribution, or more importantly, its impact in theatre bolstered Canadian credibility. "We had to shoulder our way into the international SOF community with reps from the British SAS and U.S. Delta," Colonel Clyde Russell, the CO of JTF 2 at the time, explained "but once we got our seat at the table, now we can hold our own."[108]

Participation in OEF also finalized the debate back at Dwyer Hill in Ottawa. One JTF 2 detachment commander explained, "9/11 put us full throttle into the war-fighting game and allowed us to pass a number of hurdles that would have taken years in a peacetime environment." Brigadier-General Michael Day, one of the SOTF commanders at the time and the current Commander of Canadian Special Operations Command at time of writing, assessed, "We progressed the unit in maturity decades that first year [in Afghanistan]."

Quite simply, the operation planted the seeds of CANSOF growth and maturation. "It allowed us to move into a kinetic mode," asserted Day, "it showed the connection of the counter-terrorism/ hostage rescue piece to the expeditionary capability." It not only revitalized the unit, but it also revealed a very potent international capability.[109] "Stepping out onto the world stage was our first big show," commented Colonel Russell. "From a strategic perspective," he added, "it opened the eyes of the grown ups of how SOF can be used as a bit of a strategic place marker in a crisis." Russell explained, "we had a small footprint but a large impact. The country got a lot of credit."

Consistently, CANSOF leadership attest to the fact that JTF 2's participation in OEF in 2001-2002 was a seminal event for the unit and CANSOF. "9/11 and Afghanistan allowed CANSOFCOM to grow into a mature combat capable force," explained Brigadier-General Day, "It was instrumental in shaping our ability to field kinetic forces, which we now use to leverage our ability to shape a theatre." He concluded, "our first deployment will remain the defining moment of who we are."[110]

The CANSOF commanders were not the only ones who recognized the importance of JTF 2's first combat deployment. On 7 December 2004, George W. Bush, the President of the United States, awarded the JTF 2 component of CJSOTF-S/Task Force (TF) K-Bar a Secretary of the Navy, Presidential Unit Citation. American officials sent the request for Canadian approval prior to its actual presentation to the CF members. DND issued a press release the following day to announce the presentation. The Canadian

Governor General congratulated JTF 2 on the award on 10 December 2004 through a media advisory.

The narrative of the citation read:

> *For extraordinary heroism and outstanding performance of duty in action against the enemy in Afghanistan from 17 October 2001 to 30 March 2002. Throughout this period, Combined Joint Special Operations Task Force – SOUTH/ Task Force K-BAR, operating first from Oman and then from forward locations throughout the southern and eastern regions of Afghanistan successfully executed its primary mission to conduct special operations in support of the US efforts as delegated to Commander US CENTCOM through the Joint Forces Special Operations Component Command (JFSOCC) to destroy, degrade and neutralize the TB [Taliban] and AQ [Al-Qaeda] leadership and military. During its six month existence TF K-Bar was the driving force behind myriad combat missions conducted in Combined Joint Operation Area Afghanistan. These precedent setting and extremely high-risk missions included search and rescue, recovery die ops, non-compliant boarding of high interest vessels, special reconnaissance, hydrographic reconnaissance, SSE [Sensitive Site Exploitation], DA missions apprehension of military and political detainees, destruction of multiple cave and tunnel complexes, identification and destruction of several known AQ training camps, explosion of thousands of pounds of enemy ordnance and successful coordination of UW operations for Afghanistan. The sailors, soldiers, Airmen, Marines and coalition partners of CJSOTF (S)/TF K-Bar set an unprecedented 100 percent mission success rate across a broad spectrum of special operations missions while operating under extremely difficult and constantly dangerous conditions. They established benchmark standards of professionalism, tenacity, courage tactical brilliance and*

operational excellence while demonstrating superb esprit de corps and maintaining the highest measures of combat readiness.[111]

In the aftermath of the award, the Canadian leadership took the opportunity to heap praise on the shadow warriors. "This citation from the U.S.," Bill Graham, the MND, announced "signifies the outstanding counter-terrorism and special operations capability that has been developed by the Canadian Forces." He added, "JTF 2 has played a critical role in Canada's contribution to the war against terrorism and will continue to be an important part of our domestic security."[112]

Similarly, General Ray Henault, the CDS at the time, asserted, "The presentation of the US Presidential Unit Citation to members of JTF 2 brings important recognition to a group of incredible CF members whose accomplishments normally cannot be publicly recognized in the interest of national security."[113] He concluded, "Canadians should be very proud of this specialized Canadian military unit."[114]

The importance of the mission and the recognition of the CANSOF contribution was also evident in the governmental decision to double the size of JTF 2. The MND quickly realized the strategic impact, at a relatively low cost, that even a small SOF task force could achieve. As such, he pushed for expansion.[115]

Despite the great effort and incredible results, the JTF 2 initial deployment to Afghanistan ended rather quickly. By late 2002, with the Taliban largely routed and the country entering what appeared to be a period of relative calm, Canada withdrew all of its forces from Afghanistan. However, it returned the following year as a contributor to the International Security Assistance Force (ISAF) in Kabul. As part of the redeployment, Canadian SOF also maintained a footprint in Afghanistan. Then in 2004, a request from the Americans prompted Canada to deploy another Canadian SOTF. This was no surprise since JTF 2's performance had elicited praise from the American ambassador Paul Cellucci. He publicly stated, "Canada's elite Tier 1 JTF 2 is as capable as any Tier 1 Special Forces in the world [and it] makes a significant contribution whenever deployed."[116]

The request to deploy the SOTF was strongly supported by both the CDS General Rick Hillier and the deputy minister, D. M. Elcock. They explained, "The deployment of Canadian special operations forces to Afghanistan would make evident our ongoing commitment to an active engagement in the Campaign Against Terrorism and it would also demonstrate our direct burden sharing with our closest allies." The deployment was also in consonance with ongoing strategic objectives for the CF in the global war on terrorism (GWoT). The deployment would assist the government of Afghanistan in providing security and stability in the country and in supporting reconstruction activities; it would assist with the elimination of Al-Qaeda, the Taliban and other anti-coalition militants as continuing terrorist threats to international peace and security; and it would support efforts to address the humanitarian needs of Afghans.

Nevertheless, the high-level support was not surprising. After all, they were well-versed in the strength of the unit. "One of my first visits," acknowledged General Hillier, "was to Joint Task Force 2, our special forces unit based near Ottawa, no strangers to me after the many operations." He explained:

> JTF 2 troopers are the Olympic athletes of soldiering, our version of gold medalists, taking on the most difficult missions and tasks with a level of skill and professionalism that has earned the respect of special forces units around the world. Like the U.S. Delta Force or the British Special Air Service (SAS), they get the most

dangerous and demanding of missions, from hostage rescues to acting as bodyguards for VIPs (like me!) to operating for long periods of time on their own in enemy territory.[117]

By 2005, the JTF 2 SOTF was back in country supporting OEF. Although originally committed for only a year, the mandate was repeatedly extended up until the time of writing. Their mission, however, remained largely unchanged. General Hillier affirmed that Canadian SOF had established a presence on Afghanistan battlefields and that they were effective in disrupting the Taliban leadership.[118] He declared, "What we want to do is take out the [Taliban] commanders who are engaged in orchestrating, facilitating, paying, leading, planning and driving folks to attack us or attack the Afghans or attack the innocent." He added, "And our special forces are focused very much on that. ... I said, during a recent speech, that we had removed from the battlefield six commanders who were responsible for the deaths of 21 Canadian soldiers." Hillier explained, "Well that's changed. We've removed seven commanders who have been responsible for the deaths of 27 soldiers."[119]

Canadian scholars have reinforced Hillier's revelations. A team studying operations in Kandahar province noted that "insurgent operations in 2007 were increasingly characterized by lack of coordination and poor planning, which could be attributed to the growing effectiveness of ISAF's Special Operations Forces." They explained, "SOF units from all ISAF contributor nations in the south were pooled for the task of arresting known bombmaking cell leaders, drug lords, and a legal case prepared for their arrest, Canadian (and other ISAF) SOF troops would be deployed to apprehend the suspect. As often as not, if the target was a Tier 1 Taliban leader, he would try to shoot his way out, with predictable results. Consequently, Taliban command-and-control capacity in the south in 2007 was less effective than the previous fall."[120]

In addition, conventional commanders also spoke to the influence CANSOF was exerting in theatre. A Canadian battle group commander noted the impressive effect SOF had on his area of operations in Kandahar. "The SOF strikes had a chilling effect on the Taliban. In one strike they killed an important leader and 16 of his fighters. The Taliban leadership in Kandahar City felt a lot of pressure from SOF. They were moving every day so we saw a reduction in activity. They [Taliban] were being disrupted – they were on the move, on the run."[121]

And this was exactly the effect the CDS expected from his CANSOF SOTF. "Without the proactive operations necessary to precisely track [Taliban leaders] locate them and attack them," General Hillier insisted, "they with their forces would still be trying to kill us."[122] And so, as the campaign in the Canadian theatre of operations evolved from 2005 to 2011, so too did the specific CANSOF tasks, as well as their tactics, techniques and procedures (TTPs), to ensure that the standing CANSOF SOTF in Afghanistan provided the necessary effects to support the ongoing counter-insurgency efforts.

CANADIAN SPECIAL OPERATIONS FORCES COMMAND

The Afghanistan experience, as already noted, proved to be a watershed for CANSOF. Very quickly the tempo of operations, as well as the execution of the myriad of missions, clearly highlighted force structure concerns that prevented JTF 2 from reaching its full potential. A 2003 study written by CANSOF staff examined the lessons learned from the 2001-2002 mission in Afghanistan. It identified the need for a Tier 2 SOF capability within Canada to support JTF 2 operations. This call for additional resources did not fall on deaf ears.

In February 2005, General Hillier, the CDS, told his general officers at a special general/flag officer seminar in Cornwall, Ontario that "We need an integrated Canadian Forces that consists of maritime, air, land and special forces, woven together to make a more effective military."[123] This was the first time that a CDS spoke of Canada's SOF capability within the context as a fourth environment within the CF. Later that year, on 19 April 2005, General Hillier declared that he intended "on bringing JTF 2, along with all the enablers that it would need, to conduct operations successfully into one organization with one commander."[124] This would prove to be a major step for CANSOF. As a result, on 1 February 2006, as part of the CF's transformation program, CANSOFCOM was created.[125]

The purpose of CANSOFCOM was clearly articulated as the need "to force develop, generate and, where required, employ and sustain Special Operations Task Forces capable of achieving tactical, operational and strategic effects required by the Government of Canada."[126] The command consisted of a small headquarters, JTF 2, a new "Tier 2" combatant unit called the Canadian Special Operations Regiment (CSOR), 427 Special Operations Aviation Squadron (SOAS) and the Joint Nuclear, Biological Chemical Defence Company (JNBCD Company), which was officially renamed in September 2007 to the Canadian Joint Incident Response Unit (CJIRU).[127] The respective unit responsibilities were given as:

1. JTF 2 – Its mission is to provide a force capable of rendering armed assistance and surgical, precise effects in the resolution of an issue that is, or has the potential of, affecting the national interest. The primary focus is counter-terrorism; however, the unit is employed on other high value tasks such as special reconnaissance, DA and Defence, Diplomacy and Military Assistance (DDMA);[128]

2. CSOR – Its mission is to provide high readiness special operations forces capable of force generating for, and conducting, integrated SOTFs to execute operations on behalf

of the Government of Canada. It is also responsible for conducting DA, Non-Combatant Evacuation Operations (NEO) and DDMA;

3. 427 Special Operations Aviation Squadron – Its mission is to generate and employ the integrated aviation element of CANSOFCOM high-readiness SOTFs for the conduct of domestic and international operations. Its range of tasks include CT, DA and DDMA;

4. CJIRU – Its mission is provide timely and agile broad-based Chemical, Biological, Radiological, Nuclear (CBRN) support to the GoC in order to prevent, control and mitigate CBRN threats to Canada, Canadians and Canadian interests. The unit is a core member of the National CBRN Response Team, and is also responsible for conducting CT, SR and Counter Proliferation (CP). The unit has three key mandates:

    a. Respond to CBRN events in conjunction with other elements of the National CBRNE [explosive] Response Team;

    b. Provide an agile integral part of the CANSOFCOM Immediate Reaction Task Force (IRTF); and

    c. Specialized support to CF expeditionary operations.[129]

Although initially the core of CANSOFCOM was JTF 2, the Command has evolved. "We don't talk about deploying units," CANSOFCOM Commander Brigadier-General Mike Day explained, "We talk about deploying special operation task forces, which are absolutely an amalgam of all the parts of this command."[130] One such example was the publicly announced SOTF called "Arrowhead." This task force was not created for a long-term mission, but instead was designed to allow the Canadian military to quickly put a "footprint" into a crisis area.[131] "Arrowhead will be the precursor" to a larger special forces task force if needed, Day explained.[132] He stated that CSOR would be responsible for creating the necessary command team to coordinate the response to an international crisis or mission. However, the task force would be able to draw from personnel in various CANSOFCOM units as needed, and those assigned to TF Arrowhead would be on 24/7 alert to move out.[133]

The solidification of CANSOFCOM as the fourth service was also advanced when, on 4 February 2008, the CDS granted Honour Bearing status to JTF 2 and CSOR. This honour is "afforded to combatant units whose functional purpose is to close with and conquer, neutralize or destroy the enemy as an effective fighting force. Only combatant military units are entitled to be publicly recognized for active participation in battle against a formed and armed enemy through the award of battle honours and honorary distinctions."[134] Moreover, the CDS also approved that the 1st Canadian Special Service Battalion (better known as the Canadian component of the FSSF) be perpetuated by CSOR. This meant that CSOR would carry the battles honours of the FSSF from the Second World War.[135]

Five years into its existence, CANSOFCOM has proven itself as an integral national capability. It has conducted operations domestically and around the world and throughout has demonstrated a high level of professionalism and expertise. It has provided DND and the GoC with a unique capability that is unmatched elsewhere in the CF or any other governmental department. "I think it is fair to say the worth of Canada's special forces has been so completely proven to the chain of command – the Canadian Forces and the government of Canada – that the question is not, 'Does it survive? What is its structure?'" Brigadier-General Day opined, but rather, "the question is, 'How much do we want it to grow by?'"[136]

These were not hollow words. Others outside of the command agreed. "There is not a more tactically agile capability in the world," retired Lieutenant-General Michel Gauthier, a former commander of the Canadian Expeditionary Command, said. "They are," he insisted, "as good as any in the world, and what they do is function effectively in chaotic and complex environments."[137] A former CDS, Vice-Admiral Larry Murray insisted, "I don't know where we would be today if we didn't develop that [SOF] capability back in the 1990s."[138]

The current CDS apparently agreed. General Walter Natynczyk has "praised the work of the country's SOF," and stated, "they've proven their worth during the past 17 years in war zones from Bosnia to Afghanistan."[139] Natynczyk insisted, "The units will remain essential in the future [since] we see that irregular warfare, the counterinsurgency we are seeing in Afghanistan, is occurring and could occur in other parts of the world." He noted, "The one strong aspect of special forces is that it is very surgical in nature. They need a high level of ... competence."[140]

And the national SOF legacy has shown that Canada's SOF organizations throughout their history have demonstrated exactly that. From the earliest Ranger Tradition, through the Second World War and the Cold War, to the current campaign against terrorism, Canada's SOF capability has proven to be amongst the best in the world. CANSOFCOM continues this tradition at home and on the front lines in Afghanistan and other trouble spots around the world. Moreover, it continues to evolve and adapt to meet the future threats to the nation. In the end, the command lives the words of its motto – "*Viam Inveniemus*" ("We will find a way.")

NOTES

1   *Canada, Canadian Special Operations Command – 2008* (Ottawa: DND, 2008); and Canada, *CANSOFCOM Capstone Concept for Special Operations 2009* (Ottawa: DND, 2009), 8.

2   See Bernd Horn, "La Petite Guerre: A Strategy of Survival," in B. Horn, ed. *The Canadian Way of War. Serving the National Interest* (Toronto: Dundurn, 2006), 21-56; Bernd Horn, "Marin and Langy – Master Practitioners of la petite guerre," in B. Horn and Roch Legault, eds., *Loyal Service: Perspectives of French-Canadian Military Leaders* (Toronto: Dundurn, 2007), 53-86; Bernd Horn, "Only for the Strong of Heart: Ranging and the Practice of La Petite Guerre During the Struggle for North America," in B. Horn, ed., *Show No Fear: Daring Actions in Canadian Military History* (Toronto: Dundurn, 2008), 17-64; and B. Horn, "Terror on the Frontier: The Role of the Indians in the Struggle for North America," in B. Horn, ed. *Forging a Nation: Perspectives on the Canadian Military Experience* (St. Catharines: Vanwell Publishers, 2002), 43-64.

3   With a population of only 60,000, New France faced the danger of being engulfed by its larger neighbour to the south, namely the English colonies that numbered approximately 1,500,000. The scale of the threat was enormous. During the French and Indian War, the English colonies outnumbered New France in manpower by nearly 25 to one. George F. Stanley, *Canada's Soldiers. The Military History of an Unmilitary People* (Toronto: The Macmillan Company of Canada Limited, 1960), 61; W.J. Eccles, "The French forces in North America during the Seven Years' War," in *Dictionary of Canadian Biography* [henceforth *DCB*], *Vol III, 1741 to 1770* (Toronto: University of Toronto Press, 1974), xx; Robert Leckie, *A Few Acres of Snow - The Saga of the French and Indian Wars* (Toronto: John Wiley & Sons, 1999), 103; and A. Doughty, *The Siege of Quebec and the Battle of the Plains of Abraham, Vol I* (Quebec: Dussault & Proulx, 1901), 158.

4   Impartial Hand. *The Contest in America Between Great Britain and France with Its Consequences and Importance* (London: Strand, 1757), 128. The writer also notes that the Indians and Canadians who travel without baggage, support themselves with stores and magazines and who maintain themselves in the woods "do more execution ... than four or fives time

their number of our men." Ibid., 138. See also W.J. Eccles, *The French in North America 1500-1783* (Markham, ON: Fitzheny & Whiteside, 1998), 208; Edward P. Hamilton, ed., *Adventures in the Wilderness. The American Journals of Louis Antoine de Bougainville, 1756-1760* (University of Oklahoma Press, 1990), 333; and M. Pouchot, *Memoirs on the Late War in North America between France and England* (originally Yverdon, 1781 – reprint Youngstown, NY: Old Fort Niagara Association, Inc., 1994), 78.

5   Walter O'Meara, *Guns at the Forks* (Pittsburg: University of Pittsburg Press, 1965), 85. See also Stephen Brumwell, *Redcoats. British Soldiers and War in the Americas, 1755-63* (Cambridge: University of Cambridge, 2002); and Ian K. Steele, *Guerillas and Grenadiers* (Toronto: Ryerson Press, 1969).

6   "Memoir on the Defense of the Fort of Carillon," *The Bulletin of the Fort Ticonderoga Museum*, Vol. 13, No. 3, 1972, 200-201; Ian K. Steele, *Betrayals. Fort William Henry & the Massacre* (New York: Oxford University Press, 1990), 96; and Fred Anderson, *Crucible of War* (New York: Vintage Books, 2001), 187.

7   The deep strikes into English territory during the Seven Year's War consistently disrupted British campaign plans and kept them on the defensive from the summer of 1755 until 1758. Moreover, it ravaged frontier settlements, economies and public morale. The raids terrorized the frontier and tied down large numbers of troops for rear security. The plight of the English colonists could not be ignored by their political leaders. The incursions into Virginia alone caused the governor there to raise 10 militia companies, a total of 1,000 men, for internal defence. Similarly, Pennsylvania raised 1,500 provincial troops and built a string of forts extending from New Jersey to Maryland in an attempt to try and impede the raiders. See Letter from General Shirley to Major-General Abercromby, 27 June 1756, Public Records Office (PRO), War Office (WO) 1/4, Correspondence, 1755-1763. See also Robert C. Alberts, *The Most Extraordinary Adventures of Major Robert Stobo* (Boston: Houghton Mifflin Company Boston, 1965), 152. See also Anderson, 637; Leckie, 101; Letter From William Shirley (New York) to Principal Secretary of War, 20 December 1755, PRO, WO 1/4, Correspondence, 1755-1763; H.R. Casgrain, ed., *Lettres du Chevalier De Lévis concernant La Guerre du Canada 1756-1760* (Montreal: C.O. Beauchemin & Fils, 1889), 75; Steele,

Guerillas and Grenadiers, 24; Le Comte Gabriel de Maurès de Malartic, *Journal des Campagnes au Canada de 1755 à 1760* (Paris: Librairie Plon, 1902), 52-53; 232; and O'Meara, 161.

8   *DCB, Vol III*, 260.

9   Ibid., 261.

10   *DCB, Vol IV, 1771-1800* (Toronto: University of Toronto, 1979), 308.

11   Rogers was a smuggler prior to the war. On Robert Rogers and his rangers the definitive work is Burt G. Loescher, *The History of Rogers Rangers. Volume I - The Beginnings Jan 1755 - 6 April 1758* (Bowie, Maryland: Heritage Books, Inc., 1946, reprint 2001) and *Genesis Rogers Rangers. Volume II - The First Green Berets* (San Mateo, California, 1969. Reprint - Bowie, Maryland: Heritage Books, Inc., 2000). See also John R. Cuneo, *Robert Rogers of the Rangers* (New York: Oxford University Press, 1959); *DCB, Vol IV, 1771-1800*, 679-682; Timothy J. Todish, *The Annotated and Illustrated Journals of Major Robert Rogers* (Fleischmanns, NY: Purple Mountain Press, 2002); and *Warfare on the Colonial American Frontier: The Journals of Major Robert Rogers* [*Rogers' Journal*] & *An Historical Account of the Expedition Against the Ohio Indians in the year 1764, Under the Command of Henry Bouquet, Esq.* (Reprinted from an original 1769 Edition - Bargersville, IN: Dreslar Publishing, 2001).

12   Cuneo, 33.

13   See *Rogers' Journal*, 13-14; Loescher, Vol 1, 63-64 and 87; Brumwell, 213; and Cuneo, 32-33.

14   Quoted in René Chartrand, *Canadian Military Heritage, Vol II, 1000-1754* (Montreal: Art Global Inc., 1993), 49; and Letter, Thomas Gage to Amherst, Albany, 18 February 1759. PRO, WO 34/46A, Amherst Papers.

15   See *DCB, Vol IV*, 308; and Chartrand, *Canadian Military Heritage*, Vol II, 49.

16   Ironically, despite the apparent utility and arguable success of rangers, as well as the constant calls for their employment, they never

became fully accepted by their professional counterparts. During the war they were never taken on to the official strength of the British Army. Moreover, their lax discipline, disheveled if not unruly appearance, as well as their manner of war-making were simply unacceptable to most British officers. "I am afraid," lamented Lord Loudoun, "[that] I shall be blamed for the ranging companies." Quoted in Loescher, Vol 1, 164.

17   The last of the British troops were evacuated from the beaches of Dunkirk on 2 June 1940. 53,000 French troops were evacuated 3-4 June. The British Admiralty estimated that approximately 338,226 men were evacuated between 26 May and 3 June. The British left behind 2,000 guns, 60,000 trucks, 76,000 tons of ammunition and 600,000 tons of fuel and supplies. Cesare Salmaggi and Alfredo Pallavisini, *2194 Days of War* (New York: Gallery Books, 1988), 4 June 1940; and I.C.R. Dear, ed., *The Oxford Companion to World War II* (Oxford: Oxford University Press, 1995), 312-313. Another account gives the losses as 475 tanks, 38,000 vehicles, 12,000 motorcycles, 8,000 telephones, 1,855 wireless sets, 7,000 tonnes of ammunition, 90,000 rifles, 1,000 heavy guns, 2,000 tractors, 8,000 Bren guns and 400 antitank guns. On 6 June the War Cabinet was informed that there were fewer than 600,000 rifles and only 12,000 Bren guns in the whole of the UK. John Parker, *Commandos. The Inside Story of Britain's Most Elite Fighting Force* (London: Headline Book Publishing, 2000), 15. Yet another source gives the losses as: stores and equipment for 500,000 men, about 100 tanks, 2,000 other vehicles, 600 guns, and large stocks of ammunition . A.J. Barker, *Dunkirk: The Great Escape* (London: J.M. Dent & Sons Ltd., 1977), 224. A major problem with determining numbers is the actual categorization of equipments.

18   Cecil Aspinall-Oglander, *Roger Keyes. Being the Biography of Admiral of the Fleet Lord Keyes of Zeebrugge and Dover* (London: Hogarth Press, 1951), 380.

19   Ibid., 380.

20   Quoted in John Terraine, *The Life and Times of Lord Mountbatten* (London: Arrow Books, 1980), 83.

21   Hilary St. George Saunders, *The Green Beret. The Story of the Commandos* (London: Michael Joseph, 1956), 118.

22   Winston S. Churchill, *The Second World War. Their Finest Hour* (Boston: Houghton Mifflin Company, 1949), 246-247. See also Colonel J.W. Hackett, "The Employment of Special Forces," *Royal United Services Institute* (RUSI), Vol. 97, No. 585, (February 1952), 28. Churchill later penned a note to President Franklin D. Roosevelt that revealed his mindset. "[The] essence of defence," he asserted, "is to attack the enemy upon us - leap at his throat and keep the grip until the life is out of him." Quoted in William Stevenson, *A Man Called Intrepid* (Guilford, CT: The Lyons Press, 2000), 131.

23   William Mackenzie, *The Secret History of SOE* (London: St Ermin's Press, 2000), xvii.

24   Ibid., 754. The SOE operated worldwide with the exception of the Soviet Union. It consisted of two branches – one to provide facilities (i.e. money, clothing, forged papers, training, weapons, ciphers and signals), the other to execute missions.

25   Denis Riggin, *SOE Syllabus. Lessons in Ungentlemanly Warfare*, WWII (London: Public Records Office, 2001), 1.

26   Ibid., 11. Once the US was in the war the second function became the most important. Camp X and its staff assisted large numbers of Americans from the Office of Strategic Services (OSS) and the Office of War Information to set up their own schools and train their own staff. The OSS was created in June 1942. It functioned as the principal US intelligence organization in all theatres for remainder of the Second World War. It was the counterpart to British intelligence service MI6 and the SOE. See also Lynn-Philip Hodgson, *Inside Camp X* (Port Perry, ON: Blake Book Distribution, 2000).

27   Roy Maclaren, *Canadians Behind Enemy Lines, 1939-1945* (Vancouver: UBC Press, 2004), 150, 172. 199-200. Approximately 3,226 personnel including all services and civilian employees were employed in the SOE by 1942. By 30 April 1944, the total strength rose to 11,752. Mackenzie, 717-719.

28   Cited in Peter Wilkinson and Joan Bright Astley, *Gubbins & SOE* (London: Leo Cooper, 1997), i. The SOE disbanded in January 1946.

29   *Combined Operations. The Official Story of the Commandos* (New York: The Macmillan Company, 1943), 16; and Aspinall-Oglander, 381.

30   "Hand-out to Press Party Visiting The Commando Depot Achnacarry, 9-12 January 1943," 2. PRO, DEFE 2/5, War Diary COC.

31   Brigadier T.B.L. Churchill, "The Value of Commandos," *RUSI*, Vol. 65, No. 577, (February 1950), 85.

32   Charles Messenger, *The Commandos 1940-1946* (London: William Kimber, 1985), 411. For a detailed account of the British raiding policy and the creation of the commandos see Bernd Horn, "Strength Born From Weakness: The Establishment of the Raiding Concept and the British Commandos," *Canadian Military Journal*, Vol. 6, No. 3, (Autumn 2005), 59-68.

33   George Kerr, "Viking Force. Canada's Unknown Commandos," *Canadian Military History*, Vol. 9, No. 4, (Autumn 2000), 28.

34   Ibid., 29.

35   In December 1940, the commandos were renamed Special Service Units. However, by February 1941 the Special Service Units were split up and commandos, as independent units, emerged once again. This was a result of the decision to deploy a number of commandos to the Middle East. Nonetheless, the eleven commandos which existed were grouped in a Special Service (SS) Brigade. The SS Brigade's primary mission remained that of carrying out raids. However, it was also given the secondary tasks of acting as an elite or shock assault brigade to seize and hold a bridgehead to cover a landing in force, as well as providing especially trained covering forces for any operation. "Organization and Training of British Commandos," *Intelligence Training Bulletin No. 3*, Headquarters First Special Service Force, 11 November 1942, 2. Department of Defence Directorate of History and Heritage (DHH), file 145.3009 (D5), Organization and Instructions for the 1st Canadian Special Service Battalion, July 1944-December 1944.

36   Kerr, 30.

37   Ibid., 33.

38   The ill-fated Dieppe Raid led to recriminations of callousness, in-
competence, negligence and security violations. The original raid, code
named Rutter, was cancelled on 7 July 1942 because of bad weather.
Mountbatten later resurrected it, under questionable authority, under
the code name Jubilee on 19 August. In total, 4,963 Canadians, 1,075
British and 50 American Rangers took part. In short, a lack of adequate
air support and naval gunfire (due to the absence of battleships), as
well as the failure of the armour to gain lodgement, compounded by
communication errors, the very narrow channelled approaches over open
ground for the assaulting forces and the strong German fortifications,
led to an unmitigated disaster. The Canadians suffered 3,367 (killed,
wounded or captured) casualties of the 4,963 that participated. The British casualties amounted to 275. The Royal Navy lost one destroyer and
33 landing craft and the RAF lost 106 aircraft. See Brian Loring Villa,
Mountbatten and the Dieppe Raid (Don Mills, ON: Oxford University
Press, 1994); Brigadier-General Denis Whitaker and Shelagh Whitaker,
Dieppe – Tragedy to Triumph (Toronto: McGraw-Hill Ryerson, 1992); and
Will Fowler, *The Commandos At Dieppe: Rehearsal for D-Day* (London:
Harper-Collins, 2002).

39   E.G. Finley, *RCN Beach Commando 'W'* (Ottawa: Gilmour Repro-
ductions, 1994), 1.

40   Ibid., 2. The RCN Beach Commandos are divided into three beach
parties each commanded by a beach master. Due to the arduous requirements of employment special medical requirements (relative to those
imposed on other RCN volunteers) were imposed on volunteers:

    1.   Under 35 years of age;
    2.   Mental stability, with no family history of mental disease or
         disorder;
    3.   No history of chronic illness (e.g. bronchitis, asthma, TB,
         rheumatism, arthritis, heart, ear);
    4.   Standard visual acuity and hearing; and
    5.   Free from VD.
Ibid., 10.

41   Ibid., viii-5.

42   The conceptual model for selection was such that one journalist quipped, "You've practically got to be Superman's 2IC [Second-in-Command] in order to get in." "Canada's Jumping Jacks!" *Khaki. The Army Bulletin*, Vol. 1, No. 22, (29 September 1943), 1. For a detailed examination of 1 Cdn Para Bn see Bernd Horn and Michel Wycyznski, *Canadian Airborne Forces since 1942* (London: Osprey, 2006); B. Horn and M. Wycyznski, *Paras Versus the Reich. Canada's Paratroopers at War, 1942-1945* (Toronto: Dundurn Press, 2003); B. Horn and M. Wycyznski, *Tip of the Spear - An Intimate Portrait of the First Canadian Parachute Battalion, 1942-1945* (Toronto: Dundurn Press, 2002); and B. Horn and M. Wycyznski, *In Search of Pegasus - The Canadian Airborne Experience, 1942 - 1999* (St. Catharines: Vanwell Publishing, 2000).

43   Robert Taylor, "Paratroop Van Eager to be Tip of Army 'Dagger,'" *Toronto Daily Star*, 12 August 1942. 1 Cdn Para Bn Association (Assn) Archives, Lockyer, Mark, file 10-3.

44   James C. Anderson, "Tough, Hard-As-Nails Paratroopers Arrive to Open Shilo School," 22 September 1942, 1. Cdn Para Bn Assn Archives, Firlotte, Robert, file 2-11; "Toughest in Canada's Army Back for Paratroop Course," *The Star*, 21 September 1942. 1 Cdn Para Bn Assn Archives, Firlotte, Robert, file 2-11; and Ronald K Keith, "Sky Troops," *Maclean's Magazine*, 1 August 1943, 18-20 & 28. This is simply a representative sample. Virtually every article in newspapers nation-wide used similar adjectives to describe Canada's "newest corps elite." See also . "Assembling Paratroopers at Calgary," *Globe and Mail*, Vol. XCIX, No. 28916, (18 August 1942), 13. LAC, microfilm N-20035; and Robert Taylor, "Paratroop Van Eager to be Tip of Army 'Dagger,'" *Toronto Daily Star*, 12 August 1942. 1 Cdn Para Bn Assn Archives, Lockyer, Mark, file 10-3.

45   "Assembling Paratroopers at Calgary," *Globe and Mail*, Vol. XCIX, No. 28916, (18 August 1942), 13. LAC, microfilm N-20035; and Robert Taylor, "Paratroop Van Eager to be Tip of Army 'Dagger,'" *Toronto Daily Star*, 12 August 1942. 1 Cdn Para Bn Assn Archives, Lockyer, Mark, file 10-3.

46   "Assembling Paratroopers at Calgary," *Globe and Mail*, Vol. XCIX, No. 28916, (18 August 1942), 13. LAC, microfilm N-20035.

47   James C. Anderson, "Canada's Paratroopers Don't Have Stage Fright," *Saturday Night*, No. 11, (12 December 1942), 11. LAC, microfilm 56A.

48   2 Cdn Para Bn was the higher priority of the two units. National Defence Headquarters directed the commanding officer of 1 Cdn Para Bn to transfer all jump qualified personnel who volunteered to 2 Cdn Para Bn. The rumour that 1 Cdn Para Bn's supposed sister unit would see action before they would quickly circulated through the ranks of 1 Cdn Para Bn. Predictably, many of the aggressive and action-seeking paratroopers transferred to 2 Cdn Para Bn.

49   The definitive history on the FSSF to date is Lieutenant-Colonel Robert D. Burhans, *The First Special Service Force. A War History of the North Americans 1942-1944* (Nashville: The Battery Press, 1996). He was the FSSF S2 (intelligence officer). See Major J.W. Ostiguy, Army Historical Section, "The First Special Service Force," 14 March 1951, 1, DND, DHH, file 145.3003 (D1); Joseph A. Springer, *The Black Devil Brigade. The True Story of the First Special Service Force in World War II* (Pacifica, CA: Military History, 2001); Robert Todd Ross, *The Supercommandos. First Special Service Force - 1942-1944* (Atglen, PA: Schiffer Military History, 2000); Colonel George Walton, The Devil's Brigade (Philadelphia: Chilton Books, 1966); and James A. Wood, *We Move Only Forward. Canada, the United States and the First Special Service Force 1942-1944* (St. Catharines, ON: Vanwell, 2006).

50   Norway represented an important source of scarce ores vital to the war effort. For example, Norwegian molybdenum was an important steel-hardening alloy and it represented 70 percent of the German supply, 95 percent of which came from deposits from the Knaben mine in the south of Norway. In addition, Finnish nickel refined in Norway represented 70 percent of the German intake; Norwegian aluminum and copper, 8 percent respectively. Burhans, 33.

51   The Rumanian and Italian missions were quickly ruled out. In the case of Rumania, approximately three million tons of oil were annually supplied to the Axis powers. The oil emanated from approximately 5,000 oils wells clustered in various fields within a 50-mile radius of Ploesti. The magnitude of the objective and the manpower required to effectively neutralize the target (i.e. thousands of wells) particularly in light of the

heavy defences in the area proved no less resource intensive than using a strategic bombing campaign. Therefore, these factors combined with the fact that there was no reasonable extraction plan for the raiding force, it was dropped as a possible target. The Italian option was no less problematic. This hydro-electric capacity was concentrated in only 12 power stations, but, they extended along the northern Po River watershed from the French border to across Italy. More importantly, the actually impact of a temporary stoppage on the German war effort would be minimal. Burhans, 30-33.

52   The actual breakdown of the 697 was: *Colonel (2IC) - 1; Lieutenant-Colonels or Majors — 4; Majors or Captains — 6; Lieutenants — 36; Other Ranks — 650.* Message from Canadian Military Attaché to Defensor, Washington, 16 July 1942. LAC, RG 24, file HQS 20-4-32, Mobilization and Organization, (Vol 1), Plough Project, (1 CSSBN). Microfilm reel C-5436.

53   Letter from Lieutenant-Colonel C.M. Drury, Assistant Military Attaché, Canadian Legation, Washington to the Directorate of Military Operations & Intelligence, NDHQ, Washington, 7 July 1942. LAC, RG 24, Vol 15301, 1st Canadian Special Service Battalion, [Hereafter 1 CSSBN] War Diary, August 1942.

54   The average age of the Forcemen between July 1942 and December 1943 was 26 years old. This was considerably higher that other US Army units. Lieutenant-Colonel Paul Adams, the Force's executive officer, later pointed out that this was a very important factor in the Force's cohesion and maturity. Major Scott R. McMichael, "The First Special Service Force," in *A Historical Perspective on Light Infantry*, (Fort Leavenworth, KS: Combat Studies Institute, Research Survey No. 6, US Army Command and General Staff College, 1987), 172.

55   Ross Munro, "Albertan Second in Command of Allies' Super-Commandos," Unidentified Canadian newspaper clipping, 6 August 1942, LAC, RG 24, Vol 15301, August 1942. 1st Canadian Special Service Battalion, [Hereafter 1 CSSBN] War Diary, Serial 1354, August 1942.

56   Memorandum, CCO to CCHQ, "Plough Scheme," 19 January 1943. PRO, DEFE 2/6, COC War Diary.

57   Don Mason, "'Air Commandos' Will Strike Hard at Axis," newspaper clipping, unknown publication, 2nd Canadian Parachute Battalion War Diary, LAC, RG 24, Vol 15301, August 1942.

58   Quoted in Burhans, 35. See also: Memorandum, McQueen to CGS, 8 October 1942. LAC, RG 24, HQS 20-4-32, "Mobilization Organization (1 Special Service Battalion), Reel C-5436; Message, Canmilitry to Defensor (Stuart to Murchie), GSD 2088, 8 October 1942. LAC, RG 24, CMHQ, Vol 12,305, File 3/Plough/1 "Organization and Operation of Proposed Plough Project."

59   Memorandum, McQueen to CGS, 8 October 1942. LAC, RG 24, HQS 20-4-32, "Mobilization Organization (1 Special Service Battalion), Reel C-5436. See also Message, Canmilitry to Defensor (Stuart to Murchie), GSD 2088, 8 October 1942. LAC, RG 24, CMHQ, Vol 12,305, File 3/Plough/1 "Organization and Operation of Proposed Plough Project." James Wood, "'Matters Canadian' and the Problem with Being Special. Robert T. Frederick on the First Special Service Force," *Canadian Military History*, Vol. 12, No. 4, (Autumn 2003), 21.

60   See Message, Military Attaché to Defensor, Ottawa, MA1286 16/7, 12 July 1942. LAC, RG 24, HQS 20-4-32, Mobilization Organization Plough Project (1st SS Bn), Reel C-5436; "Minutes of Meeting Held at C.O.H.Q. On 4.1.43 To Discuss Long – and Short – Term Policy Regarding Norwegian Operations," para 4., "Cobblestone Operations." PRO, DEFE 2/6, COC War Diary; Peter Layton Cottingham, *Once Upon A Wartime. A Canadian Who Survived the Devil's Brigade* (Private Printing, 1996), 49; and Burhans, 36.

61   Burhans, 37; Letter, Marshall to Pope, "Second Canadian Parachute Battalion," 17 October 1942. LAC, RG 24, HQS-2-32, Employment and Movement Operations, 1st Special Service Battalion, Reel C-5489.

62   Telegram DEFENSOR to CANMILITRY, No. G.S.D. 2088, 8 October 1942. LAC, RG 24, HQS-2-32, Employment and Movement Operations, 1st Special Service Battalion.

63   Ibid. Not surprisingly the CGS suggested that McNaughton determine whether the British would welcome the 2nd Parachute Battalion in their Airborne Division, or if he would consider adding it to the First

Canadian Army so as to develop options in the event the Americans cancelled their participation.

64   Letter, Marshall to Pope, "Second Canadian Parachute Battalion," 17 October 1942. LAC, RG 24, HQS-2-32, Employment and Movement Operations, 1st Special Service Battalion, Reel C-5489.

65   Letter, Pope to CGS, "Second Canadian Parachute Battalion," 20 October 1942. LAC, RG 24, HQS-2-32, Employment and Movement Operations, 1st Special Service Battalion, Reel C-5489. See also Telegram DEFENSOR to CANMILITRY, No. G.S.D. 2088, 8 October 1942. LAC, RG 24, HQS-2-32, Employment and Movement Operations, 1st Special Service Battalion.

66   *Minutes of the War Cabinet Committee*, 28 October 1942. LAC, RG 2, Series A-5-B Cabinet War Committee, Minutes and Documents of the Cabinet War Committee, Vol. 11, Meeting no. 201, 28 October 1942, Reel C-4874.

67   The success of the various SOF raids at the onset of the war drove Hitler to extreme reaction. On 18 October 1942, he issued his famous "Commando Order" that directed that "all men operating against German troops in so-called Commando raids in Europe or in Africa are to be annihilated to the last man." Enemy intelligence summaries bluntly acknowledged that "men selected for this sort of Commando [mission] by the enemy are well trained and equipped for their task." So incensed was the German dictator by their constant attacks that he ordered them killed "whether they be soldiers in uniform...whether fighting or seeking to escape...even if these individuals on discovery make obvious their intention of giving themselves up as prisoners." He insisted that "no pardon is on any account to be given." See 10 Pz Div Circular, "Sabotage and Commando Operations," 10 January 1943. PRO, DEFE 2/6, War Diary, COC; John Parker, *Commandos. The Inside Story of Britain's Most Elite Fighting Force* (London: Headline Book Publishing, 2000), 2-3; and Julian Thompson, *War Behind Enemy Lines* (Washington D.C.: Brassey's, 2001), 127.

68   Letter, Lieutenant-General McNaughton to Major-General Crerar, 19 August 1941. LAC, RG 24, Vol 12260, File: 1 Para Tps / 1, Message (G.S. 1647).

69   The school itself faced a tenuous future. Its survival hung in the air pending the final decision on the structure of the postwar army.

70   The JAS/CJATC mission included:
   a. Research in Airportability of Army personnel and equipment;
   b. User Trials of equipment, especially under cold weather conditions;
   c. Limited Development and Assessment of Airborne equipment; and
   d. Training of Paratroop volunteers; training in Airportability of personnel and equipment; training in maintenance of air; advanced training of Glider pilots in exercises with troops; training in some of the uses of light aircraft.
See "The Organization of an Army Air Centre In Canada," 29 November & 27 December 1945. DHH 168.009 (D45).

71   For a detailed history of the Cdn SAS Coy, see Bernd Horn, "A Military Enigma: The Canadian Special Air Service Company, 1948-49," *Canadian Military History*, Vol. 10, No. 1, (Winter 2001), 21-30.

72   "SAS Company - JAS (Army)", 13 June 1947. LAC, RG 24, Reel C-8255, File HQS 88-60-2.

73   "SAS Company," 30 October 1947, 4 and "Requested Amendment to Interim Plan – SAR," 11 September 1947. LAC, RG 24, Reel C-8255, File HQS 88-60-2.

74   "SAS Company - JAS (Army)", 13 June 1947, Appendix A. LAC, RG 24, Reel C-8255, File HQS 88-60-2.

75   "Special Air Service Company - Implementation Policy," 12 September 1947. NAC, RG 24, Reel C-8255, File HQS 88-60-2.

76   "SAS Company," 30 October 1947 (Air S94), LAC, RG 24, Reel C-8255, File HQS 88-60-2.

77   "SAS Terms of Reference," 16 April 1948; "Duties of the SAS Coy," 29 January 1948; SAS Coy - Air Training Directive," December 1948. LAC, RG 24, Reel C-8255, File HQS 88-60-2.

78   "SAS Company," 27 October 1948. LAC, RG 24, Reel C-8255, File HQS 88-60-2.

79   Luc Charron, "Loss of a Canadian Hero," *The Maroon Beret*, Vol. 4 No. 2, (August 1999), 28.

80   Interviews of former serving members by author.

81   See Bernd Horn, *Bastard Sons: A Critical Examination of the Canadian Airborne Experience, 1942-1995* (St. Catharines: Vanwell Publishers, 2001); George Kitching, *Mud and Green Fields. The Memoirs of Major-General George Kitching* (St. Catherines, ON: Vanwell Publishing Ltd., 1986), 248; "Command, Mobile Striking Force," 21 October 1948. DHH 112.3M2 (D369); and Sean Maloney, "The Mobile Striking Force and Continental Defence 1948-1955," *Canadian Military History*, Vol. 2, No. 2, (August 1993), 78.

82   "Special Parachute Force is Planned," *The Gazette*, 7 December 1966, 1.

83   Special Committee on Defence. *Minutes of Proceedings and Evidence*, 21 June 1966, 298-299.

84   Colonel D.H. Rochester, "The Birth of a Regiment," *The Maroon Beret*, 20th Anniversary Issue, 1988, 34.

85   For a definitive history of the Cdn AB Regt see Bernd Horn, *Bastard Sons: A Critical Examination of the Canadian Airborne Experience, 1942-1995* (St. Catharines: Vanwell Publishers, 2001).

86   "Formation of the Canadian Airborne Regiment - Activation and Terms of Reference," 15 May 1967, 3.

87   Ibid., 3.

88   Ibid., 2.

89   The official CF magazine announced the creation of the Cdn AB Regt and underlined its special mandate. It noted, "Some personnel will be trained to carry out deep penetration patrols, while others in all arms of the regiment will be trained in underwater diving techniques. There will be jumpers who specialize in High Altitude Low Opening (HALO) techniques for infiltrations patrols or pathfinder duties. ....Scattered throughout the Regiment will be soldiers who speak a variety of second languages." Major K.G. Roberts, "Canadian Airborne Regiment," *Sentinel*, June 1968, 2.

90   "Canadian Airborne Regiment - Operational Concept, Annex C" (written by the Cdn AB Regt planning staff) and *CFP 310 (1) - Airborne, Volume 1, The Canadian Airborne Regiment*, 1968, Chapter 1, Sect 2, "Role, Capabilities and Employment."

91   The move and reorganization, however, became a defining moment for the Cdn AB Regt. It signaled nothing short of the organization's eventual demise. Of prime importance, and instrumental to the Regiment's subsequent decline, was the loss of independent formation status. It was now simply an integral part of the newly created SSF. The Cdn AB Regt became nothing more than just another infantry unit, albeit an airborne one. It lost its special exemption from taskings and was now given assignments in the same manner as the other units within the SSF. However, there was a more serious consequence. As the Regiment became defined and viewed as just another infantry unit, its claim on seasoned officers and soldiers was dismissed. Tragically, it lost its preferred manning. It was no longer in the envious position of receiving only experienced and mature leaders and soldiers. Prior to the reorganization all riflemen within the commandos had to be qualified to the rank of corporal. This of course meant that those soldiers were generally more mature and experienced. However, after the move to CFB Petawawa, the former pre-requisite was no longer followed. The resultant influx of younger, immature and junior soldiers had an eventual impact on the character and reputation of the Cdn AB Regt. See Horn, *Bastard Sons*, 143-184.

92   The SSF was formerly 2 Canadian Mechanized Brigade Group (CMBG). It reverted back to 2 CMBG in 1995.

93   Incidents included: the mistreatment of prisoners on several occasions; the alleged unjustified shooting and resultant death of an

intruder; and the torture death of an apprehended thief. These occurrences ultimately defined the Airborne's achievements in the public consciousness. For additional details see Horn, *Bastard Sons*, 185-248.

94   See Horn, *Bastard Sons*, 185-209.

95   See Ibid., 217-248.

96   Brigadier-General Jim Cox, interview with author, 27 April 2010.

97   See Peter Harclerode, *Secret Soldiers. Special Forces in the War Against Terrorism* (London: Cassell & Co, 2000); Paul de B. Taillon, *The Evolution of Special Forces in Counter-Terrorism* (Westport: Praeger, 2001); Benjamin Netanyahu, *Fighting Terrorism* (New York: Noonday Press, 1995); Christopher Dobson and Ronald Payne, *The Terrorists* (New York: Facts on File, 1995); Landau, 187-201; Marquis, 62-65; and Brian MacDonald, ed., *Terror* (Toronto: The Canadian Institute of Strategic Studies, 1986).

98   New units were created or existing ones assigned new tasks. For example, the Germans established *Grenzshutzgruppe* 9 (GSG 9) in September 1972; the British assigned the Counter-Terrorist role to the SAS that year same year; the French formed the *Groupe d'Intervention de la Gendarmerie Nationale* (GIGN) two years later; the Belgiums created the *Escadron Special D'Intervention* (ESI) also in 1974; the United States formed its premier CT unit, the 1st Special Forces Operational Detachment (DELTA) in 1977; and the Italians raised the *Gruppo d'Intervento Speziale* (GIS) in 1978. In the end, most countries developed specialist CT organizations to deal with the problem. See Major-General Ulrich Wegener, "The Evolution of Grenzschutzgruppe (GSG) 9 and the Lessons of 'Operation Magic Fire' in Mogadishu," in Bernd Horn, David Last and Paul B. de Taillon, *Force of Choice - Perspectives on Special Operations* (Montreal: McGill-Queens Press, 2004), Chapter 7; David Miller, *Special Forces* (London: Salamander Books, 2001), 18-73; Harclerode, 264-285 & 411; Adams, 160-162; Marquis, 63-65; Weale, 201-235; Colonel Charlie Beckwith, *Delta Force* (New York: Dell, 1983); Connor, 262-356; Neillands, 204-246; and Leroy Thompson, *The Rescuers. The World's Top Anti-Terrorist Units* (London: A David & Charles Military Book, 1986).

99   Discussion between author and a former lieutenant-governor of Ontario who was a member of the Federal government at the time, 21 June 2006. This speaks to the perceptions of many senior conventional leaders with regards to SOF at that point in time.

100   Brigadier-General Ray Romses, the first JTF 2 CO, stated that part of the rationale for the transfer was the government's emphasis on "economizing how it did business." As such, with the Cold War over and DND looking for new roles, the Deputy Ministers of the various departments rationalized that the 75 RCMP officers at SERT, who only trained, would be more beneficial doing actual police work, while DND, which was effective at training and looking for a new role, could do HR/CT. Interview with author, 21 June 2008.

101   DND News Release NR-04.098, dated 8 December 2004, "Joint Task Force Two Members Receive U.S. Presidential Unit Citation." Direct Action, which are short duration strikes and other precise small-scale offensive actions conducted by special operation forces to seize, destroy, capture, exploit, recover or damage designated targets. Direct action differs from conventional offensive actions in the level of physical and political risk, operational techniques, and the degree of discriminate and precise use of force to achieve specific objectives. Special Reconnaissance, which are missions conducted to collect or verify information of strategic or operational significance. These actions complement and refine other collection methods but are normally directed upon extremely significant areas of interest. Sensitive Sight Exploitation (SSE) is a type of direct action operation involving the gathering of intelligence and/or evidence from a specific area or location. SSEs may be conducted in friendly, hostile, denied or politically sensitive territory. SSEs may include the destruction of weapons, munitions or equipment if the aforementioned items cannot be recovered. If there is no reasonable expectation of encountering enemy or hostile forces, SOF would not be required.

102   CANSOF utilizes an integrated operating concept that is based on SOTFs. The concept is predicated on a broad spectrum of SOF capabilities, which in the event of a deliberate deployment or crisis, are tailored and scaled into an integrated force package. SOTFs are developed, generated and, where required, force employed in order to achieve tactical,

operational and strategic effects required by the Government of Canada. See Canada, *Canadian Special Operations Command – 2008* (Ottawa: DND, 2008); and Canada, *CANSOFCOM Capstone Concept for Special Operations 2009* (Ottawa: DND, 2009), 11 for additional detail.

103   Allan Woods, "Canada's elite commandos and the invasion of Afghanistan," The Star.Com, <http://www.thestar.com/news/canada/afghanmission/article/800296--forged-in-the-fire-of-afghanistan>, accessed 25 April 2010

104   "Ottawa: Canadian Commandos Were on Afghan Frontlines," <http://circ.jmellon.com/docs/html/jtf2_canada_super_commandos.html>, accessed 12 March 2004.

105   Ibid.

106   Martin O'Malley, "JTF 2: Canadas Super-Secret Commandos," CBC News, <http://circ.jmellon.com/docs/html/jtf2_canada_super_commandos. html>, accessed 12 March 2004.

107   Cited in Allan Woods, "Canada's elite commandos and the invasion of Afghanistan," The Star.Com, <http://www.thestar.com/news/canada/afghanmission/article/800296--forged-in-the-fire-of-afghanistan>, accessed 25 April 2010.

108   All non-attributed quotes are based on interviews with author.

109   Day noted, "we went through a pretty low period before Clyde [Russell] came in [as CO]. We started to suffer training fatigue – we were among the best, if not the best in the world at hostage rescue." But the problem was – they were never deployed. Many worried they had inherited some RCMP cultural affectations – a police mentality in many ways. The "two way range in Afghanistan forced us to adopt a more warrior mentality."

110   Colonel Mike Day, 5 March 2008. Day became the second commander of Canadian Special Operations Command, in July 2008.

111   The citation package also provided a brief history of CJSOTF (South): CJSOTF(S)/TF K-Bar – in October 2001 in response to the terrorist attacks of 9/11 Commander US Central Command (CENTCOM) directed the establishment of a combined joint special operation task force to conduct special operations in Southern Afghanistan to destroy, degrade and neutralize Taliban and Al-Qaeda forces. Captain (Navy) Robert Harward, US Navy Commander Naval Special Warfare Group One/Commander TF K-Bar began conducting maritime interception operations in the Arabian Sea. Ground combat operations began on 22 November 2001 when attached units conducted a 96 hour clandestine SR in advance of a United States marine corps (USMC) assault on landing zone (LZ) Rhino in Southern Afghanistan while other units conducted advance force operations, reconnaissance and assessment of alternate landing zones. On 24 November his Naval Special Warfare Task Force provided terminal guidance for the USMC assault on LZ Rhino. After seizure of LZ Rhino, Captain Harward stood up CJSOTF(S) on 26 November and forces conducted a series of SR, DA and SSE missions to detect, apprehend and destroy Taliban and AQ forces. The TF provided critical SR in support of conventional forces during Operation Anaconda in March 2002. From October 2001 to March 2002, CJSOTF-SOUTH conducted 42 SR, 23 DA and SSE missions, directed 147 close air support missions, intercepted and searched 12 ships, apprehended 112 detainees and inflicted over 115 enemy casualties. All at a cost of three friendly casualties – one dead – two wounded.

112   DND News Release NR-04.098, dated 8 December 2004, "Joint Task Force Two Members Receive U.S. Presidential Unit Citation."

113   Six awards (1 Meritorious Service Cross (MSC), 1 Meritorious Service Medal (MSM) and 6 Mention in Dispatches (MiD)) were eventually given. Lieutenant-Colonel Mike Beaudette received a MSC; Paul, Devin, Mike and Bruce all received MiDs.

114   DND News Release NR-04.098, dated 8 December 2004, "Joint Task Force Two Members Receive U.S. Presidential Unit Citation."

115   Canadian Alliance, "Expansion of JTF 2 Dangerous," 7 February 2002, http://circ.jmellon.com/docs/txt/joint_task_force_2_expansion_dangerous.txt, accessed 12 March 2004.

116   Ambassador Paul Cellucci, Conference of Defence Associates Conference, Ottawa, 7 March 2005.

117   General Rick Hillier, A *Soldier First: Bullets, Bureaucrats and the Politics of War* (Toronto: HarperCollins Publishers Ltd., 2009), 368.

118   David Pugliese, "Canadian Forces Make Mark in Afghanistan," *Defence News*, 19 May 2008, 18.

119   Paul Robinson, "We can't just take them out; It's tempting to simply fire a missile or sniper bullet and be done with suspected terrorist leaders – but it's a lot more complicated than that", *The Ottawa Citizen*, 27 May 2008.

120   Lee Winsor, David Charters and Brent Wilson, *Kandahar Tour: The Turning Point in Canada's Afghan Mission* (Mississauga: John Wiley & Sons Canada, Ltd., 2008), 167. Tier 1 Taliban refers to the hard-line insurgents who fight for ideological, political and/or religious reasons, as opposed to Tier 2 insurgents who are considered guns for hire, young men driven largely to fight due to monetary considerations or coercion.

121   Lieutenant-Colonel Rob Walker, interview with author, 5 October 2008.

122   David Pugliese, "Canadian Forces Make Mark in Afghanistan," *Defence News*, 19 May 2008, 18.

123   "Talking Points. CF Transformation Initiative," CDS GO/FO Symposium, Cornwall, February 2005, 3.

124   *Canadian Special Operations Command – 2008*; and *CANSOFCOM Capstone Concept for Special Operations 2009*, 8.

125   Hillier's desire to transform the CF was based on his perception that the CF had to become more responsive, adaptive and relevant. He declared, "We need to transform the Canadian Forces completely, from a Cold War-oriented, bureaucratic, process-focused organization into a modern, combat-capable force, where the three elements – navy, army

and air force, enabled by Special Forces – all worked together as one team to protect Canada by conducting operations effectively at home and abroad. I envisioned a flexible, agile and quick-thinking military that would be able to bring exactly the right kind of forces to accomplish whatever mission they were given, whether it was responding to a natural disaster like a tsunami or an ice storm or fighting a counter-insurgency war in southern Afghanistan." General Rick Hillier, *A Soldier First: Bullets, Bureaucrats and the Politics of War* (Toronto: HarperCollins Publishers Ltd., 2009), 323.

126   Canada, *Canadian Special Operations Command – 2008* (Ottawa: DND, 2008); and Canada, *CANSOFCOM Capstone Concept for Special Operations 2009* (Ottawa: DND, 2009), 8.

127   The events of 11 September 2001, led to the immediate CBRN response capability of the CF to be assigned to a new dedicated high readiness unit, the Joint Nuclear, Biological Chemical Defence Company (JNBCD Company). By June 2002, the MND had approved the project that enabled the creation of the unit as well as a stand-alone CBRN Response Team (RT) to form the CF component of the National CBRN RT with the RCMP and Public Health Canada partners. Since 1 February 2006 the unit has been a part of CANSOFCOM. Its name was officially changed to the CJIRU-CBRN in September 2007.

128   High Value Tasks (HVT) tasks are defined as follows:

Special Reconnaissance, which are missions conducted to collect or verify information of strategic or operational significance. These actions complement and refine other collection methods but are normally directed upon extremely significant areas of interest.

Direct Action, which are short duration strikes and other precise small-scale offensive actions conducted by special operation forces to seize, destroy, capture, exploit, recover or damage designated targets. Direct action differs from conventional offensive actions in the level of physical and political risk, operational techniques, and the degree of discriminate and precise use of force to achieve specific objectives.

Counter-proliferation, which refers to actions to limit the possession, use, acquisition or transit of weapons of mass effect (WME). It includes actions to locate, seize, capture and recover WME and in some instances under the Proliferation Security Initiative prevent the improper employment of dual use materials.

Non-Combatant Evacuation Operations, which refer to operations that are conducted to assist the Department of Foreign Affairs in the evacuations of Canadians from foreign host nations. SOTF can play a key-supporting role through the provision of early special reconnaissance, providing strategic communications links and security advice.

Defence, Diplomacy, and Military Assistance, which refers to operations that contribute to nation building through assistance to select states through the provision of specialized military advice, training and assistance (e.g., Candidate Physical Ability Test (CPAT), Military Training Assistance Program (MTAP)). CANSOFCOM contributions are managed within the Command's areas of expertise.

129   Canada, *Canadian Special Operations Command – 2008* (Ottawa: DND, 2008); and *Canada, CANSOFCOM Capstone Concept for Special Operations 2009* (Ottawa: DND, 2009).

130   David Pugliese, "Canadian Forces Make Mark in Afghanistan," *Defence News*, 19 May 2008, 18.

131   David Pugliese, "Military Forms New Quick Reaction Task Force," *The Ottawa Citizen*, <http://www.ottawacitizen.com/news/Military+forms+quick+reaction+task+force/3290244/story.html>, accessed 18 July 2010.

132   Ibid.

133   Ibid.

134   CANFORGEN 030/08 CDS 003/08, 041846Z Feb 08.

135   CANFORGEN 029/08 CDS 002/08, 041846Z Feb 08.

136   David Pugliese, "Getting the drop on Special Ops," *The Ottawa Citizen,* 17 July, 2010.

CHAPTER 1

137   Ian Elliot, "Special forces different from video game portrayal," *The Whig-Standard*, <http://www.thewhig.com/ArticleDisplay aspx?e=2882136>, accessed 26 January 2011.

138   Vice-Admiral Larry Murray, interview with Colonel Bernd Horn and Dr. Bill Bentley, 6 October 2010.

139   Cited in David Pugliese, "Getting the drop on Special Ops," *The Ottawa Citizen,* July 17, 2010.

140   Cited in Ibid.

CHAPTER 2

SPECIAL OPERATIONS FORCES
FORCE DEVELOPMENT

COLONEL BOB KELLY

Within the discussion of Special Operations Forces as a national enabler, it is important to explore the topic of force development. Force development can be defined as "the ability to conceive, design, build and, eventually, manage new and renewed capabilities." As such, its relationship to SOF as a national enabler is clear: through force development, Canadian Special Operations Forces Command is able to continually evolve to meet current and upcoming challenges.

First, it is prudent to dispel some myths and provide some facts about Canadian Special Operations Forces. The first widely circulated myth is that SOF and their activities are extremely expensive. The truth is that SOF are quite cost-effective. Since they are not equipment platform based (i.e. they do not rely on ships, planes, light armoured vehicles (LAVs), etc.), there are, in fact, significant efficiencies in cost.

The second myth is that there are not enough quality personnel to fill SOF should growth be required, subsequently making growth impossible. Rather, the truth is that there are many personnel in the Canadian Forces sea, land and air environments who have the proper talents and skill sets to aptly fill SOF positions. Though SOF cannot be built quickly, it can currently be done from within the CF population.

The third myth is that SOF are agile because they cut corners and bypass normal governance procedures and approvals. Conversely, the truth is that CANSOFCOM is bound by all the same mandated procedures and approvals as any other member of the CF, Department of National Defence and Government of Canada. For day to day procurement, the same competitive process and dollar thresholds apply to CANSOFCOM as to any other government organization.

A final widely circulated myth is that CANSOFCOM overdoes operational security (OPSEC) to avoid scrutiny and hide the fact that it does not follow accepted governance and policy. The truth is that CANSOFCOM follows all GoC policies and procedures. OPSEC is driven by the reality that there are individuals/groups or other nations that seek to exploit weaknesses. Professionalism, credibility and trust – as well as, on occasion, a degree of "invisibility" – are required for inclusion in working with our allies. Simply put, OPSEC is mandatory in enabling and allowing the safe and effective sharing of information between partners.

These truths about CANSOF underscore the importance of good force development. The building blocks of force development can be described using the acronym PRICIE:

> Personnel;
> Research & Development;
> Infrastructure and Organization;
> Concepts, Doctrine & Collective Training;
> Information Management; and
> Equipment, Supplies and Services.

Each aforementioned element represents a crucial link in the force development chain. First, the correct personnel need to be selected, trained and retained. Indeed, the core strength of CANSOF is their people, be they operators or supporters. Next, to remain on the cutting edge of new technologies, ideas, and tactics, techniques and procedures demands that research and development be continuously undertaken. Having the proper infrastructure and organizational development facilitates this process and is reflected in SOF concepts, doctrine and collective training. Information management is also key to successful SOF as having accurate, complete information at the correct time can mean the difference between success and failure in operations. Moreover, ensuring the correct equipment and supplies are available facilitates CANSOFCOM's ability to supply an essential and unique service to the GoC.

Enabled with resources and good practices, CANSOFCOM's first priority is to support security, which includes planned events, to pre-empt potentially catastrophic events from occurring. If this first priority is not met, CANSOFCOM's next major objective is to provide the GoC with an immediate and effective response to unplanned events. As such, the things that drive and support high readiness must be considered in all force design work. This requirement means that: training must always be current; travel limitations must be adhered to in order to meet recall timings; equipment must be kept operationally ready and available to accommodate any environment; personnel must have both specific and generic skill sets in order to cover a maximum range of tasks; geographic prepositioning is required so as to provide intelligence and early warning; and personnel must always be fit to deploy.

In order to meet these requirements, CANSOFCOM's main outputs are Special Operations Task Forces, which are produced through an Integrated Operating Concept. Each of the four units of the Command (Joint Task Force Two, Canadian Special Operations Regiment, 427 Special Operations Aviation Squadron and Canadian Joint Incident Response Unit – Chemical, Biological, Radiological and Nuclear) have a role in Force Generating aspects of the SOTFs, which are the Force Employment entities used in operations. The four current SOTFs are:

Immediate Reaction Task Force, which is domestically focused, globally deployable and led by JTF 2; Chemical, Biological, Radiological, Nuclear and Explosives Task Force, which is domestically focused, globally deployable and CJIRU-led; Standing Deployed Task Force (SDTF), which is globally focused with a rotating lead; and ARROWHEAD, a globally focused, domestically deployable, CSOR-led SOTF.

These four types of SOTFs align nicely with the CFDS, which provides a roadmap for the modernization of the CF. As described by the GoC, the CFDS "puts forward clear roles and missions for the Canadian Forces, outlining a level of ambition that will enable the CF to maintain the ability to deliver excellence at home, be a strong and reliable partner in the defence of North America, and project leadership abroad by making meaningful contributions to operations overseas."[1] As part of its mandate, the CFDS outlines six core missions. The missions and SOTF matches to the missions assigned by the CFDS are as follows:

CFDS Missions:	Type of Task Force
1. Conduct daily domestic and continental operations, including in the Arctic and through NORAD	IRTF, CBRNE TF
2. Support a major international event in Canada, such as the 2010 Olympics	IRTF, CBRNE TF
3. Respond to a major terrorist attack	IRTF, CBRNE TF
4. Support civilian authorities during a crisis in Canada, such as a natural disaster	As required
5. Lead and/or conduct a major international operation for an extended period	SDTF
6. Deploy forces in response to crises elsewhere in the world for shorter periods	TF ARROWHEAD or IRTF, CBRNE TF

Given these missions and CANSOFCOM's mandate to be there when the government calls, several conclusions can be drawn about present and future SOF operations and force development requirements. First, it is clear that the SOF area of responsibility is global. As such, command needs to have expertise in all environments. In order to accomplish this task, there is a need to have certain units specialized for specific environments rather than all units trying to cover all environments. Moreover, SOF may be required to operate in a pandemic/contaminated environment for extended periods. In this type of operating environment, and in fact most of the operating environments in which SOF will find themselves, there needs to be both dedicated enablers and resources pre-positioned to reduce the time-to-effect ratio. Research and development funding, including cyber development, will help facilitate this goal. Additionally, where possible, the use of machines instead of humans contributes to economy of forces and can also act as a force multiplier. Indeed, personnel capacity must allow for a training and reconstitution cycle. Recognizing demographic realities by recruiting from the street in addition to the CF stream, as well as ensuring a reasonable operational tempo for personnel, will help facilitate this objective.

In order to be effectively employed and to help to delineate where SOF are best suited and where the larger conventional force is a more logical choice, it is important to keep the four SOF "truths" in mind: first, humans are more important than hardware; second, quality is better than quantity; third, SOF cannot be mass-produced; and, finally, competent SOF cannot be created after emergencies occur. As such, SOF should be employed to shape the operating environment early, preferably pre-positioned before warning, either permanently or temporarily, to help counter time and space limitations. They should be used for precision, non-routine operations where a higher than normal skill level is required, such as an environment where unique equipment and training are needed or where the situation is politically sensitive.

SOF must have the ability to overwhelm any adversary through overmatch as well as more than one method to achieve outcomes through an arsenal approach to capabilities.

SOF are at ease in both a technologically rich or technologically denied environment, and they excel in ambiguous and volatile situations. Intelligence led at all levels, SOF are able to seize and maintain the initiative. In fact, SOF can be seen as a "wild card" or "Force '19'", which implies that of the 18 scenarios prepared by the CF, SOF are prepared for the yet to be written 19th scenario.

In sum, CANSOF provide the GoC with a unique and essential service, and clearly serve as an important national enabler. As such, force development, or the ability to conceive, design, build and eventually manage new and renewed capabilities, is a vital function in keeping CANSOFCOM able to support the GoC. Force development in the areas of personnel, equipment and organization allow CANSOF to meet challenges facing the government. Thus, enabled by motivated and talented personnel, CANSOF provide an economically savvy defence option to the GoC that is particularly valuable in high risk, rapid response and/or politically sensitive areas.

NOTES

1   Government of Canada, *Canada First Defence Strategy*, <http://www.forces.gc.ca/site/pri/first-premier/index-eng.asp>, accessed 12 January 2011.

CHAPTER 3

SPECIAL OPERATIONS FORCES: SHAPING THE AREA OF OPERATIONS

LIEUTENANT-COLONEL MIKE ROULEAU

Research and current practice indicates that disproportionate demands will be placed on high-utility, low-density joint enablers like Special Operations Forces in the future security environment. As such, it is important to understand how SOF shape the area of operations and how this effect can be maximized in the future.

Fundamentally, SOF shape the area of operations by providing cognitive responses to complex situations. This capability is primarily enabled due to the high calibre of their personnel and their capability to perform unique tasks. Beyond simply being effective, however, SOF must be seen as a trustworthy and credible partner by today's defence community and that of the future. Thus, in order to maintain their competitive edge, SOF must continue to be innovative and capable in a variety of tasks, as well as monitor growth and media communications effectively.

PROVIDING COGNITIVE RESPONSES TO COMPLEX SITUATIONS

SOF cannot shape the battle-space if they do not first understand the complexities of the contemporary operating environment. As such, cognitive responses to complex situations provide the backdrop to how SOF shape the COE.[1] Notably, there are many issues at play in the COE. First, the subtleties of an adaptive "threatscape" must be understood. Hybrid threats comprised of non-state actors with access to dangerous technologies are an issue. More to the point, trans-national constituencies of radicalized and radi-calizing extremists who competently leverage the global virtual commons to hone their craft represent a threat.[2] Additionally, not only has globalization shrunk the world, it is also shrinking the time and space that national security practitioners have to see, recognize and exploit opportunities. Superimpose on these issues the pervasive media environment and a requirement for enhanced transparency and we begin to understand the challenges facing national security practitioners.

Consequently, today's military officer must fundamentally un-derstand the interplay between policy, strategy and execution in order to manage the interdependencies among them. Possessing a well-developed appreciation for how the machinery of govern-ment works is thus essential for achieving optimal effects in the COE. It is not sufficient to merely be "on receive"; rather, SOF must shape the context of what is possible and, more importantly, what is not.

SOF are particularly suited to this task. SOF's uniqueness in the national security environment lies partly in their breadth across the defence, security and intelligence domains. We must be smart on where Canadian national security strengths lie in order to le-verage for "best fit / best results". We must also be smart on where challenge areas exist so as to contribute to collective improvement. As such, SOF must be, and be seen to be, a productive national security partner.

Indeed, SOF rely on integration. Commanders must persist in their call for the most streamlined, vertical integration possible. Eliminating non-contributing layers of decision-makers enhances clarity, agility and speed across all phases and all activities. Inso-far as horizontal integration is concerned, smartly placing finite human capital across organizations is the only way to get the levels of integrated SOF, whole-of-government, and coalition fusion that today's operating environment requires. Comprehensive solutions require painfully comprehensive and necessary investments.

Seeing national security through a far more expansive lens than just nations, security and defence is what is demanded. National security in a 21st century context is about demography, monetary and fiscal policies, energy resources and climate change, to name just a few. The "so what?" for today's national security practitioner is that we must continually expand our personal portfolios in order to both shape our operations and be successful on the ground.

SPECIAL FORCES WITH SPECIAL MISSIONS

SOF forces are comprised of high-calibre individuals who execute demanding tasks. SOF do things others can do, but to a higher degree of fidelity (eg. Direct Action, Strategic Reconnaissance, Recce-in-Force and insertion methods, just to mention a few). Moreover, they do things that others cannot. A unique individual is required to accomplish these tasks.

These intelligent, motivated, fit, committed, humorous (if at times slightly irreverent) troops thrive in ambiguity. Literally and figuratively, they see clearly in the dark, make workable sense out of chaos, and make appropriate and timely decisions absent of the ability to "call home" in order to achieve the desired effect.

Collectively, these highly motivated and skilled personnel provide the Government of Canada with a value-added national security partner in the form of Canadian Special Operations Forces, thereby enriching the dialogue at the political-military and military-strategic levels and enabling operational and tactical successes. Strategically, SOF are a unique asset in the GoC toolbox and are always available, remaining constantly on very high readiness. Furthermore, they are able to provide invaluable politically informed military advice that allows political leaders to make informed decisions. Moreover, they have the personal where-withal and technology to move in high risk, politically sensitive areas. Additionally, militarily, SOF act as a vanguard force for tactics, techniques and procedures, with doctrinal advancement and equipment matters often cascading onto field forces. Importantly, SOF also act as a joint binding agent regularly interacting with air, maritime and land forces making the Canadian Forces whole greater than the sum of its parts.

Operationally, SOF impedes enemy time, space and will. Centred completely on the intelligence discipline (and please note the use of the word "discipline" vice "function," underscoring the criticality of intelligence), they strike, or are feared to be planning to strike, enemy command and control (C2) and key enablers. This ability keeps enemy leaders on the move in order to avoid becoming geo-located and helps to erode their influence. Moreover, SOF contribute a level of sophistication to the intelligence, surveillance and reconnaissance (ISR) battle through integrated and inter-agency cooperation that enables the overall campaign. It is interesting to note the open source reporting of US white SOF elements working in tandem with the United States Agency for International Development (USAID) in Afghanistan in areas beyond the reach of Provincial Reconstruction Teams. Here we see the seeds of pragmatism over purism flourishing.

Tactically, SOF enter the enemy's observation, orientation, decision, and action (OODA)-loop and, on the basis of creativity and audaciousness in the battle-space, they leverage superior TTPs, shock action, unparalleled warrior spirit and technological over-match to render the asymmetric battle-space more symmetric. Strategic reconnaissance and direct action strikes help set local conditions for main force success. Well-synchronized and properly sequenced, these mission-sets contribute across the clear, hold and build continuum. That being said, such operations should not be viewed as decisive in the context of counter-insurgency (COIN).

Through all of these processes, however, tactical SOF commanders will be challenged to assess demand against supply. They must apply the fundamental tests of: appropriateness; feasibility; justifiability; and sustainability. In order to determine their advice to superior commanders, they must ask: is it a SOF mission?; is it doable?; do the potential rewards warrant the risks?; and, is it logistically manageable? And, of course, all of these decisions are superimposed on the *prima facie* requirement of adhering to the Geneva Conventions and Laws of Armed Conflict.

To summarize, the assumption must be that the SOF operator's ability to shoot, move and communicate is beyond reproach. But the SOF commander, from detachment to formation, is the one who must carry the greatest personal burden. He/she must be dexterous and critical in thought, decisive and bold in action, and resilient enough to wake up the next day and set new conditions all over again, whether on operations or back at home garrisons in the office.

MAINTAINING A COMPETITIVE EDGE

Without laying down the details of the future security environment, it suffices to say that: wars of choice will increasingly cede to wars of necessity; military engagements whose enterprise centres on state-building will be increasingly scrutinized; and precision effects will continue to be in high demand.

As such, SOF need to be relentless in investing to establish themselves as trusted and credible partners within the defence community. Failure to do so allows for mythology to set in where negative stigmas can become accepted truisms. In order to prevent this process from happening, investments in time, people and tailored information is essential.

SOF must also retain a deliberate dual track focus of excellence. First, they must ensure that current operational outputs squarely aligned with CF, and subsequently SOF, core values. Next, while still aligning with core values, they must focus on stimulating progress for tomorrow's enhanced capabilities.

Being small and nimble with minimal institutional overhead is a SOF strength because it allows for agility; but it is also a SOF weakness because it makes it difficult to marshal one's position in the face of a complex military bureaucracy.

All of these issues are factors that need to be considered in order to maintain the relevance of SOF in the COE. But it is not just about innovating. It is about innovating how SOF innovate. Bottom up, top down or hybrid groupings all have a place at the table. If everything SOF are experimenting with works, it should tell us we lack a culture of risk-taking and audacity; conversely, if too little works, we are wasting resources and need to re-scale our efforts.

Balancing precision capabilities against the tyranny of "niche" capabilities, those likely to only be used in exceedingly low-probability circumstances, is something SOF cannot afford. The demand/supply dilemma suggests that marginal utility capabilities, sexy and fun though they may be, need to be sacrificed on the altar of necessity.

Moreover, SOF must be watchful of growth and expansion. Retaining an edge or high reliability organizational (HRO) status requires that allocation of decision rights, incentive structures, information flows and unique organizational design be catered to, all of which are dampened to some degree by growth.

Moreover, SOF must continue to have a robust internal debate and dialogue about the balance between communications outreach and operations security. SOF need to fully understand the opportunity cost in support and goodwill that they absorb every time they fail to tell about their many successes.

In conclusion, SOF and their leaders must, above all, remain pragmatic. Do we design to capability or design to cost? The answer is probably a bit of both. There is no room for a purist approach moving forward and I am pleased, as an interested SOF observer, to see that this is largely the track CANSOF is on.

NOTES

1   In this chapter this theme will focus on the Canadian national security context.

2   Marc Sageman, the noted American terrorism scholar, speaks at length on this phenomenon.

CHAPTER 4

SHAPING OPERATIONS:
SPECIAL OPERATIONS FORCES
AS A NATIONAL ENABLER

US COLONEL (RETIRED) JAMES F. POWERS, JR.

Regardless of nationality or trade, many people within the defence community recognize the enabling characteristics of Special Operations Forces. These enabling characteristics are less easily identifiable, however, by non-SOF members – including conventional military operators and planners – at the operational and strategic levels. In fact, at the strategic level of policy/strategy development (including resource allocation), most decision-makers and resource providers lack sufficient knowledge of the enabling capabilities of SOF to the contemporary operating environment. This dearth of knowledge hinders a full appreciation and utilization of SOF to assess, consider and, potentially, shape strategies, plans and emerging concepts. This lack of understanding at higher levels of military planning represents a serious challenge to the effective employment of SOF in the COE, as well as the future operating environment. Thankfully, however, through a conscious effort on the part of the Special Operations community, this gap is beginning to close.

Notably, and increasingly since the end of the Vietnam War, the numbers of US Congressmen and Staffers having prior military experience, and thus a degree of familiarization with SOF capabilities and limitations, have been decreasing. While this relationship is perhaps not unexpected, it does mean that a liaison needs to be nurtured through which those savvy with the codified, implied and emerging Special Operations activities and enabling characteristics can inform national policy and decision-makers. Indeed, much can be learned by looking at SOF from an historical context. Such an appreciation will serve to inform emerging plans and highlight considerations for future activities.

SPECIAL OPERATIONS FORCES

As a frame of reference, it is first important to identify those specific activities which SOF are legally charged to execute. The following activities, codified in the US Code (Title X – Armed Forces), are currently specified for US SOF. According to the US Code, Special Operations activities include each of the following insofar as it relates to Special Operations:

- Direct Action

- Strategic Reconnaissance

- Unconventional Warfare

- Foreign Internal Defense

- Civil Affairs

- Psychological Operations

- Counterterrorism

- Humanitarian Assistance

- Theatre Search and Rescue

- Other activities as may be specified by the President or the Secretary of Defense.

Notably, the last specific point allows for a broad application of SOF at the discretion of key individuals as the situation dictates. As such, it is important to explore some of the probable tenets of the FOE.

THE FUTURE OPERATING ENVIRONMENT

Looking historically across the experiences of the world's militaries, several assumptions concerning the FOE can be posited. Importantly, each suggests a strong need for a rapid, responsive, and capable force able to perform unconventional or special tasks – in today's lexicon, unconventional/special forces.

First, it is quite probable that contemporary, emerging and future conflicts will continue to highlight western military doctrinal gaps. This disconnect should not be surprising, particularly to those having an avid interest in military history, lessons derived from case studies, and the process whereby operations affect doctrine. Notably, these gaps are derived through no lack of effort as the US spends a lot of time and energy developing doctrine to generally serve as a foundation for operations, training, equipment requirements, and force development. Nonetheless, there will always be situations that arise for which there is no stated doctrinal protocol and/or appropriate equipment. The gaps that emerge between doctrinal principles, associated equipment requirements and battlefield situations provide the rationale and genesis for unconventional/special activities. The simple fact is that planners at every level will never be able to totally anticipate every conceivable requirement – there will always be gaps between doctrine and the requirements dictated by battlefield realities. This lack of symmetry is not a human frailty; we must simply remain cognizant that these gaps will emerge. Moreover, while belligerents generally rely initially on doctrine, in the chaos of conflict and war, they usually resort to *ad hoc*, expedient measures if required. This is just the nature of conflict where the unexpected is to be expected. This situation simply underscores the need for an adaptive force such as SOF.

Second, it is likely that the reality of a national level *grand strategy* will remain remote in the FOE. American professional military educational institutions belabour the tenets of strategy (i.e., ends, ways and means) but, unfortunately, most politicians have not been afforded the same privileges and/or education. A *grand strategy* developed theoretically by the National Security Council and tasking each of the departments within the Executive Branch with specific associated supporting tasks has appeared to have eluded the US capability or desire. The diplomatic, informational, economic, financial, intelligence and law enforcement tasks suggested for a comprehensive *grand strategy* appear to have been somehow omitted from American defense strategy. Consequently, the US Armed Forces is directed to execute operations sometimes without the benefit of knowing where their actions fit into the overall strategy (if, in fact, there is one). In other words, synchronization of military actions with non-military activities appears to range from little to non-existent. An understanding of the roles and capabilities of the US Armed Forces and, in particular US SOF, by government planners could help to mitigate any further widening of the aforementioned gap.

Finally, the FOE will likely require a military force that is capable of operating between the *seams* of specified tasks. This tenet of the FOE is particularly valid for SOF since, on occasion, it has been quite broad. Moreover, there are natural seams that develop between conventional missions, the capabilities of general purpose forces and strategic goals that lie just outside of the reach of any one agency or department of the US federal government. In order to decrease/lessen any friction, orchestration of operations and activities within these seams requires a high level of cohesion between conventional forces and SOF. More importantly, where specific legal guidance is either absent or unspecified, these operations demand that the spirit of the US Code be followed at all times.

THE LEGAL BASIS OF SOF AND STATUTORY GAPS

Each nation has its own processes and protocols for determining the basis for its unconventional forces whether they be resources-constrained, mission-focused or strategy-based. Thus, individual nations are responsible for the assessment and justification of, and the establishment of a legal basis for, their unconventional/special forces.[1] Although there are many names for these forces and operations depending on the country, their purpose is uniform: to execute those emerging tasks not previously assigned to general purpose/conventional forces.

Generally, each nation has enacted laws prescribing roles, functions and missions for its armed forces. However, para-military, criminal/terrorist organizations may elect to not follow any prescribed laws of armed conflict. This situation presents a tactical dilemma for US Armed Forces. To fight in the same manner as the belligerents may inherently require the US Armed Forces to break national and international laws regarding armed conflict; to not fight in the same manner allows the belligerents to have a distinct asymmetric advantage. Notably, US protocols may require a Presidential Finding in order to facilitate military operations against these types of belligerents, whereas other nations may not require such a process.

Regardless, every nation's military strategists will likely continue to experience three ever-present gaps concerning what their armed forces and, particularly SOF, are prescribed to do and the constraints under which they perform. The first such gap concerns the essential tasks versus the available resources. When this situation occurs, the US military generally derives another course of action that considers this constraint or seeks relief from higher authority of that task unless assets can be provided.

The second gap reflects statutory responsibilities versus doctrinal roles and functions. Each may morph over time according to stimuli, but the dilemma occurs when the statutory responsibilities are not reflected in the doctrine/equipment and *vice versa*. Simply stated, a legal "responsibility" to act may exceed the current capability, whereas, on the other hand, a statutory/legal responsibility may prevent the execution of a certain task previously directed.

Third, national imperatives for action compared with roles, functions and resources will also almost always be separated by a chasm. Sometimes a decision by the National Command Authorities (in the US the President and Secretary of Defense) for national action takes precedence over all else and military units are thrust into an action for which they may have neither sufficient training nor the proper time to prepare – usually the latter. It is up to the civilian leadership, based on input from the military advisors, to decide whether or not a military presence is worth that risk. Certainly, historical examples can be used to argue either side.

A SELECTED HISTORY OF SOF

Office of Strategic Services

Canadian and American SOF have a common ancestor: the British Special Operations Executive. The foundations of today's US SOF doctrine, founded in historical vignettes from as early as the Revolutionary War's Francis Marion, "The Swamp Fox," through "Merrill's Marauders," to the Civilian Irregular Defense Group Program in Vietnam and continuing through to today's operations in Afghanistan, Iraq and the Philippines, are linked to the Second World War organization established to develop strategic intelligence: the Office of Strategic Services. The United States Special Operations Command (USSOCOM) still maintains that important relationship with former members via close partnership and coordination with the OSS Society. The efforts and exploits of these innovative and clever men and women enabled the Allies during the Second World War to exploit economy of force missions throughout Europe and the Pacific theatres and later Indo-China through their small foot-print, intelligence-gathering and advisory methodologies.

First Special Service Force

Designated as the First Special Service Force, the *Devil's Brigade* was a joint Second World War American-Canadian commando unit trained at Fort Harrison near Helena, Montana in the US.

Civilian Irregular Defense Group Program (Vietnam)

In the early days of US advisory assistance to the South Vietnamese Government, the US believed that paramilitary forces should be developed from the mountain/highland minority groups of South Vietnam in order to strengthen and broaden the counter-insurgency effort of the Vietnamese government. Secondly, the Montagnards, Rhade, Nung and other minority groups appeared to be prime targets for North Vietnamese Communist propaganda, partly because of their dissatisfaction with the South Vietnamese government; it was thus important to prevent the Viet Cong from recruiting them and taking complete control of their large and strategic land holdings.

Forty villages were assessed and designated for incorporation into a trial program entitled the Civilian Irregular Defense Group (CIDG) Program. In a joint effort, US and Vietnamese Special Forces troops incorporated recruits for both village defence and the local security force through local village leaders. Before a village could be accepted as a part of the development program, the village chief was required to affirm that everyone in the village would participate in the program and that a sufficient number of people would volunteer for training to provide adequate protection for the village. The program was so popular that villagers soon began recruiting among themselves. Part of the project's popularity undoubtedly stemmed from the fact that the Montagnards could have their weapons back. In the late 1950s all weapons, including the crossbow, had been denied them by the government as reprisal for Viet Cong depredations, and only bamboo spears were allowed until the second week in December 1961, when the government finally gave permission to train and arm the village defenders and strike forces. The strike force would maintain itself in a camp, while the village defenders would return to their homes after receiving training and arms.

Activities within the operational area established in coordination with the province chief and Vietnam Army units in the vicinity consisted of:

- Small local security patrols;

- Ambushes;

- Village defence patrols;

- Local intelligence nets; and

- An alert system in which local men, women, and children reported suspicious movement in the area.

All villages were lightly fortified, with evacuation the primary defensive measure and some use of family shelters for women and children. Strike force troops remained on the alert in the base centre at Buon Enao to serve as a reaction force and the villages maintained a mutually supporting defensive system wherein village defenders rushed to each other's assistance. The system included Vietnamese villages as well.

Logistical support was provided directly by US agencies outside Vietnamese and US Army supply channels. US Special Forces served as the vehicle for providing this support at village level, although US participation was *indirect* in that distribution of weapons and pay of troops were accomplished through local leaders.

In the field of civic assistance, the Village Self-Defense Program provided community development along with military security. Village defenders and strike force medics conducted clinics, sometimes moving into new villages and thus expanding the project.

The program was considered a resounding success. Village defenders and strike forces accepted the training and weapons enthusiastically and became strongly motivated to oppose the Viet Cong, against whom they fought well. Programs such as the CIDG program enabled both the US and South Vietnamese Governments to implement economy of force measures and thus weight other, more important operations in the overall campaign.

Operation IVORY COAST (North Vietnam, Son Tay Raid)

In 1970, the US identified the names of over 500 American prisoners of war (POW) who were being held by the North Vietnamese. Sources indicated the location of the prisoners was in the vicinity of Son Tay, North Vietnam. The conditions under which these prisoners were being held were reportedly atrocious; sources further indicated cruel punishment by their captors. A planning group studied the possibility of conducting a night raid on a North Vietnamese POW camp and found that an attack on the camp at Son Tay was feasible and should be attempted.

Two months later, Operation IVORY COAST commenced to organize, plan, and train for the mission. Brilliantly executed, American casualties for the raid were one wounded; in addition, two aircraft were lost in the operation. North Vietnamese casualties were estimated at 100-200 killed. Intelligence later revealed that the prisoners originally held at Son Tay had been moved earlier to a camp fifteen miles away. While some intelligence indicated this immediately prior to the raid, there was not time to change the target. Despite this intelligence failure, the raid was deemed a tactical success due to its near flawless execution.

The inherent skills possessed by the members of the 6th and 7th Special Forces Groups facilitated the rapid train-up and rehearsals for this operation. Investing the ground combat planning and execution phases in SOF enabled this strategic raid. Without this on-hand capability, the National Command Authorities would have had two other choices: form an *ad hoc* force from either a single or multiple Service components; or assign the mission to the general purpose/conventional forces.

Operation EAGLE CLAW (Iran)

In November 1979, Iranian militant students seized the American Embassy in Teheran. By December 1979, a rescue force was selected and a training program was under way. Training exercises were conducted through March 1980 and the Joint Chiefs of Staff (JCS) approved mission execution on 16 April 1980. Between 19 and 23 April, the forces deployed to Southwest Asia.

On 24 April 1980, after six months of failed negotiations, the National Command Authorities executed Operation EAGLE CLAW to free the American hostages.

The plan called for eight US Navy RH-53D helicopters to fly 600 miles to a forward refueling point designated as *Desert One* and, under the cover of darkness, refuel from KC-130 tankers, load a 120-person US Army assault team and proceed to two additional hide sites. One of the GO/NO-GO parameters for the mission was a minimum of six operational helicopters. Within four hours, two helicopters aborted due to mechanical failure. The remaining aircraft were delayed due to weather, with one of them not operational due to a hydraulic leak.

While repositioning to refuel from the C-130s, one helicopter collided with a C-130. The two aircraft were quickly engulfed in flames. The on-scene commander decided at that point to load the survivors of the collision and all the other helicopter crews in the C-130s and depart. Eight men had been killed and five more injured. Five intact helicopters, the burned wreckage of the helicopter and C-130, and the dead, were left behind.

Unlike Operation IVORY COAST, analysis of the mission concluded that there were significant problems. Command and control during the execution of the operation was flawed. Violating the principle of unity of command, there was no designated mission commander for six months, hampering the training, planning, and execution of the operation. There were separate commanders for site security, helicopter force, ground force, KC-130, and landing support. The ground force commander had GO/NO-GO authority, but he was not known to the rest of the force. Joint training as we know today, was not conducted; it was conducted at the individual and unit level within each component. Although there were a few rehearsals that assessed specific portions of the operation, there was no full dress rehearsal. Compounding the problem were communications inter-operability and procedural restraints.

Appointed by the JCS to study the operation, a six-member commission concluded that the Navy and Marine pilots selected for the operation had little experience in long-range overland navigation or refueling from C-130s yet were selected though more than a hundred qualified Air Force H-53 pilots were available. Another issue was the lack of a comprehensive readiness evaluation and mission rehearsal program. From the beginning, training was not conducted in a truly joint manner; it was compartmentalized and held at scattered locations throughout the US. The limited rehearsals that were conducted assessed only portions of the total mission. Also at issue was the number of helicopters used. The commission concluded that at least ten and perhaps as many as twelve helicopters should have been launched to guarantee the minimum of six required for completion of the mission. The plan was also criticized for using the hopscotch method of ground refueling instead of air refueling as was used for the Son Tay raid. By air refueling en route, the commission thought the entire Desert One scenario could have been avoided.

No one likes failure, but in this case the Holloway Commission Report provided the impetus and path to forge a new paradigm for ensuring these violated principles never occurred again through *ad hoc*, Service-driven arrangements. Without the individual failures and doctrinal violations of Operation EAGLE CLAW, we would not have the USSOCOM today. In this particular operation, the inherent capabilities of SOF were not permitted to flourish and become a force multiplier. The old ways of cobbling together a force, conducting compartmented training and then attempting to orchestrate the mission without a full rehearsal proved to be the telltale flaw. The new model, established over the objections of each sitting and former Service chief, was a new command for Special Operations Forces – USSOCOM.

Operation PROVIDE COMFORT (Southern Turkey/Northern Iraq)

In the aftermath of allied combat operations during Operation DESERT STORM, Saddam Hussein drove the Kurdish peoples of Iraq towards the Turkish and Iranian borders. From best accounts, approx 1.5 million Kurds fled their homes with little to no sustaining supplies and were scattered in groups along the southern Turkish and northern Iraqi borders. The allied operation executed to stabilize, coordinate and synchronize humanitarian assistance relief efforts and set the conditions for their return to Iraq was called Operation PROVIDE COMFORT. Commanded initially by a Joint Special Operations Task Force (JSOTF) established from Special Operations Command – Europe (SOCEOR), assets (10th Special Forces Group and 39th Special Operations Wing) were inserted into these scattered groups and organized the Kurds into *de facto* camps whereby assessments of what was needed and where could be made. The inherent capabilities of these SOCEUR SOF to rapidly establish a JSOTF and deploy with familiar command and control systems and structures enabled the US European Command to then bring in Allied ground and air units for the large-scale recovery efforts.

Combined Joint Special Operations Task Force (Philippines)

Following the tragic events of 9/11, the USSOCOM deployed elements of the 1st Special Forces Group to the Philippines to facilitate counter-terrorism training and assistance to the ongoing efforts of the Philippine Government. The capabilities of American SOF, already well-known to the Philippine armed forces, thus enabled the Commander, US Pacific Command, to advise, influence and monitor counter-terrorism efforts while saving assigned and apportioned general purpose forces for normal operations, training and other military-to-military initiatives. This resident, in-theatre capability regarding CT provides each of our Geographic Combatant Commanders with an unsurpassed entry point with the nations in their respective areas of responsibility.

Operation IRAQI FREEDOM (Iraq)

The situation in Iraq following initial combat operations set the stage for opening a second front in the North using indigenous forces as a para-military force. This task – not one generically associated with general purpose forces – provided the classic Unconventional Warfare opportunity for American SOF to assist the Joint Force Ground Component Commander to implement yet another economy of force strategy and thus general purpose forces for their doctrinal tasks.

Operation ENDURING FREEDOM (Afghanistan)

Of all the enabling activities executed in Afghanistan thus far, the one most likely to capture the attention of the media and other militaries studying the successes and failures are the Provincial Reconstruction Teams (PRTs). These composite teams – built largely around SOF elements but including not only general purpose forces but also other US Government agency personnel and teams – are returning normalcy to the countryside and thus freeing the larger combat/general purpose forces for other combat and stability operations. The success of these teams, using innovative and culturally-based strategies, has been one of the major successes of the Afghanistan Campaign.

CONCLUSION

These selective vignettes illustrate how SOF can enable national military and national security strategies. They illustrate the challenges that can occur when the unique capabilities of SOF are not recognized by military strategists and politicians, as well as the benefits that can be derived when SOF are appropriately tasked. While gaps in the FOE concerning doctrine and the employment of *grand strategy* will without doubt remain, the proper employment of SOF can help to bridge these gaps, as well as establish a near seamless interface between SOF and conventional forces. Moreover, the proper employment of SOF also helps to mitigate statutory gaps including: essential tasks versus available resources; statutory responsibilities versus doctrinal roles and functions; and national imperatives for actions compared with roles, functions and resources. While many decision-makers and resource providers at the strategic level of policy and strategy development may continue to gain and maintain sufficient knowledge of the enabling capabilities of SOF to the COE, due to a conscious effort on behalf of the Special Operations community, this situation is improving. Clearly, part of the role of SOF as a national enabler is also as a national educator.

NOTES

1   For purposes of this chapter, "unconventional" refers to irregular, special, commando and other non-general purpose forces or concepts.

CHAPTER 5

SPECIAL OPERATIONS FORCES: AN ECONOMY OF FORCE OPTION FOR CANADA?

DR. DAVID A. CHARTERS

"Never in the field of human conflict
was so much owed by so many to so few."
WINSTON CHURCHILL

Winston Churchill's wartime tribute to the success of the Air Force RAF in the Battle of Britain spoke of military actions that were not only successful, but effective in a manner disproportionate to the resources applied. In spite of being outnumbered, RAF Fighter Command delivered a decisive victory that yielded strategic effects significant for the conduct of the rest of the war. In this respect, Churchill's words capture the essence of that fundamental principle of war: Economy of Force (EOF).

The aim of this chapter is to examine whether Special Operations Forces can provide Canada with an EOF option. To analyze this issue, the chapter will discuss four questions. First, what do we mean by Economy of Force? Second, why and under what circumstances does EOF matter? Third, what EOF capabilities do SOF bring to the battlefield and to the decision-makers? This latter question will be answered in part by using a series of case studies to illustrate the EOF capabilities of SOF. These case studies will also demonstrate the benefits and drawbacks of SOF/EOF operations. The remainder of the chapter will be devoted to answering a fourth question: does Canada need an EOF/SOF capability. In response to this fourth question, a series of sub-questions will also be posed:

1. What kinds of crises and conflicts are likely to emerge over the next decade (2010-2020), and which of these are most likely to engage the Canadian Forces?

2. What constraints are likely to shape CF organization, capabilities, and operations and Canadian SOF structures and capabilities?

3. What kinds of expeditionary operations are the CF likely to undertake?

4. How could SOF be used to ensure that these are conducted with EOF?

5. What are the minimum capabilities required to allow Canadian SOF to support the likely future EOF contingencies?

6. What steps do the Department of National Defence and Canadian Special Operations Force Command need to take to meet those requirements?

Ultimately, it is argued that Special Operations Forces offer Canada an Economy of Force option that is a strategic asset in an era of fiscal and political uncertainty at home and abroad.

WHAT IS ECONOMY OF FORCE?

This basic principle of war is at once both simple and complex. On one hand, it could be taken to suggest that one should use no more force than is needed to achieve the goal. The term "minimum force" – often applied to internal security or counter-insurgency operations – is usually conceived in those terms. Importantly, however, minimum force does not necessarily mean the same thing as EOF. Indeed, for Carl von Clausewitz, Military Strategist, EOF meant that all forces should be used *efficiently* and *effectively* to achieve victory in war.[1] Modern American military doctrine relies heavily on Clausewitz's interpretation. Here, EOF means applying maximum force at the decisive point. If that force is used efficiently and effectively there, it will ensure economy of effort by overwhelming the enemy and preserving most of one's forces rather than wasting them in piecemeal attacks.[2] But it is important to bear in mind that the maximum force needed depends on the nature of the target and the enemy. If these are limited in scope and scale, then the force applied against them could be quite small. Indeed, the cases cited later in this study illustrate this point exactly. It is not the size of the force that matters; rather, it is how well you use it.

WHEN AND WHY DOES EOF MATTER?

Clausewitz made the case for EOF in terms of war in general; he saw it as a universal principle. But the argument for EOF can be put in more specific terms. The first is a simple cost-benefit analysis, which Clausewitz himself asserted. It is a waste of resources to use force inefficiently – in effect, "using a hammer to swat a fly." Even for a major power the amount of force it can bring to bear in any campaign short of nuclear war is usually limited by logistics, by terrain, by other commitments and by economics. Rarely are there forces to spare. Therefore, EOF is not normally a mere option; rather it is a necessity.

Second, war is unpredictable. The clash of arms often generates unexpected outcomes and demands. The enemy may act in unanticipated ways, creating risks and/or opportunities. Profligate use of forces may denude one side's reserves, leaving it unable to exploit openings or vulnerable to unexpected enemy action.

Applying EOF, by contrast, can provide flexibility by freeing up forces that may be needed to respond to such threats and opportunities.

Third, circumstances may arise where the use of force is required, but political conditions – domestic or international – may demand quick resolution of the situation. Rapid and efficient use of overwhelming force may be more strategically effective and politically palatable than a prolonged, gradual escalation that leaves the outcome unclear. EOF is thus implicitly linked to decisive actions and outcomes, and to deterrence.

Finally – and closely related to the previous point – political considerations might dictate that "using a hammer to swat a fly" would be seen (at home and abroad) as unjust. Disproportionate use of force is often politically unpalatable. Therefore, in some conflicts EOF operations might yield better public relations (PR) and effective Information Operations (IO).

WHAT EOF CAPABILITIES DO SOF BRING TO THE BATTLEFIELD?

By their very nature Special Operations Forces appear to embody EOF. SOF normally comprise small units and formations, so they start with economies of scale. Nevertheless, they are specially trained and equipped to deliver unconventional combat power (and other military skills) at a tempo and level disproportionate to their size. Thus, in some circumstances they may offset shortfalls in conventional units. Being small but powerful gives SOF flexibility; they can deploy almost anywhere and bring force to bear quickly. That ability could allow them to deter or contain an escalating crisis or conflict or an enemy breakthrough, or to exploit an unexpected opportunity. Finally, SOF normally display a low profile and they can be deployed discreetly.[3] But, even where its role is known, a small force delivering a decisive punch may offer better PR/IO "optics" than a large force overwhelming the opposition with excess numbers and firepower. In an era when a sense of "fair play" seems to pervade the public discourse about the conduct of war, using SOF could be seen as a way of "leveling the playing field."

But it is one thing to suggest these possibilities in the abstract, and quite another to prove the points being made. Fortunately, the historical record provides numerous examples of SOF conducting effective EOF actions from the actions of ranger units in the Seven Years War to the St. Nazaire raid during the Second World War. In fact, seconding T. E. Lawrence to assist and advise the Arab forces during the First World War may have been one of the most decisive and cost-effective EOF/SOF operations of all time, since it helped Britain to assert itself as the dominant foreign influence in the region for nearly half a century – which is a "lifetime" in diplomatic affairs. The following selected case studies, drawn exclusively from the post-1945 era, also prove these key assertions more than adequately.

CASE STUDIES

Operation DRAGON ROUGE, Congo 1964

On 5 August 1964 during the Congo civil war "Simba" rebels captured more than 1,600 foreign nationals and held them as prisoners in Stanleyville in the eastern Congo. Over the following 111 days they became pawns in the struggle between the Simba rebels, who had captured much of eastern and central Congo, and the Congolese government, which was attempting to recapture it with Belgian and American military assistance and mercenaries. These actions put the foreign hostages at risk; some at other locations were killed, while others used as human shields. Rescue planning had begun early but was complicated by distance, terrain, and poor intelligence on the Simbas and their hostages. The initial

US rescue plans were either too small to succeed or too large and unwieldy. In the end, Belgium dispatched a para-commando force of 340 troops, which was deployed in a United States Air Force (USAF) C-130 transport aircraft, staging through the British air base at Ascension Island in the south Atlantic and the airport at Kamina in the Congo. The first wave of troops parachuted onto Stanleyville airport at 0600 hours on 24 November, secured it and cleared the runways by 0650 hours, at which point the remainder of the force was air-landed. They then moved into the town, fought off the Simbas, and rescued the hostages and Congolese nationals. By the end of the day, 1,400 had been evacuated; the remainder flew out the next day. On the 26th, a second operation was mounted to rescue 375 hostages in Paulis, some 200 miles northeast of Stanleyville. In all, about 60 hostages were killed before they could be rescued. The Belgian force suffered 7 casualties, including 2 fatalities. The casualty figures for the Simbas is not known with certainty, but was high. The rescue force withdrew quickly, as anger and protests mounted in many Third World capitals. While falling well short of perfect, the operation largely achieved its objectives.[4]

The narrative above simplifies what was, in fact, a complex, contentious, and politically sensitive operation. It took place in a volatile and dynamic environment, made fraught with disagreement between the Belgians and the US about its aims and planning. The Americans were primarily concerned about the rescue of their nationals, and pursued a negotiated diplomatic solution up to the last minute. The Belgians saw the operation as a strategic effort that would not only rescue the hostages but help to stop or reverse the Simba revolt, which threatened their economic interests in the country. No one had ever before attempted such a large-scale rescue by air over such a long distance. Strategic surprise had been lost because four days before the operation the Belgian foreign minister leaked the existence of the rescue force. The Simbas, therefore, expected a rescue attempt and planned to kill their hostages once the operation began. Only their confusion about the landings and a shortage of time prevented a larger massacre. The rescue operation did not end the Simba rebellion, but probably weakened it; it did not expand further, and the Congolese army and its foreign mercenary auxiliary force defeated it a few months later.[5]

The essential points raised by Operation DRAGON ROUGE are that in spite of the advantages identified above, SOF EOF operations are not the easy options, militarily or politically. They are fraught with risks and cannot guarantee total success, especially in the circumstances which often necessitate them and under which they are planned: political and military chaos; unfamiliar cultures and terrain; poor intelligence; and hasty planning, with last-minute changes being made "on the fly." Nevertheless, in this case the forces involved demonstrated the value of such operations and the qualities required for them to succeed: improvisation, flexibility, initiative, and courage. They largely succeeded in spite of the many obstacles that jeopardized their potential for success.

CLARET Operations, Borneo 1964-66

Between 1963 and 1966, Britain, Malaysia, Australia and New Zealand were engaged in an undeclared war with Indonesia in Borneo. Indonesia's leader, Achmed Sukarno, had opposed the creation of Malaysia, which the British had rushed into being in 1963 against the advice of its allies (including Australia and the United States). Not only did this disrupt Sukarno's plans for a more grandiose federation called Maphilindo – a union of Malaya, the Philippines, and Indonesia under his leadership – but it allowed Britain to retain a significant presence and influence in the region, something he had hoped to supplant with his own. In response, he declared a policy of *Konfrontasi* – confrontation –

which manifested itself as a low-intensity conflict characterized by cross-border raids and the attempt to stimulate an insurgency in the Malaysian part of Borneo.[6]

When the Indonesian raids began in April 1963, the British had few troops ready to defend a jungle border some 1,500 km long. So, while they reinforced the area with up to 30,000 British and Commonwealth troops, they used standard counter-insurgency methods to root out and eliminate the domestic insurgent organization. Simultaneously, they absorbed but contained the Indonesian attacks, which increasingly involved some of their best regular forces. Then in 1964, with the border and rear areas relatively secure, the British went over to the offensive. The method chosen was Special Operations – covert raids against Indonesian bases near the border – and the principal instrument was SOF: the SAS Regiment. But since the SAS could deploy only one squadron, later reinforced by SAS from Australia and New Zealand, it also created and trained special operations companies within line battalions of the regular British Army and the Gurkhas. These operations were conducted under the code name CLARET.[7]

The intent of these Special Operations was complex and nuanced. While Britain and its allies wanted to stop the Indonesian campaign against Malaysia they did not want and could not sustain – militarily or diplomatically – a large-scale war to achieve that goal. Therefore, inflicting a high-profile military defeat on Indonesia was neither practical nor desirable. Indeed, humiliating Sukarno could actually escalate the conflict – the very effect they were trying to avoid. So, the purpose of the cross-border operations was to apply just enough military pressure to force the Indonesians onto the defensive and to discourage further incursions into Malaysian Borneo.[8] In essence, it was an exercise in what might be called "pro-active deterrence."

Following covert surveillance, SOF units would conduct carefully planned raids on the Indonesian bases, making good use of stealth, surprise and shock effect with their sudden attacks. Initially the raids were limited to a maximum depth of 3,000 yards across the border, but were later extended to 5,000 and then 10,000 yards. To ensure secrecy and British plausible deniability they were governed by strict guidelines, known as the "Golden Rules". These determined that each raid had to be approved by the Director of Operations; each one had to be planned and rehearsed using only trained and tested troops; operational security had to be absolute; there would be no air support except in case of the most extreme emergency; and no one would be left behind dead or alive.[9]

The CLARET special operations succeeded. By August 1965 Indonesian forces had been pushed back at least 10,000 yards from the border and had ceased offensive operations into Malaysian Borneo. Political turmoil inside Indonesia, starting with a failed coup by the communist party in September, weakened Sukarno's hold on power and preoccupied the Indonesian military for the next few months. In March 1966 the Indonesian government indicated that it wished to end the Confrontation campaign. CLARET operations ceased in May, peace talks began in June and the war ended by agreement in August 1966.[10]

A number of key features explain the operational outcome. First, from the outset the political and military leadership were clear and agreed on the intent of the campaign – that it was a limited war in which armed force was used to achieve limited political ends. Military means, the special operations in particular, were tailored, constrained, and applied in a carefully calibrated manner intended to achieve those ends and no more. Second, decision-making and command were exercised through a unified structure that integrated all Commonwealth forces and civil and police authorities under the direction of the Malaysian National Defence Council, chaired by the Malaysian Prime Minister. The British government itself was responsible for some key decisions surrounding the operations of British forces, however, consultation and contact with

the Malaysian government and close personal working relationships that had developed during the earlier Malayan Emergency
campaign allowed the two governments to "de-conflict" any issues
that might have derailed the campaign.[11]

That said, ending the war still proved to be a challenge. Escalation was politically unacceptable and would have imposed severe
demands on Britain's forces. Negotiations offered no incentive to
Sukarno who believed he benefited politically from Konfrontasi,
and Malaysia and Singapore would oppose making a deal with
him. Prolonging the war was costly for Britain and it was not clear
that attrition alone would bring about an Indonesian ceasefire. But
it did prevent Indonesia from achieving its objectives and, as one
historian suggests, in doing so it may have influenced the emerging political crisis inside Indonesia in a way that ultimately solved
Britain's strategic problem. It did not have to escalate or negotiate.
The Indonesians simply decided to end the Confrontation.

The British campaign was a good example of "strategic coping"
but was also very much "a near run thing."[12] Even so, if military
operations are intended to advance and achieve strategic aims,
then the CLARET special operations bear the hallmarks of success. Using limited means they achieved the goals set out for them,
and helped to shape the overall campaign in a way that favoured
Britain and Malaysia when the changed political conditions inside
Indonesia tipped military thinking there toward war termination.
This lends weight to the contemporary assessment of then-
Minister of Defence Denis Healey, who described the Borneo campaign as a "textbook demonstration of how to apply economy of
force, under political guidance for political ends."[13]

The Dhofar Campaign, 1970-75

Between 1970 and 1975 the British fought and won a low-profile
counter-insurgency campaign in the desolate and forbidding Dhofar province of the Sultanate of Oman in the Arabian Peninsula.

It was a victory of considerable strategic significance. Had the insurgency succeeded there was a risk that a pro-Soviet regime would have gained control of the mouth of the Persian Gulf: a vital chokepoint in the flow of oil to the West.[14] The British military commitment to the Dhofar War was a classic EOF exercise, and SOF played a significant role in the British strategy and its success.

From 1932 to 1970 Oman had been ruled by Sultan Sa'id Ibn Taimour, a reclusive autocrat completely out of touch with change in the region and in his country. He had done little to develop the country and had neglected the population of Dhofar in particular. Tribal groups there decided to fight for secession. By 1970, rebels supported by the People's Democratic Republic of Yemen (PDRY), a radical Marxist state aligned with the Soviet Union, controlled most of Dhofar province and the Sultan's regime itself was facing defeat. In July he was deposed in a nearly bloodless coup by his son Qaboos, assisted by British officers and officials serving in the Omani government and military. Qaboos, a reformer trained at Sandhurst, was committed to defeating the insurgency.[15]

Guided by his British advisors, the new Sultan devised a counter-insurgency strategy based on two key weapons: money and information. First, the government created a Dhofar Development Committee (DDC) that integrated the civil, military, and police agencies into unified team working to a common purpose – providing economic benefits to the volatile province. Using the country's oil wealth, the DDC poured massive resources into Dhofar, building roads, schools and mosques, establishing medical clinics, and digging water wells, the latter being an asset of inestimable value in a desert area. Over the six-year period, the government spent in excess of one billion pounds on social and economic development. This was a weapon the insurgents simply could not match.[16]

Second, in concert with the development effort, the government launched an Information Operation designed to regain the allegiance of the population and to win over at least some of the rebels. The IO drew their attention to the economic benefits the government was providing. It pointed out that the insurgents had nothing comparable to offer the people. It also offered amnesty to the rebels, promising a share in those benefits if they switched sides and fought for the government. Underlying both of these messages was an appeal to Islam, firmly placing the government on the side of God and defining Communism as his enemy. Reinforced by material benefits it was a powerful message.[17]

However, to persuade people to switch allegiances, both the development and IO programs and the Dhofari people themselves would have to be protected from disruption and intimidation by the insurgents. For both political and resource-scarcity reasons, the British military commitment to Oman/Dhofar was severely constrained. There was little enthusiasm, even within the newly elected Conservative government, for involvement in another small war in a remnant of an empire. Insofar as possible, the conflict would be kept at arm's length. This consideration was aided by the facts that much of the British military was tied to Britain and Europe by North Atlantic Treaty Organization (NATO) commitments, and that the growing conflict in Northern Ireland was absorbing most of the remaining army units. So, Britain limited its liability and its visibility by providing small specialized units and individual soldiers on loan or contract who filled key leadership posts in the Omani forces. Thus, at any one time the number of British troops serving in Oman never exceeded 750. The brunt of the fighting was borne by about 10,000 troops from Oman, Jordan, Iran, and Pakistan.[18]

The SOF contribution comprised two SAS squadrons, deployed on four-month rotations under the innocuous cover of British Army Training Teams (BATT). The BATT conducted their own operations (patrols, direct action), trained the Sultan's army, provided intelligence, and carried out civil affairs "hearts and minds" operations. They also apparently trained exiled Yemeni tribesmen in cross-border raids into the PDRY. But their most important contribution lay in training and leading *Firqats* – counter-gangs of local Dhofaris and former insurgents who had surrendered under the amnesty and agreed to fight for the Sultan. By the end of the campaign the *Firqats* totaled nearly 2,000, including 800 former insurgents. Since the insurgents' peak strength comprised about 2,000 full-time and 3,000-4,000 part-time fighters, the defections were a serious blow.[19]

The SAS also fought in the most significant single engagement of the campaign, the battle of Mirbat on 19 July 1972. In a fiercely fought battle that lasted many hours, an eight-man BATT, supported by 30-40 Omani gendarmerie, fought off a determined attack by 200-300 insurgents. The outcome was uncertain until an Omani air force air strike and an airmobile assault by elements of a newly-arrived SAS squadron routed the insurgents. The insurgents had hoped to score a propaganda victory by capturing the town, but instead suffered a blow from which they never recovered. Owing to domestic political concerns, the battle went unreported in Britain for several weeks. Subsequent engagements and the counter-insurgency campaign as a whole gradually eroded the insurgents' strength to about 850 by the spring of 1975, and in December the war was declared over and won.[20]

It is probably fair to describe the entire Dhofar campaign as an EOF operation, driven as much by political, economic and resource constraints as by the demands of the campaign itself. It was EOF by necessity. One analyst singled out the value of providing specialist personnel, particularly, but not only, the SAS. Still, by raising and leading the *Firqats* and in the rural development work of the civil affairs teams, the SAS "filled a niche that neither Omanis nor regular British soldiers could provide."[21] This action, it was argued, allowed the government to gain the upper hand over the insurgents. The SAS were also invaluable in training the Omani forces,[22] and, as noted above, they played a key role in the battle that turned the tide of the war. They demonstrated the capabilities so often associated with SOF: flexibility; adaptability to harsh operational environments and unfamiliar cultures; small unit leadership; courage; and initiative. So, a small investment in SOF had yielded disproportionate results – the very essence of EOF.

Operation URGENT FURY, Grenada 1983

In October 1983, the United States invaded the Caribbean island state of Grenada, ostensibly to restore order in the wake of a bloody coup and to rescue American students caught up in the unrest. Grenadian-American relations had been strained before the coup, because the US perceived the ruling New Jewel Movement (NJM) as too friendly with Cuba. So the coup which installed an even more radical regime provided a pretext for an invasion that was also meant to ensure that a new pro-US government emerged from the chaos.[23] This admittedly is a bare-bones summary, but the pre- and post-invasion politics and legal debates need not concern us further in this study.

American SOF played a central role in the invasion, but did not perform as effectively as required. The purpose of this analysis is not to find fault or place blame, but rather to use the case to illustrate some of the limitations and challenges confronting SOF in hastily planned operations where EOF is not a central principle.

Grenada is a tiny, oval-shaped island (344 sq km) located at the eastern edge of the Caribbean, about 160 km north of Venezuela and about 2,400 km southeast of Miami. At the time of the invasion it had a population of about 90,000, about one-third of whom lived in or near the capital St. George's on the southwest coast. The main airport was located south of the capital at Point Salines, with a single 3,000 metre runway lying on an east-west axis at the southwestern tip of the island. A second, smaller airport was located at Pearls on the northeast coast. The medical school had two campuses south of St. George's about 2.5 km apart, one of them beside the airport. The island is hilly with the highest point being about 840 metres above sea level. The island is no more than 20 km wide at its widest point. Much of the island is densely forested. The climate is tropical.

The Grenadian military, called at the time the People's Revolutionary Armed Forces (PRAF), included the regular army and militia and the police and security services. By any standard of measure it was a tiny force, and neither well-trained nor well-equipped. The regime was able to deploy only about 450-475 regulars and less than 250 militia at the time of the invasion. Most of the population declined to mobilize. So the regime was forced to abandon any notion of defending the whole island and concentrated its forces in four company groups in the southwest, around St. George's and the Point Salines airport. Cuba, which supported the NJM, had since 1979 provided a modest amount of small arms, crew-served weapons (including mortars and anti-aircraft guns), trucks and light armoured vehicles. It sent 40 military advisers to train the PRAF, and also had deployed a construction battalion of 650 that was working on the airport at Point Salines. But, they were under strict orders from Cuba only to defend themselves if attacked, and President Castro had told the Grenadian regime that sending Cuban reinforcements to help defend Grenada against an American invasion was "impossible and unthinkable."[24] In fact, during the invasion, the US and Cuban governments maintained a "backchannel" to try to "de-conflict" their forces. In the event that that failed and they did engage in combat against each other,[25] that the intent of both sides was to prevent this was noteworthy.

By contrast, the US mounted a massive invasion force: two brigades of the 82nd Airborne Division, a Marine Amphibious Unit, two Ranger battalions, Delta Force, and three Sea Air Land (SEAL) teams. They were supported by a Carrier Air Wing, an amphibious task force, air transport, and the US Air Force's 1st Special Operations Wing, totaling some 20,000 servicemen.[26] Thus, SOF comprised the majority of the forces used in the invasion. But this was not an EOF operation; it was "overkill." As such, it is a useful counter-example to the previous case studies.

As events in Grenada unfolded quickly, American military planning was equally rapid. The invasion plan was drafted in four days, which proved insufficient for effective planning.[27] The basic plan involved US forces seizing the two airfields (Point Salines and Pearls), rescuing American students, freeing the Governor General and some political prisoners, and deploying a Caribbean peacekeeping force. The Rangers, Marines and SOF would go in first but would depart quickly, leaving the 82nd Airborne and the Caribbean force to restore calm and order. The SOF were assigned several key missions. Two SEAL teams were to recce the Point Salines airport and beaches where the Marines would land. Elements of the two Ranger battalions would airdrop onto the Point Salines airport and secure it so that troops from the 82nd could be air-landed there. The Rangers would also rescue the students. At the same time, the Marines would capture Pearls airport by air-landing assault and then secure the town of Grenville just south of the airport. A third SEAL team would rescue the Governor General, who was being held at his official residence. A fourth SEAL team would capture and temporarily disable the government radio transmitter. A Delta Force squadron was to capture the main prison and free political prisoners being held there. H-hour was 0500 on 25 October.[28]

The overall mission succeeded, but the execution of the plan was severely flawed: a fiasco that narrowly averted disaster. It was a nearly perfect example of Murphy's Law – almost everything that could go wrong did. And SOF were not spared; in fact, some of their failures placed the operation in jeopardy. Only the SEAL beach recce near Pearls went off as planned; they warned the Marines about dangerous surf and beach defences. The SEALs assigned to recce the Point Salines airport never reached their objective. Part of the team drowned after parachuting into heavy seas; the others were rescued after their rubber inflatable boat (RIB)'s motor was swamped. Instead, an MC-130 did the airfield recce and found that the runway had been blocked. But it did not detect the PRAF and Cuban defensive positions, so the airborne assault encountered unexpectedly heavy fire. All but one plane in the first wave aborted the first pass over the drop zone (DZ) then became jumbled among the second wave. Thus the two Ranger battalions were mixed up upon landing, causing some confusion. Moreover, the plan had called for the airborne assault to be completed in about thirty minutes at dawn, but delays in launching the operation and the need for a second pass over the DZ meant that the landings started a half-hour late and were spread out over ninety minutes, with the final drop being conducted in broad daylight and under fire.[29]

The SEALs captured the radio transmitter and took it off the air. But the Grenadian militia drove them off, and an AC-130 gunship then destroyed the transmitter, which had not been the plan. Likewise, the raids to rescue the Governor General and the prisoners both failed. The SEALs secured Government House by rappelling from helicopters. They and the Governor General were meant to be extracted quickly by ground forces, but were trapped by PRAF counter attacks, including an armored personnel carrier (APC), until rescued by the Marines twenty-four hours later. The attack on the prison fared even worse. The prison was a formidable walled target sitting on a narrow ridge with no flat ground nearby for an LZ. Moreover, it was over-watched about 300 metres to the east by Fort Frederick, where the PRAF had two anti-aircraft guns. The helicopter-borne Delta Force/Ranger team arrived seventy-five minutes late and faced intense fire from the fort. Lacking any air support they suffered heavy casualties and the loss of one Blackhawk helicopter, and their attack was driven off. A hasty raid on the PRAF's Calvigny Barracks succeeded, but at a cost of three crashed helicopters and three dead and five seriously wounded Rangers.[30]

The rescue of American medical students that was the main declared aim of the operation did succeed but more by good luck than good management. Until the operation was underway, US forces were unaware that there were two campuses, so they did not know the whereabouts of more than half of the students, nor how many there were – some 100 were at the True Blue campus by the airport; more than 230 lived at Grand Anse 2.5 km away on the west coast, and 200 others lived elsewhere. Then the problems with the air assault delayed the rescue at the True Blue campus. Fortunately the fighting there was minimal and neither the students nor the Rangers suffered any casualties. The "rescue" at Grand Anse took place 33 hours after the initial landings, with the Rangers deploying from Marine helicopters following a massive bombardment of suspected PRAF positions around the campus. Just like the assault at Point Salines the Ranger companies got mixed up because the helicopters took off out of sequence and then put them down at the wrong LZ. The Grand Anse students were evacuated without incident, but most of those who lived off-campus were not extracted until 28 and 29 October, and twenty-one students and staff members were not located and thus left behind.[31]

Clearly the entire operation, and not just its SOF elements, left much to be desired. So how do we explain this failure? First, URGENT FURY was a large and complex operation. It involved some 20,000 US military personnel from all four services organized into five task forces, plus a Caribbean contingent of about 350. The size of the force was dictated by multiple, changing objectives: rescuing American students and the Governor General; capturing vital points; overthrowing the Grenadian regime; and installing a stabilization force. These competing objectives divided the force and weakened it, placing each element of the mission in jeopardy. As a result it became the very antithesis of EOF.

Second, for political reasons the operation was planned and launched on short notice. The short planning phase – four days – allowed no time for the overall force commander; Admiral Wesley McDonald, Atlantic Command, and his subordinate commanders, formations and units to resolve a host of planning problems, such as coordination, communications, and logistics. Planning and preparations were notable for a lack of "joint-ness;" everything was "stove-piped," and orders were issued with little inter-service consultation. There was no rehearsal, and coordination was improvised on the spot, being dependent on the initiative of individual commanders. The most serious casualty of the truncated and uncoordinated planning process was communications. Once in action, the Army and Marines could not talk to each other. Many of these problems imposed the delays on the launching of the operation, which turned it into much more dangerous mission than might have been the case had it begun on time (before dawn).[32]

If the foregoing issues were not serious enough in their own right, they were exacerbated by poor intelligence. American commanders knew very little about Grenada, lacked good maps, and had little time to acquire and absorb much needed information. First, they were unaware that the students did not need to be rescued. They were not in danger; in fact, the regime had gone out of its way to ensure that they were safe. Second, as noted above, US forces did not know where most of the students were, rendering rescue planning difficult. Third, enemy and target intelligence was poor. The invasion forces did not know the location of hostile forces and underestimated the resistance they would offer. Likewise, poor recce and intelligence left the US forces without an LZ at the prison and unable to find the LZ easily at Government House, delaying their landing there. Thus they were driven off from the prison and the radio transmitter and surrounded at Government House.[33]

Finally, the US did not gain strategic or tactical surprise. At the strategic level, US posturing and visible preparations meant that the Grenadians were expecting an attack.[34] They used the time they had to prepare for it as best they could with the limited resources at their disposal. Those proved sufficient to disrupt and delay US operations although not enough to prevent the US from ultimately prevailing. The delays caused by US planning and deployment problems meant that American forces landed mostly in broad daylight, losing the advantage of tactical surprise that would have been conferred by night attack.

One result of all of these deficiencies was that the various SOF that might have been sufficient to conduct EOF operations under optimal conditions proved insufficient to the tasks they were assigned when those conditions failed to materialize. Moreover, they were poorly supported by conventional US forces in spite of the preponderance of such forces deployed in the theatre.

SOF EOF LESSONS FROM THE CASE STUDIES

These four cases are by no means exhaustive and one could easily choose examples from other more distant or more recent conflicts. The role of SOF in the toppling of the Taliban regime in 2001 is a case in point. It was a remarkable and cost-effective use of SOF, and it is hardly surprising that it has been touted as a "model" of future war.[35] That said, it is important not to rely on singular successes which may be exceptions to the rule. A great deal of value can be learned about SOF EOF by studying operations that did not work perfectly, even if they succeeded in the end. The cases employed here, while perhaps less familiar than some more recent examples may have been, nonetheless highlight both the strengths and limitations of SOF EOF operations.

The first thing that stands out from these examples is the complexity of these operations. They usually take place in unfamiliar cultures and terrain, in situations of political and military chaos or uncertainty. They are often politically sensitive; public disclosure of the operations could compromise them or cause strategic complications. Thus a "low profile" is preferred, if not essential. They place a high premium on surprise, yet it is often difficult to achieve it. Some, such as hostage rescue operations, occur on short notice with little time for planning and preparation. The attendant risks are high; there are no guarantees of success. But the potential "payoffs" are equally high.

Given these conditions, the success of SOF EOF operations seems to depend on the following:

1. Clarity of operational aims – and a limited number of them. It is hard to apply EOF if there are too many objectives, requiring too many units to achieve them;

2. Unity of command. Clarifies authority and responsibility, simplifies planning and reporting, and eliminates duplication of effort;

3. Accurate and timely intelligence on enemy, targets, terrain, weather, culture, and hostages/evacuees (if any). Good intelligence makes it easier to plan for EOF. This fact, in turn, puts a premium on intelligence-sharing among all participating forces and supporting agencies (domestic and foreign);

4. The highest quality troops, extremely well-trained, and capable of improvisation, flexibility, initiative, daring, and courage, in numbers sufficient to achieve goals;

5. Clear Rules of Engagement;

6. Rehearsals if possible, involving all forces participating, conventional and SOF, to familiarize and harmonize/de-conflict procedures, orders, and plans;

7. Close cooperation with conventional forces, especially for fire support and mobility, and with civilian and non-governmental organizations (NGOs) where appropriate;

8. Reliable, secure, interoperable, redundant communications;

9. Political authorities thoroughly briefed, committed to the mission, with enough confidence in their military leaders to avoid micro-managing operations, and willing to accept responsibility for errors, failures and political fallout; and

10. An Information Operations program to provide cover if needed, and to explain the operation if not.

There are no surprises here, since many of these items are fundamental tenets to all military actions. But the high yield/high risk nature of SOF EOF missions makes them doubly important. That said, the foregoing represent the ideal circumstances, which rarely prevail in reality. Nonetheless, the political decision to employ SOF for EOF missions requires a careful analysis and weighing of benefits and risks.

DOES CANADA NEED A SOF EOF CAPABILITY?

To answer this question requires answers to the series of sub-questions identified at the start of this paper. In several "strategic vision" papers, the Canadian government and the Canadian Forces have already attempted to answer them.[36] Nonetheless, the following responses provide a unique view that, while speculative, is not out of step with widely held perspectives.

Question 1. What kinds of crises and conflicts are likely to emerge over the next decade (2010-2020), and which of these are most likely to engage the CF?

The answer to this is deceptively easy: everything we have seen in the past decade, and then some. While the past is not always a reliable guide to the future, it is likely that certain trends will continue and certain kinds of events will be repeated. Clearly, for example, we have not yet seen the end of the Al-Qaeda problem and the corresponding War on Terrorism. Many parts of the Developing World are still plagued by local and regional instabilities, crises, and wars: Afghanistan, Pakistan, the Middle East, Somalia, Sudan, Congo, and Mexico, just to name a few. The threat of major wars lingers over several long-standing crisis areas: India and Pakistan; the Korean peninsula; and the Middle East. Additionally each of the latter carries with it the prospect of a nuclear exchange. Major natural disasters are likely to be a frequent occurrence, perhaps increasingly so if climate change has the predicted impacts.

But trying to answer this question also should force us to "think outside the box" of the familiar and to consider some "alternative universes." What, for example, would be the strategic implications of complete state failure in Mexico, rendering it as chaotic as Somalia is today? The same question could be posed about a post-communist Cuba or a Venezuela under or after Chavez. Indeed, the gloomier among us might ponder the prospect of a United States torn by civil strife arising from economic crisis and political paralysis. One implication of these scenarios is that we do not have to look far abroad to find an ugly future; it could happen right in Canada's backyard.

With the notable exceptions of the October Crisis and the Air India bombing Canada has thus far been spared the worst ravages of terrorism.[37] Should we assume that lucky streak will continue?

The evidence presented at the trials of the so-called "Toronto 18" demonstrated that the threat from this group was more serious than initial media reporting suggested.[38] This and similar cases should serve as "wake-up calls;" home-grown terrorism is a real (though not yet large) problem even in Canada,[39] and we cannot assume that we have seen the last of it. There are various groups that have grievances against the Canadian government or against foreign entities inside Canada, and it would be foolish to assume that none will resort to terrorism. It has happened before and can happen again. We should be aware that emergent groups may try to adopt and employ terrorist tactics, techniques and procedures that seemed to work elsewhere.

In the aftermath of 9/11, Deputy Prime Minister John Manley observed that the worst scenario for Canada was not a terrorist attack on Canada, but one on the US that had some link to Canada.[40] Arguably, Manley was both right and wrong. It is possible that any serious attack inside Canada could result in dire consequences arising from reactions south of the border. Even if that attack did not target American interests, it could seriously impact trade, travel, tourism, and Canadian sovereignty generally.

Nonetheless, the reverse is also true: another major attack in the US could impact Canada severely even if there is no Canadian connection to the event. On the one hand, there could be increased pressure to seal all American borders or to create a "Fortress North America."[41] On the other hand, if an attack that employed some kind of mass destruction weapon (nuclear, chemical or biological) occurred close to the Canadian border (Detroit or Seattle) the immediate and post-event effects could impact Canada directly in ways and on a scale that we are probably not prepared for: tens of thousands of injured and sick, for example. The same could be said for some natural disasters, such as a major earthquake that levels Seattle and Vancouver. Additionally, disputes over resources and sovereignty in the Arctic have the potential to generate crises, if not conflict. Certainly, the answers to question 1 suggest an almost "infinite field" of potential crises and conflicts and any one of them could require the deployment of Canadian Forces.

Question 2. What constraints are likely to shape CF organization, capabilities, and operations and Canadian SOF structures and capabilities?

The first is budgetary. With the war in Afghanistan winding down and economic concerns reducing federal spending it is likely that defence budgets will be constrained, if not reduced, for the foreseeable future by successor governments, regardless of party affiliation. Only an event of severe national or international significance would change that. If this is correct, then the CF will probably experience yet another era of downsizing and reorganization. There will be a loss of experienced personnel, and some capabilities will be eliminated or moth-balled while others may simply atrophy. Some long-term projects may be shelved. Governments may be tempted to retain only the capabilities that they feel they can afford, rather than ones that they might actually need. In short, expect "defence on the cheap."

The second constraint is political and social. Defence and foreign affairs rarely figure prominently in Canadian political discourse, but that changed during the Afghan war. While there was much public admiration for the military as an institution, the steady stream of casualties took its toll. The war became a divisive political and social issue. Indeed, the decision to end Canada's combat role in 2011 was driven entirely by domestic political discontent, not by the state of the conflict or the needs of the mission. The expressed desire that Canada return to its "traditional peacekeeping role" may not reflect global realities, but it is no less real for that in the minds of critics of Canada's Afghan role. Again, short of a global or national crisis of almost existential proportions it will be difficult for any future government to find a national political consensus that would support even a relatively short-term commitment of the CF to combat. Thus, for budgetary and political reasons, EOF may be the defining feature of future CF missions.

Question 3. What kinds of expeditionary operations are the CF likely to undertake?

While the answer to Question 1 suggested a wide range of possible missions, the answers to Question 2 suggest otherwise. For political reasons future governments are likely to avoid commitments to major conflicts, and the effects of budgetary constraints are likely to make such decisions easier. After all, if you do not have enough troops to spare, if you cannot deploy them or sustain them in a mid-high intensity conflict, then it is easy to avoid a commitment that is likely to be politically divisive. Clearly there will be a preference for UN-sanctioned missions, in particular those that more closely resemble "traditional" peacekeeping. There will, of course, be countervailing pressures from our allies to contribute to missions that matter to them. Canadian governments will find they have to go some way to meet those requests, if only to avoid problems in other aspects of bilateral and multilateral relationships, such as trade. This suggests that governments will seek a "minimalist" approach that maximizes visibility but limits exposure, risks, and costs (material and human). By definition then, EOF will be the "order of the day." This situation suggests that the CF will be tasked with the following types of operations:

- Peacekeeping – "traditional" inter-pository and observer missions. This could include filling headquarters staff positions, providing communications, engineer, and logistic support, providing unarmed observers, police, reconnaissance capabilities (vehicle- and unmanned aerial vehicle (UAV)-borne), medical teams, and – if absolutely necessary – lightly armed troops in company to battalion strength;

- Peace-building – Post-conflict political and social recon-struction, including monitoring cease-fires, supervising and securing elections, mine-clearance, disarmament of belligerents, security sector reform, and civil-military co-operation (CIMIC);

- Counter-Terrorism – siege-breaking, hostage rescue, co-vert surveillance and tracking, "snatch" operations. These may be domestic or foreign operations;

- Stability Operations, including counter-insurgency, but in primarily non-combat roles: Provincial Reconstruction Teams, training teams, Information Operations, recon-naissance and intelligence, mobility, and some staff and support functions;

- Disaster Response – immediate humanitarian relief (food and water, medical, etc.) and long-term reconstruction. Some short-term security tasks may be required; and

- Sovereignty Operations – deployment of CF units to the Arctic, airspace control over Canadian territory, and sea control of territorial water and approaches.

Limiting the CF to these types of missions would represent a re-turn to the 1990s, but probably would impose some coherence on defence policy, defence spending, military capabilities, and public expectations. That would provide EOF at the strategic level.

Of course, Canada may be invited to join international coalitions for Chapter 7 Peace-Restoring Operations in the event of severe international crises, such as a war in Korea. As suggested above, the Canadian government might find it difficult to deflect pressure to participate. But it could easily meet those demands with a "limited liability" commitment such as a naval task group, as was done in the 1991 Gulf War. Avoiding a direct combat role would minimize risks, costs, and political dissent at home, while showing enough support to mollify our allies and keep "a seat at the table."

The answer to Question 3 is not meant to suggest that it is the most desirable approach. "Defence on the cheap" is likely to prove a short-sighted policy. However, if politics is "the art of the possible," then it behooves us to consider soberly what may be politically, financially, and militarily possible in post-Afghanistan Canada.

Question 4. How could SOF be used to ensure that these types of missions are conducted with EOF?

First, it is important to acknowledge that it would be a mistake to oversell SOF as the EOF solution to all of Canada's defence needs over the next decade. The political and fiscal constraints that define the limited range of operations identified above will impose limits on the utility of Canada's SOF. If the CF themselves go through force reductions, then it is likely that CANSOFCOM will also experience a decline in size, budget, and capabilities.

That said, even a smaller SOF component would provide a useful resource. The Counter-Terrorism task described above is "made to measure" for SOF. As for the rest, SOF could provide certain niche capabilities: covert surveillance and intelligence collection in peace-keeping operations; CIMIC tasks in peace-building; training teams, IO, intelligence and reconnaissance in stability operations; close protection for very important persons (VIPs) in disaster relief missions; presence patrols in remote areas and boarding parties (including counter-narcotics) in sovereignty operations. In most of these they would work alongside conventional forces,

CHAPTER 5

Canadian or foreign. Of course, conventional units could perform most of these tasks. But at relatively little added cost, the special skills that SOF deploy enhance the capabilities of units and formations to which they are attached. Their presence and skills would be appreciated by our allies, while their low visibility would be appreciated by Canadian government leaders.

Noticeably absent from the list above are the kinds of Direct Action missions so commonly associated with SOF such as, for example, the cross-border raids of the Confrontation Campaign. These have been excluded because future Canadian governments may seek to avoid commitments that entail serious political risks and the potential for high casualties or for Canadians being captured and held hostage.

Question 5. What are the minimum capabilities required to allow Canadian SOF to support the likely future EOF contingencies?

At a minimum this requires a dedicated unit with the appropriate training, skills, equipment, command and control structure, and mobility. These exist at present in the Canadian Special Operations Regiment.[42] Beyond this SOF require a logistics sustainment capability for distant deployments, strategic lift to get them there and support them, intelligence from national and allied agencies, robust and secure strategic communications links, and a recruitment/selection/training establishment to ensure the SOF can maintain needed force levels and capabilities.

Question 6. What steps do DND and CANSOFCOM need to take to meet those requirements?

The first task confronting DND, and this and succeeding governments, is to decide what missions its wants the Canadian Forces, including its SOF, to be able to perform. As suggested earlier, these will be defined by political and financial concerns, and it is possible that the range of missions will be quite limited. Second, DND will have to advise the government on the kinds of forces those missions will require – both what and how much. Then, between them they will have to decide how much they can afford. Inevitably, some missions may have to be shelved or the requirements scaled back to bring forces and capabilities into line with fiscal realities. Thus, future Canadian SOF will have to be considered in light of the entire package of affordable CF capabilities. As suggested earlier, if the CF themselves are reduced in size there is likely to be pressure to scale back SOF as well. Similarly, changes in funding priorities within the CF, such as allocating more resources to major capital projects (ships or fighter aircraft), could limit the CF's ability to justify and maintain their SOF. In the past in other countries it often has been difficult to maintain SOF when core military capabilities are being cut.[43]

CANSOFCOM's main challenge, therefore, will be to convince DND and, ultimately, the government that SOF *are a core* capability, not a luxury. For the Counter-Terrorism mission this goal should be easy. Beyond that it gets more challenging, but not impossible. It should be possible to make the case on financial grounds – that SOF provide "a bigger bang for the buck," even if that "bang" is non-kinetic. Likewise, since modern conflicts and crises tend to "morph" from one form to another, deployed forces need to be able adapt to changing circumstances. The flexibility of SOF can allow them to adapt perhaps somewhat easier and quicker than larger conventional formations. The ability of SOF to "multi-task" this way promises economies of scale and investment.

From a political perspective, if one goal is to make a significant contribution to coalition operations without attracting a lot of attention to it, then SOF fills that niche. SOF combine the virtues of low public visibility with a high operational impact. But their small size also limits the liability of engagement, and makes it easy to extract them if it becomes politically necessary to do so. SOF, therefore, would appear to fit neatly into the political and financial future of Canadian defence envisaged above. In sum, Special Operations Forces offer Canada an Economy of Force option that is a strategic asset in an era of fiscal and political uncertainty at home and abroad.

NOTES

1   Carl von Clausewitz, *On War*.

2   U. S. Army, *Field Manual FM 3-0 Operations* (Washington, DC: Headquarters, United States Department of the Army, 14 June 2001), Chapter 4, 13, <http://www.dtic.mil/doctrine/jel/service_pubs/fm3_0a.pdf>, accessed 30 November 2010.

3   Bernd Horn, "Special Operations Forces: Uncloaking an Enigma," in Colonel Bernd Horn and Major Tony Balasevicius, *Casting Light on the Shadows: Canadian Perspectives on Special Operations Forces* (Toronto: The Dundurn Group and the Canadian Defence Academy Press, 2007), 24, 26, 28, 30.

4   Major Thomas P. Odom, *Dragon Operations: Hostage Rescues in the Congo, 1964-1965. Leavenworth Papers no. 14* (Fort Leavenworth, Kansas: Combat Studies Institute, 1988), 9-10, 15, 17, 19-20, 22-23, 25-28, 34-40, 65-71, 74, 78, 81, 84-96, 101-119, 124, 126-145.

5   Ibid., 5-6, 13-17, 30-32, 38, 42-43, 61, 63, 69, 74, 77, 150, 153-55.

6   Christopher Tuck, "Borneo 1963-66: Counter-Insurgency Operations and War Termination," *Small Wars and Insurgency*, Vol. 15, No. 3 (Winter 2004), 90-92.

7   Ibid., 92-93, 95-97. See also, Bob Hall and Andrew Ross, "The Political and Military Effectiveness of Commonwealth Forces in Confrontation, 1963-66," *Small Wars and Insurgency*, Vol. 19, No. 2 (June 2008),

241-242; and Raffi Gregorian, "CLARET Operations and Confrontation, 1964-66," *Conflict Quarterly*, Vol. 11, No. 1 (Winter 1991), 50.

8   Tuck, 93-95, 97, 100-101.

9   Gregorian, 53-56

10   Ibid., 59-61; Tuck, 95, 98, 106-107; Hall and Ross, 246-249, 251. Hall and Ross put the total number of CLARET raids at 50.

11   Tuck, 98-100.

12   Ibid., 102-108.

13   Cited in Gregorian, 65.

14   Geraint Hughes, "A 'Model Campaign' Reappraised: The Counter-Insurgency War in Dhofar, Oman, 1965-1975," *The Journal of Strategic Studies*, Vol. 32, No. 2 (April 2009), 277-278; Walter C. Ladwig III, "Supporting Allies in Counterinsurgency: Britain and the Dhofar Rebellion," Small Wars and Insurgencies, Vol. 19, No. 1 (March 2008), 63-64.

15   Hughes, 279-281; Ladwig III, 66-67, 70-71; Ian Beckett and John Pimlott, *Directed Reading and Project Scheme: The Dhofar Campaign, 1965-1965* (Royal Military Academy, Junior Command and Staff Course, Sandhurst, UK , undated), 10-11, copy in Dhofar Campaign Box, Gregg Centre Archive, UNB.

16   Hughes, 289-290.

17   Ibid., 291; Beckett and Pimlott, 14-15. The organization of the IO from 1970 to 1976 is sketched out in a hand-drafted schematic, marked "Oman", copy in Dhofar Campaign Box, Gregg Centre Archive. A British Army Information Team and a Psyops specialist aided the IO.

18   Ladwig III, 63, 68, 71, 76; Hughes, 277, 282.

19   Hughes, 283, 294-295.

20   Ibid, 271-272, 284-285.

21   Ladwig III, 79.

22   Ibid, 79.

23   Richard W. Stewart, *Operation Urgent Fury: the Invasion of Grenada, October 1983 CMH PUB 70-114-1* (Washington, DC: US Army Center of Military History, 2008), 7-8; Major Mark Adkin, *Urgent Fury: The Battle for Grenada* (Lexington, MA: Lexington Books, 1989), 89, 107-111.

24   Adkin, 20-24, 90-91, 152-158, 161, 162.

25   Ibid, 160.

26   Ibid., 119, 131, 133-134, 136-139, 143.

27   Ibid., 126-128; Daniel P. Bolger, "Special Operations and the Grenada Campaign," *Parameters*, Vol. 18, No. 4 (December 1988), 53.

28   Thomas K. Adams, *US Special Operations Forces in Action: The Challenge of Unconventional Warfare* (London: Frank Cass, 1998), 189-190. Bolger identifies thirteen separate SOF tasks, including psychological operation (PSYOP), Civil Affairs, and SOW gunship support to ground operations. But some so-called SOF tasks, such as the capture of the airport, were − even by Bolger's criteria − really conventional operations. Bolger, 56.

29   Adams, 190; Adkin, 198-204, 208-212.

30   Stewart, 19, 24-25; Adams, 191; Adkin, 186-189.

31   Adkin, 130, 264-272, 305.

32   Colonel Stephen Anno and Lt-Colonel William E. Einspahr, *Command, Control and Communications Lessons Learned: Iranian Rescue, Falklands Conflict, Grenadan Invasion, Libya Raid. Research Report AU-AWC-88-043* (Maxwell Air Force Base: Air War College, 1988), 41-44,

<http://handle.dtic.mil/100-2/ADA202091>, accessed 21 Novemeber 2010; Stewart, 10-12, 30, 31, 32-36.

33 Anno and Einspahr, 37-38; Adkin, 88-89, 100-101, 129-131.

34 Adkin, 120-122.

35 Warren Chin, "Operation 'Enduring Freedom': A Victory for a Conventional Force Fighting an Unconventional War," *Small Wars and Insurgency*, Vol. 14, No. 1 (2003), 57, 64. Citing numerous problems with the campaign Chin is skeptical of the OEF model.

36 See, for example, Chief of the Defence Staff, *Shaping the Future of the Canadian Forces: A Strategy for 2020* (Ottawa: Department of National Defence, 11 September 2006), <http://www.cds.forces.gc.ca/str/index-eng.asp>, accessed 30 November 2010.

37 David A. Charters, "The (Un) Peaceable Kingdom? Terrorism and Canada Before 9/11," *Policy Matters*, Vol. 9, No. 4 (October 2008), 3, 14-21.

38 "Toronto 18 Video Evidence Released," <http://www.cbc.ca/canada/toronto/story/2009/10/20/toronto-18-amara-video963.html>, accessed 30 November 2010.

39 Canadian Security Intelligence Service, *Public Report 2008-2009* (Ottawa: Public Works and Government Services Canada, 2009), 8-9, <http://www.csis-scrs.gc.ca/pblctns/nnlrprt/2008/Final_PR_08-09.pdf>, accessed 30 November 2010.

40 Manley quoted on CBC News, 2002.

41 David A. Charters, "'Defence Against Help': Canadian-American Cooperation in the War on Terrorism," in David A. Charters and Graham F. Walker, eds., *After 9/11: Terrorism and Crime in a Globalised World* (Halifax: Centre for Foreign Policy Studies, 2005), 300.

42 "Canadian Special Operations Regiment Background Information," <http://www.csor-rosc.forces.gc.ca/bi-rg/index-eng.asp>, accessed 30 November 2010.

43   David A. Charters, "From Palestine to Northern Ireland: British Adaptation to Low-Intensity Operations," in David Charters and Maurice Tugwell, eds., *Armies in Low Intensity Conflict* (London: Brassey's, 1989), 208; Tim Jones, *SAS: The First Secret Wars. The Unknown Years of Combat and Counter-Insurgency* (London: I.I. Taurus, 2005), 17, 19-23, 26-27, 34, 38-39; Adams, 156-160.

CHAPTER 6

FINDING THE RIGHT BALANCE: SPECIAL OPERATIONS FORCES AS AN ECONOMY OF FORCE CAPABILITY

US CAPTAIN (NAVY) THOMAS C. SASS

Special Operations present an economy of force capability to national decision-makers. In fact, this is the very premise that underpins the theoretical foundations of Special Operations. The rich history of Special Operations since the Second World War reveals that nation states create and maintain selectively organized, trained, equipped, and designated SOF[1] to provide national decision-makers with an organization that expands policy choices and which provides an economy of force option at the strategic level of war.[2]

Special Operations (SO) do indeed appear to be "special." Scholar Colin Gray observed that SO comprise six distinctive characteristics. They are: clandestine, covert or overt in nature; unorthodox; small in scale; they contain high risk; are directed toward significant political and military objectives; and hold foreign policy impact. Gray articulated that at the heart of the matter, SO lie beyond the routine tasks of war; rather, they represent operations that regular forces cannot perform.[3] Academic James Kiras further asserted that SO's strategic performance is measured by their ability to enhance the performance of the general purpose forces and conventional manoeuvre.[4] These theoretical foundations are reflected in US doctrine which states that SO are "...operations with no broad conventional force requirement, conducted in denied and politically sensitive areas, may require low visibility, clandestine, or covert capabilities, intended to achieve military, political, informational and or economic objectives, can be conducted independently or in conjunction with conventional forces or other government agencies, can be conducted through, with, or by indigenous forces, and differentiated by physical and political risk."[5]

Since the Second World War, the popularity and effectiveness of SO has ebbed and flowed. As we reach a stage where SOF are currently considered the force of last resort, yet also the force of choice, it is valuable to explore the evolution of SO since the Second World War. First, it is important to assert whether or not the strategic utility of SO derived from the experience of the Second World War has held over time. Next, it is relevant to explore the current manifestation of SO's strategic performance. Finally, it is possible to ascertain whether or not SO provide contemporary national decision-makers an effective economy of force option.

Certainly, two major claims of SO strategic utility, economy of force and expansion of choice at the strategic level of war, have held over time and are enduring. Moreover, SO continue to enable conventional force manoeuvre and enhance conventional force performance across the spectrum of conflict. Indeed, in the context of a contemporary strategic environment dominated by irregular threats and a global war against violent extremist organizations and armed groups, SO serve as a catalyst to unify, extend the reach and maximize the effects of other instruments of national power. Nonetheless, SO cannot be considered as an economy of force capability in and of itself. Instead, economy of force should be directly linked to expansion of choice and the relationship between the two must be correctly balanced.

In order to defend these arguments, this chapter will begin with a review of select foundational SO experiences to illustrate the theoretical foundations for understanding SO and their context within the organizational structure of military forces, particularly with respect to the US and United Kingdom (UK).[6] Next, two geo-strategic and operationally significant inflection points relative to the development of SO will be explored and their legacies will be examined. Third, this chapter will outline some recent SOF experiences to illustrate the extension of the theoretical foundations for SO dating back to the Second World War into the current strategic environment. (See Figure 1.)

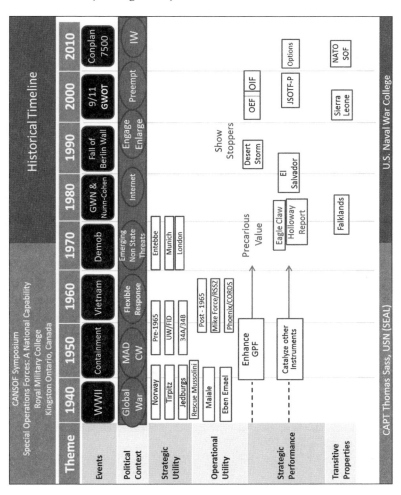

FIGURE 1. The Enduring and Evolving Character of SOF from 1940 - 2010.

CHAPTER 6

SOF FOUNDATIONAL EXPERIENCES

During the Second World War, all of the major belligerents created SOF units. These forces were roughly divided into two broad
categories. The first group of forces consisted of specialized units
within the already established military force structures that performed a broad range of independent military operations within
conventional campaigns. A second group of forces performed covert and clandestine operations outside of the conventional force
organizational structure. These operations included sabotage,
reconnaissance, PSYOPS and intelligence related activities as an
alternative means to, and in anticipation of, follow-on conventional campaigns.

The strategic utility of SOF during the Second World War can be
clearly illustrated by examining the period post-Nazi occupation
of Western Europe in June of 1940 and prior to the invasion of
Normandy four years later. During this period, Allied forces continuously attempted to leverage the natural defensive geographical
features of the English Channel in order to create the time and
space required to build forces for an invasion of Europe. In order
for an invasion to be successful, the Allies needed a means to access the denied areas of Nazi occupied Europe, and to assist and
coordinate local resistance groups in order to maintain pressure on
the enemy and bolster domestic morale.[7] Concurrently, however,
strategic threats episodically appeared and presented, at times, insurmountable challenges to allied conventional forces. Thankfully,
SOF provided alternatives outside of the scope of conventional
force capabilities in order to resolve these challenging strategic
threats. Moreover, they allowed conventional forces the ability
to maintain their principal effort and continue to prepare for the
invasion of Europe.

One way that SOF were able to resolve strategic threats beyond
the capabilities of conventional forces was by serving within

conventional campaigns. For example, SOF performed activities behind Nazi lines in Europe in preparation for the Allied invasion of Normandy of June of 1944. The Allies had developed supporting plans and conducted operations prior to D-Day intended to impede Nazi Germany's ability to oppose the amphibious landings of Operation OVERLORD and to assist the Allied forces' campaign to destroy the Nazi regime and army. Special Forces Headquarters, formed within General Eisenhower's Supreme Headquarters, Allied Expeditionary Forces, coordinated the independent, yet supporting, operations and provided operational command and control of SOF to achieve these goals. Specifically, assigned to each of the Allied Army Groups, Jedburgh Teams, the fore-runners to modern US Army SOF, were formed in 1943 to organize and control resistance elements in occupied France. Comprised of an officer, a radio operator and a linguist, the Jedburgh Teams parachuted behind enemy lines and linked up with resistance groups who then conducted guerilla warfare, sabotage and other activities in the enemy rear to disrupt their capacity to reinforce the breached perimeter at the water's edge. SOF thereby contributed to providing time and space for Allied forces to establish a beachhead, which enabled the conventional force to achieve its operational objectives more effectively.[8]

Coordinated SO in the land domain also occurred within the British force structure. For instance, British SAS elements, operating in the enemy rear, conducted a sustained offensive by attacking enemy infrastructure and their ability to counter allied movements, as well as coordinating resistance elements in Europe, Africa and the British India Burma theatres of Operations.[9]

In the maritime domain, the exploits of the Scouts and Raiders and the Naval Combat Demolition Units of the US Navy and the undersea warriors that manned the X-Craft of the Royal Navy provide excellent examples of specialized units within the naval forces' structures that performed a broad range of independent military operations within conventional campaigns. The Scouts and Raiders and Naval Combat Demolition Units, later to become the Underwater Demolition Teams and SEAL Teams of the US Navy, were firmly embedded in the operating concept of naval operations. These groups performed pre-assault cross-channel reconnaissance and follow-on assault obstacle clearance and guidance functions to support and enable the amphibious landings at the Normandy Beaches.[10]

For example, the X-Craft, a mini-submarine, which also conducted pre-assault cross channel reconnaissance in support of Operation NEPTUNE, again illustrates the theoretical foundation for SO during this period. While the Allies continued to build forces for the invasion of Normandy, Germany positioned the Battleship Tirpitz, the sister ship of the famed Bismarck, in the Keafjord anchorage, located north of the Arctic Circle and in the deep recess of the Altafjord and Sternsund sound of Norway. This location possessed overwhelming defensive advantages that presented extremely difficult challenges to the Allied forces. The intent of the Nazi imposition of a fleet-in-being strategy was to threaten the Allied convoys to Soviet Russia that kept it in the war on the Eastern Front, as well as to ensure the Tirpitz maintained unhindered access to the open sea. Consequently, the UK was forced to dedicate a disproportionate number of ships to the defence of these convoys and to the defence of the homeland, drawing them away from operational requirements elsewhere. As British Prime Minister Winston Churchill observed, "[The Tirpitz] held four times the number of British capital ships paralyzed, to say nothing of the two new American battleships retained in Atlantic... In this period, the whole strategy of the war turned on one ship."[11]

The X-Craft were specifically developed to counter this threat. Designed to be towed by a fleet submarine and overcome the defensive obstacles approaching Keafjord, the X-Craft contained innovative technology required for an operator to lockout of the submarine and emplace explosive charges. On 23 September, two of the six X-Crafts that had sailed for the attack on the Tirpitz arrived at the objective and emplaced their charges. They succeeded in crippling the Tirpitz for six months. Consequently, during the fall and winter of 1943, nineteen Allied convoys succeeded in reaching the Soviet Union, thereby enabling it to stay in the war and thus allowing the Allies to continue their principal effort of building land forces for the invasion of Europe.[12]

A second way in which SOF were able to resolve strategic threats beyond the capabilities of conventional forces during the Second World War was by performing covert and clandestine operations outside of the conventional force organizational structure. The British SOE and the American OSS illustrate the essential characteristics of this group of SOF. The defence of the Vemork Hydroelectric plant is a good example. In 1935, the hydro-electric plant in Vemork, Norway was the largest hydroelectric plant in the world. Its primary purpose was to create electricity. However, through several processes, it created heavy water or Deuterium (D_2O), which is used in the development of nuclear weapons. At the time, the facility in Vemork was the only source of heavy water in Europe. In 1940, Germany invaded Norway and took control of the Vemork Hydroelectric plant. This seizure represented an unacceptable strategic risk for the Allies. Preventing Nazi Germany form obtaining sufficient heavy water, the critical precursor element to a nuclear weapon, became an imperative.

Destroying the plant presented insurmountable challenges for conventional land, air and maritime forces, however. As an alternative, the SOE planned and conducted a series of raids, executed by Norwegian Commandos, on the Vemork Hydroelectric plant and Hydro Ferry on Lake Tinnsjoe. On 18 October 1942, four Norwegian SOE Commandos under the operation code-named "Grouse" were parachuted onto the Hardanger Plateau in Norway and patrolled many miles to conduct on-site recon of the Vemork plant and then to receive follow-on forces. Their small numbers and limited logistical requirements enabled their successful surveillance over a long period of time. The eventual follow-on forces team, code named "Gunnerside," consisted of five specially selected and trained Norwegian SOE Commandos. The team was inserted into the area by parachute on 16 February 1943. After several days, the Gunnerside team met up with the Grouse team and they patrolled the plant and executed their tactical assault. The plant suffered extensive damage and the Nazis attempted to remove the remaining stocks of D_2O back to Germany. By deploying Norwegian Commandos once again, however, the SOE interdicted these remaining stocks of heavy water. On 20 February 1944, they struck and sunk the "Hydro" ferry on Lake Tinnsjoe and thereby limited the Nazi's ability to develop nuclear weapons.

Although these selected vignettes do not offer a comprehensive look at all SOF organizations and experiences of the Second World War, they do illustrate the theoretical foundation of SO. Specifically, these examples illustrate the strategic impact of SOF as an economy of force when simultaneously evolving as an expansion of choice. Operating both within the command and control structure of Supreme Allied Headquarters Europe or operating independently and synchronized with the conventional campaign, SO activities were designed to directly support the conventional campaign. During the Second World War, there was a close relationship between those SOF that operated within the command and control structure of Supreme Allied Headquarters Europe and those that operated independently. In fact, SO personnel often migrated back and forth between the two groups. These two groups of SO continued to evolve after the Second World War into SO components of the Army and Naval service structures, and into intelligence organizations in both the US and UK models, (and generally across allied structures). Notably, however, in the postwar period the balance between SOF as an economy of effort option and an expansion of choice has not always been achieved.

Arguably, this unequal pairing has, at times, mitigated the strategic effect of SOF.

Select vignettes from the Vietnam War continue to illustrate some of the enduring foundational qualities of SO, yet also underscore some of the challenges and limitations of SOF being organized under the Army and Naval service structures, particularly in the American context. Responding as an alternative to conventional force employment, US Special Forces were institutionalized in 1957 as a branch of the US Army and deployed to Vietnam. At the time, the Eisenhower Administration employed a defence strategy that emphasized nuclear forces as part of the nuclear deterrence concept of Mutual Assured Destruction (MAD). MAD represented the military means of the Cold War national security strategy, which was fixated on containing the Soviet Union. As part of this strategy, nuclear forces were accompanied by large conventional force formations arrayed on the European plains in order to deter and defend against a Soviet incursion into Western Europe. While the principal focus of conventional forces was on its deterrent and defence roles in Europe, the Eisenhower administration also pursued covert action, unconventional warfare and foreign internal defence as the means to oppose the Communist North Vietnamese and Viet Cong incursion into the Republic of South Vietnam. These actions represented an economy of force effort that presented an alternative to direct confrontation with the Soviet Union over the expansion of communist regimes. Following its experience with nuclear brinkmanship during the Cuban Missile Crisis of October 1961, the Kennedy Administration introduced the strategy of Flexible Response and in the case of Vietnam, expanded the covert action, unconventional warfare and foreign internal defence efforts.

Disappointed over CIA covert action efforts in Vietnam, in mid-1962, President Kennedy transferred responsibility for the effort to the Department of Defense in order to access more resources and thereby increase the scale and scope of the effort.[13] Subsequently, increased USSF personnel deployed to the Military and Assistance Command Vietnam – Studies and Observation Group (MACV-SOG) where the main effort was being prosecuted. Activity focused on agent operations, cross-border reconnaissance, military deception, and PSYOPS in both land and maritime domains. This force transitioned from the Second World War model of a strike force operating behind enemy lines to a training force that developed capabilities within the Republic of South Vietnam in order to execute a COIN strategy. Although USSF saw great success organizing and training the Vietnamese Special Forces Units, the Montagnards, and the Civilian Irregular Defense Corps, arguably the effort proved to be too little and too late for the scale of the threat presented.

In 1965, the Johnson administration escalated the war to a conventional force war of manoeuvre and the majority of USSF operated within that conventional structure as tactical manoeuvre elements in mobile assault roles. The Under Water Demolition and SEAL Teams operated in the maritime environment of IV Corps and the Rung Sat Special Zone and conducted reconnaissance, direct actions and intelligence operations to deny sanctuary and attrite the Viet Cong unilaterally. In support of Naval objectives, they did so in combination with, and through, the Republic of Vietnam Special Operations Forces.[14]

In 1967, President Johnson unified the three principal efforts within the Republic of Vietnam by placing all military and civilian programs under the command and control of the military commander, Commander US Military Assistance Command Vietnam. He established the Civil Operations and Revolutionary Development Support (CORDS) to unify the efforts of all instruments of power operating in Vietnam to support the pacification of the population. CORDS also linked the military campaign against the North Vietnamese Army and the CIA's effort to counter the clandestine political infrastructure of the Viet Cong through the Intelligence Coordination and Exploitation Program (ICEX), which eventually became the Phoenix Program. It is in the Phoenix Program that elements of the SF of MACV-SOG worked in close cooperation with intelligence and police organizations in an effort to influence the population in order to counter the Viet Cong infrastructure (VCI), which had attempted to establish a shadow government and terror campaign against South Vietnamese government officials.[15]

While scholars continue to debate the nature of the Phoenix Program and its strategic effect, there is consensus that the program did create time and space for the pacification effort. Unity of command of all instruments of power addressing pacification, the military campaign, and the counter infrastructure operation provided a unique set of circumstances. Consequently, the majority of USSF were involved with both the military and the pacification efforts. Nonetheless, their exceptional tactical performance produced operational rather than strategic effects in both the maritime and land domains. Importantly, however, US SOF helped enable the main effort of conventional force manoeuvre.[16] In fact, Vietnam foreshadowed SOF developments in integrated counter-leadership and COIN operating concepts. Indeed, decades later, in the 21st century, the requirement for an intelligence capability to identify and counter the clandestine political infrastructure, ideally in cooperation with host-nation and local police forces operating under the rule of law, is still considered essential for protecting the population.

Although the Vietnam War illustrates the enduring theoretical foundation of economy of force and expansion of choice prior to the 1965 escalation, as well as the theme of SO enabling conventional force performance, the most pertinent lesson is revealed in the postwar demobilization. Both land and maritime SOF were institutionalized in 1957 and 1962 respectively. However, they were institutionalized under their service structures. In the postwar demobilization, their size and capabilities were greatly reduced in favour of each service's components that supported their principal operating concept. In the case of the Army, the operating concept focused on large formations intended to produce overwhelming combat power through the employment of combined arms. In the case of the Navy, the operating concept focused on naval platforms centred on naval presence and naval power projection functions employing carrier battle and amphibious ready groups. The precarious value of SOF was relegated to that of an enabler for conventional force manoeuvre and consequently under-resourced in favour of the principal capabilities of the services' operating concepts.[17]

In the years following the Vietnam War, the SO service components struggled for organizational survival as they grappled with articulating their strategic value to the nation. USSF gravitated toward their historical unconventional warfare missions and focused on operating behind Soviet lines in Europe. US Navy Underwater Demolition and SEAL Teams focused on supporting naval power projection roles of amphibious assault and over the beach naval strike operations. This focus on enabling roles of the service operating concept under the construct of conventional force manoeuvre in major combat operations resulted in under-resourcing by their parent services. Consequently, the scale, scope, and readiness of US SOF contracted dramatically, relegating SOF to a minor organizational status with limited capability. The extent of low prioritization and under-resourcing of SOF by the services was illustrated by the inability of the US military in the 1970s and 1980s to develop and execute an option for the national command authority to address crises that fell outside of the requirement of conventional forces.

The post-Vietnam challenge to sustaining and employing an effective SOF capability was not strictly a US phenomenon, nor was it always completely incapacitating. In fact, the British experience in the Falklands in 1982 and the US experience in El Salvador beginning in 1982 provide two good examples of the potential – and actual – benefits of SOF as an economy of force option, when also employed as an expansion of choice.

The UK's expeditionary operation to recover the Falkland Islands illustrates the enabling role of British SOF as part of the service force structure. The UK's main effort focused on the amphibious landing of the ground force and the recapture of Port Stanley on the eastern edge of East Falkland Island. Operating as part of the expeditionary task force, the SOF role was that of enabler to conventional force manoeuvre. As such, SOF tasks focused on a direct action raid against Falkland Island based fixed wing aircraft, and reconnaissance missions in support of the amphibious landings in the west and the ground movement across East Falkland Island toward Port Stanley.

Additionally, circumstances presented an opportunity not present in the conventional force for a strategic impact via an economy of force effort that that would generate options for the operational commander. Operation MIKADO was the one SO that had the potential for an independently generated strategic impact. The principal threat to the British operation was the Argentinean land based aircraft that were based on the mainland and whose Exocet missile had sunk six British ships and damaged another dozen. The British, however, had to weigh the benefits of sending conventional forces against the likelihood that this action would polarize world opinion against them. SOF, with their small footprint, provided an alternative. Operation MIKADO envisioned the insertion of SOF reconnaissance and follow-on assault elements to conduct a raid with surgical precision against the Argentinean air base of operations for the Exocet laden aircraft and assigned aircrews. A supporting element was deployed to Argentina under covered status to perform operational support functions for the assault element. The reconnaissance element launched but, unfortunately, its infiltration helicopter malfunctioned and the mission aborted. The operation was re-tasked and planned for a submarine insertion, but never executed because the war ended.[18] Although the opportunity to generate an independent strategic impact was lost, the foundational theme of enhancing conventional force manoeuvre is illustrated by this English expeditionary operation.

The deployment of the US 7th Special Forces Group to El Salvador during the waning stages of the Cold War is perhaps the classic SO centric independent economy of force operation that generated an expansion of choice at the strategic level of war. SOF, operating with a force limitation of 55 personnel, conducted foreign internal defence in an effort to counter the communist insurgency by increasing the capacity of the El Salvadorian Armed Forces. Initially, by preventing a decision on the field and later through prolonged involvement, SOF enhanced the capability of the El Salvadorian Government and enabled it to successfully counter its internal insurgency and, in the process, generated a strategic partner for the US. This limited effort presented an alternative to larger conventional force deployments for US policy-makers and provided the opportunity for the US to sustain a prolonged effort.[19]

INFLECTION POINTS

Despite some US and British SOF successes post-Vietnam, indications of a changing strategic environment began to appear in the 1970s, which challenged SOF capabilities. Specifically, terrorist attacks by Palestinian activists against Israeli athletes at the 1972 Munich Olympics and against Israeli citizens aboard commercial aircraft hijacked to Entebbe, Uganda in 1976, and Iranian revolutionaries' attack against the Iranian Embassy in London in 1980 illustrated the threat presented by terrorists and the need for competent forces capable of countering the threats posed by these non-state armed groups. However, these incidents were not enough to bring the threat of terrorism to the forefront of national security concerns in the US, which still viewed the international security environment in a Cold War context that was restricted to relationships between nation states. In fact, it was not until US citizens were taken hostage by Iranian Revolutionaries at the American Embassy in Tehran in 1979 that the US re-examined its SOF capability.[20]

Operation EAGLE CLAW was conceived as a three phase operation whose mission was to rescue and return to the US the 53 American hostages, who were ultimately held in Tehran for 353 days. The forces were organized under an *ad-hoc* command and control structure built around a contingent from the Joint Staff. SOF planned and trained separately, forgoing unit coordination and integration in order to maintain operational security. During the first phase of the operation, advance force elements accessed the denied and politically sensitive country of Iran by employing covert means. Their objectives were to reconnoitre and put into place the infrastructure needed to conduct follow-on operations. During the second phase, US Navy transport helicopter assets, piloted by US Marine Corps pilots, launched from the USS *Nimitz* operating in the Persian Gulf. They rendezvoused with Air Force Special Operations fixed wing C-130 aircraft carrying fuel and assault forces at Desert One, the first of two planned rendezvous points in the desert. At Desert One, helicopters were to refuel with the fixed wing aircraft and reposition at a hide site outside Tehran. Assault forces were to transfer to ground transport and reposition at a separate hide site, after which actions the fixed wing aircraft were to return to base. On the following day, assault forces were to move by ground transportation to the besieged embassy and rescue the hostages. The helicopters were to follow and exfiltrate both assault teams and recovered American hostages from the embassy to a second rendezvous location in the Iranian desert called Desert Two. There they would be recovered by US Air Force strategic lift, extracted out of Iran and transported back to the US.

The operation did not go as planned, however. Insurmountable troubles began on the initial helicopter infiltration leg. An unexpected sand storm producing near blackout conditions and mechanical failure provided the underlying reason behind the inability of enough of the helicopter assets to make the first rendezvous point. The decision to abort the operation occurred at Desert One with a satellite call back to the US President. To make matters worse, while attempting to return to base, a helicopter pilot drove a turning rotor blade into the fuselage of a refueling C-130 and initiated a catastrophic explosion and fire.

The legacy of Operation EAGLE CLAW is fundamental to understanding the creation of USSOCOM and the structure and capabilities of the operating forces of USSOCOM's component commands. The principal lessons learned from this catastrophic failure are captured in the post disaster Holloway Report which identified eleven major issues, articulated general conclusions surrounding the failure, and proposed two recommendations that shaped the perceptions on the state of US SOF and the resulting congressional legislation regarding this capability. Specifically, the Holloway Report validated that the operational concept centred on a small clandestine force was a desirable policy option at the national level and that, although the operation had contained significant risks, it was viable. Importantly, however, the report also identified that the US military did not have a credible capability until months after the crisis began. Organizational structure and *ad hoc* command and control arrangements prevented coordinated training during the concept and capability development phase and presented difficulties during operational execution. Additionally, the overriding prioritization of operational security directly impacted the preparations. Finally, the combination of unexpected helicopter failure and a sand storm that created low visibility flight conditions directly contributed to an insufficient number of helicopters, which resulted in the decision to abort. In the end, the commission recommended that a standing CT task force organization be created with permanently assigned command and control, staff and forces. It also recommended the establishment of an accompanying policy oversight committee with direct access to national policy-makers.

The US Congress agreed and passed legislation that reorganized the US Department of Defense through the Goldwater-Nichols Legislation. This legislation essentially forced the integration of forces from the individual services into a Joint Force by elevating the stature of the Chairman of the Joint Chiefs of Staff and providing the Geographic Combatant Commanders with the authority to command and control all military operations in their area of responsibility. The Nunn-Cohen Amendment to that legislation created USSOCOM and provided it with a unique blend of service and Unified Combatant Command-like authorities. Specifically, USSOCOM was designated a Functional Unified Combatant Command and provided with an organizational structure. This organization allowed USSOCOM the ability to select, train and assign operating forces and standing organizations imbedded in the Geographic Combatant Commander's area of responsibility which provide command and control capabilities for deployed forces during execution. The Commander of USSOCOM was provided with funding in the form of Major Force Program-11 and enabled with the authority to control the resourcing of the development and procurement of SO-specific capabilities to enable the operating forces to execute their tasks. A policy oversight position with appropriate staff was created inside the Department of Defense that oversaw all aspects of SO, as well as defined SO core activities to include the following: "direct action, strategic reconnaissance, unconventional warfare, foreign internal defense, civil affairs, psychological operations, counterterrorism, humanitarian assistance, theater search and rescue, [and] such other activities as may be specified by the President or the Secretary of Defense."[21] The force structure and capabilities of this unified command and its components largely reflect the principal tenets articulated in the

Holloway Report, which have been, over time, largely adopted by US allies as well.

In the early years after the establishment of USSOCOM, as the Command worked its way into the defense establishment, SO occurred within the context of large conventional force campaigns and major operations. In the immediate aftermath of the Cold War, the restoration of Kuwait in Operation DESERT STORM stands out as an illustration of SO's enduring strategic utility. It illustrates two interrelated tenets of SOF, specifically that they provide an economy of force option when also occurring as an expansion of choice. Moreover, DESERT STORM shows how SO continued their historically grounded measure of strategic performance: enabling conventional force performance. Notably, strong mistrust for SO by the Joint Task Force (JTF) commander restricted their employment beyond this traditional purview.

During Operation DESERT STORM, coalition SO consisted of two principal efforts. The first effort was an independent effort that placed British and US SOF in western Iraq in search of mobile transporter erector launchers (TELS) firing SCUD missiles that targeted Israel in an effort to coax them into the war and thereby break apart the coalition, arguably its strategic centre of gravity. The other SO effort focused on increasing coalition performance through coalition support teams operating with coalition land forces in an effort to synchronize coalition land formations, as well as special reconnaissance, pilot recovery, and direct action tasks in western and northern Iraq. Maritime SOF supported both the SO and the maritime functional component commander with reconnaissance, deception, direct action, defensive mine counter measure and interdiction in the maritime domain.[22]

SO that addressed the growing threat from non-state actors that employed terrorist tactics and other unconventional means and methods of violence, and confrontation did not occur, however.

A long-established mistrust for, and perception of, SOF as reckless cowboys relegated them to pariah status even after the creation of USSOCOM. Additionally, courses of action presented to the national command authority violated the principle of economy of force. The force packages and force footprint were simply too big. Moreover, senior military commanders presented their best military judgement to civilian leadership against SOF's employment in politically sensitive circumstances, particularly when the legal basis of their role and employment outside of a Joint Area of Operations became complex under multiple titles of the US Code. Most importantly, terrorism was viewed as a crime and not a tier one national security issue.[23]

The attacks on US soil by Al-Qaeda of 11 September 2001 mark the second inflection point that influenced the theoretical development of SO and frames American understandings of the utility of SO in the current strategic environment and the measure of their strategic performance. This external shock to the US altered the international security environment, the perception and urgency of the threats posed by transnational non-state actors, the national security strategy of the US to one of pre-emption, the structure of the US security establishment,[24] and, arguably, the security strategy of all nations. Terrorism, previously considered a law enforcement problem, catapulted to a tier one international security threat.

SOF IN THE CURRENT STRATEGIC ENVIRONMENT

SOF formed the core of the initial stages of Operation ENDURING FREEDOM, the US military response to 9/11. In the immediate aftermath, small elements of the Fifth Special Forces Group inserted via Special Operations Rotary Wing aircraft equipped with enhanced avionics of the 160th Special Operations Aviation Regiment into northern Afghanistan in the middle of a sand storm and met up with CIA operatives and commanders of the Northern Alliance to conduct unconventional warfare operations. Leveraging US air power, with its precision munitions and digitized information technology, SOF and indigenous ground forces commenced offensive operations to destroy the Taliban regime that had provided sanctuary to Al-Qaeda. Following in the wake of the Northern Alliance's advance, teams from the Special Operations 96th Civil Affairs Battalion distributed humanitarian assistance provided by US government and non-governmental organizations to the Afghan population. Additionally, teams from the Special Operations 9th PSYOP Battalion supported the manoeuvre elements and developed products designed to communicate to the population that the Americans presented a better option than the Taliban. Moreover, US Army Rangers conducted combat parachute assaults to secure airfields and operating bases to sustain the advancing forces.[25]

During this period, 250 SOF operators on the ground operated under the command and control of JSOTF Dagger, an organization formed around the 5th Special Forces group to develop and control an innovative operational concept that featured SO. Economy of force was its principal governing factor. SOF provided the means for the national command authority to mitigate strategic and operational risk and challenges incurred by committing large conventional formations on the ground in a location void of a base of operations from which to operate.

As the unconventional warfare campaign proceeded, a separate SOTF conducted a CT campaign with the objective of killing, capturing, and dismantling remnants the Al-Qaeda terrorist leadership and network that fled, melded into the population or evolved into a clandestine structure as their sanctuary collapsed. Leveraging technology and access to the intelligence community, the Counter-Terrorist – Joint Special Operations Task Force adapted to their operating environment and their enemy in order to fuse intelligence with operations into a common effort that synergized and enhanced the performance of each component.[26] This effort demonstrated the initial stages of the evolution of the strategic performance of SOF.

As the campaign transitioned from its initial stage of regime destruction to a phase of consolidation and establishment of an interim government, the fighting moved south. Combined Joint Special Operations Task Force K-Bar, an organization formed around Naval Special Warfare Group One, conducted direct action and special reconnaissance operations against fleeing Taliban and Al-Qaeda fighters. Joined by SOF from coalition countries, Combined Joint Special Operations Task Force provided the opportunity for individual nations to provide a national contribution while simultaneously mitigating political risk. SOF provided a capability that included the highest quality troops from a nation while at the same time representing an economy of force effort.

Operation IRAQI FREEDOM (OIF), beginning with the invasion of Iraq for the purpose of regime change in 2003, is also a significant event in the evolution of SOF. Although impossible to capture the complexity and full scope of the campaign, which lasted for close to a decade, in a single chapter, it is possible to identify and discuss several concepts which are germane to the theoretical foundations and evolution of SOF. SOF, operating within the joint force structure, demonstrated their value as enablers to the larger conventional force manoeuvre, particularly through the decisive operations phase and its ensuing major combat operations that culminated with the collapse of the regime and the capture of Saddam Hussein.[27] Additionally, in the post-regime change stability phase, ensuing simultaneous COIN and CT campaigns in the same Joint Area of Operations for extended periods highlight other valuable insights into SOF. Specifically, SOF dramatically improved their capability to fuse all sources intelligence into their tactical targeting and operational cycle, in what came to be known as the F3EA cycle (find, fix, finish, exploit and analyze). This capability enabled SOF with a better ability to generate the next target[28] for the specific function of disrupting the clandestine political infrastructure through the killing and capturing of high value targets. As such, a synergy was formed with organizations and agencies across the federal government around this singular common purpose.[29]

This "Collaborative Warfare" required three innovations: network-based targeting in the form of F3EA; improved all-source intelligence and capability provided by sharing intelligence across organizational lines through cross-functional teams supporting the F3EA cycle; and, finally, the integration of both the CT and the COIN campaigns at the tactical and operational levels.[30] The integration of the two campaigns at the tactical and operational levels provided local commanders with the opportunity to balance the costs and benefits of prioritizing the CT versus the COIN campaign at any given place and time. The CT activities provide time and space for the COIN activities to take effect.[31] The operational level commanders could then allocate resources as needed to put those tactical units in a position to succeed. Most importantly, the SO focus on CT activities provided the focus for both interagency and conventional forces cooperation and synergy.

With the priority of resources and attention dedicated to OEF-Afghanistan and the activities in the Middle East surrounding Iraq, JTF-510, later re-designated Joint Special Operations Task Force – Philippines (JSOTF-P), deployed to the Republic of the Philippines in December 2001 as an economy of force effort to conduct foreign internal defence in coordination with the US country team to increase the operational capability of the Philippine Armed Forces and Philippine National Police forces and, in the process, enhance the governance capability of the Government of the Philippines. Requested by the Republic of the Philippines, SOF built around the First Special Force Group and elements of Naval Special Warfare, operated by, with and through the host nation in an effort to assist the host nation in enforcing its sovereignty by denying sanctuary for and isolating Jamai Islamia (JI) and the Abu Sayaf Group (ASG) on Basilan and across the southern Philippine Archipelago.

This protracted campaign was broken into four phases: assessing; advising and assisting; capability building; and follow-on civic action. The first phase mapped the dislocation between the local population and the central government. This assessment identified the capability gap in the Philippine security forces and the social structure of the island by locality with respect to the relationship between the population, the central government and the ASG insurgent movement.[32] As the capability of the Philippine security forces improved, and they were able to establish security for the population, and follow-on civic action programs applied resources through the institutions of the national government to improve the underlying conditions and the lives of the local population, reconnecting the government with the population.

The small physical footprint and low signature of SOF mitigated political risk for both US and host-nation national leadership. 2006 proved to be a transition year in which the security forces of the Philippines made significant gains against JI and ASG, improving the level of security and establishing conditions for the central government to connect with the population manifested in the "Kapit Bisig Agreement" which translates as "hand in hand" and represents a commitment by the central government to the southern Philippines.[33]

The campaign in the Philippines is informative for understanding not only the theoretical evolution of SOF but also for projecting their future utility and strategic performance in an international security environment marked by irregular and transnational threats. 2011 once again marks a transition point in the campaign. Leveraging the access and relationships that the JSOTF-P organization developed over a decade of operations, economic and legal instruments of power through USAID and the Federal Bureau of Investigation (FBI) are extending their operations into the Sulu Archipelago in concert with the host nation's commitment to develop Basilan.[34] The more valuable insights to be learned from the Philippine experience may focus on the issue of sovereignty itself and the concept of economy of force. The Philippine government, its security forces, and its institutions remain in the lead. As has been noted, "Measurable progress moves at the speed of sovereignty, at the speed of governance, and at the speed of trust."[35] Sovereignty and governance are within the domain of the Philippine society, but trust extends not only to the relationship between the Philippine government and the population, but between the Government of the Philippines and the US Government, and between the various instruments of the US Government with its focus on the country team. SOF, with their functional focus, authority, organization and resources provide a vehicle to align this effort. Credibility for this trust is reinforced by the small scale of the SOF effort that is brought forward and remains linked to their larger parent organization, USSOCOM.

At the time of writing in 2011, the international security environment marked by irregular and transnational threats provides the context in which to evaluate the utility and strategic performance of SOF. Transnational crime, extremism, and migration challenge international order in general and the ability of any nation to maintain its sovereignty over its population.[36] SOF provide a potential solution. As Eric T. Olson, the current Commander of USSOCOM notes:

> The United States Special Operations Command is tasked to synchronize the planning for global operations against terrorist networks. The 7500 series of Concept Plans (CONPLANS)…continue to function as both the framework for planning within DoD [Department of Defense]

and a supporting mechanism within the interagency environment for combating global terror networks.[37]

The strategic context of CONPLAN 7500 underscores the question of whether or not SOF serve as a catalyst to unify, extend the reach and maximize the effects of other instruments of national power. As this chapter argues, however, SOF cannot be considered an economy of force capability in and of themselves. Indeed, economy of force is inextricably linked to expansion of choice with regard to SOF and thus the relationship between the two must be balanced correctly in order for SOF to be effective.

CONCLUDING REMARKS

The principal lessons of the Holloway report have been demonstrated throughout recent history. SOF require a standing organizational structure, command and control mechanism, and assigned forces to generate the capability that provides an option to national decision-makers. In the US context, this requirement resulted in the creation of USSOCOM in 1987 and this concept has been adopted in some manner amongst most US allies.[38] Moreover, as this chapter has argued repeatedly, in order to provide an effective economy of force option, SOF must also represent an expansion of choice.

For example, in the summer of 2000, Royal Irish Rangers, operating as part of a UN peacekeeping mission in war-torn Sierra Leone were captured by an armed group known as the "West Side Boys." The conventional forces on the ground did not have the capabilities to recover the hostages and, as a result, SOF were deployed. A reconnaissance element was inserted followed by a SO assault force. The British SAS team that was inserted, however, did not have its own organic tactical air assault mobility capability. Although the objective to rescue the hostages was achieved, this operation demonstrated the utility of designated forces to provide tactical manoeuvre functions to an SO assault force. In this British case, rotary wing tactical lift capability – a fundamental finding of the Holloway Report with clear transitive properties beyond the US – was required. The principle being, one needs enough force to generate an option. This deficiency contributed to the development of the UK SOF Group, which was later deployed with great success in Iraq. Various other allied nations have taken a closer look at this example and have in their own way begun reassessments in order to build organizations and capabilities to enable future SOF successes.

In sum, building on their Second World War legacy, SO lie beyond the routine tasks of war and SOF continue to enable conventional force manoeuvre and enhance conventional force performance across the spectrum of conflict. Certainly, in today's chaotic and volatile defence environment, SOF serve as a catalyst to unify, extend the reach and maximize the effects of other instruments of national power. Most importantly, however, as the examples throughout this chapter have illustrated, the ability of SOF to provide an effective economy of force effort to national decision-makers is inextricably linked to there also being enough forces and capability within the SOF organization to generate an expansion of choice. When this balance is met, they can have tactical, operational and strategic effect across the spectrum of conflict.

CHAPTER 6

NOTES

1   William McRaven identifies Special Operation Forces as those forces who are specifically selected, trained and designated in his theory of Special Operations, which focuses on how an inferior force can achieve a tactical success against an enemy in the theoretically stronger defensive position. See William H. McRaven, *Spec Ops : Case Studies in Special Operations Warfare : Theory and Practice* (Novato, CA: Presidio, 1995). Also see Spulak, who theorizes that the SOF reduce friction in war. See Robert G. Spulak, Jr., *A Theory of Special Operations* (Hurlburt Field, FL: JSOU Press, October 2007).

2   Colin S. Gray, *Explorations in Strategy, Contributions in Military Studies*, (Westport, Conn.: Greenwood Press, 1996).

3   Ibid.

4   James Kiras, *Special Operations and Strategy from World War II to the War on Terrorism*, Cass Series – Strategy and History, (London; New York: Routledge, 2006). Note that his theoretical insight is based on a strategy of attrition as opposed to a strategy of annihilation.

5   These are only a few of Special Operations' characteristics reflected in US doctrine, "Joint Special Operations Task Force Operations," (April 2007). Similar themes are reflected in NATO doctrine. *The North Atlantic Treaty Organization Special Operations Forces Study*, (North Atlantic Treaty Organization Special Operations Coordination Centre, December 2008). For relevance specific to Canada, see "Canada Special Operations Forces Command – an Overview," National Defence and the Canadian Forces, <http://www.cansofcom.forces.gc.ca/ni/index-eng.asp>, (2011).

6   Notably, case selections follow the fundamental guidelines for qualitative research in social sciences. See for example, Alexander George and Andrew Bennett, *Case Studies and Theory Development in the Social Sciences* (Cambridge: Belfer Center for Science and International Affairs, 2004).

7   Winston Churchill, *Triumph and Tragedy* (Boston: Houghton Mifflin, 1953).

8   S.J. Lewis, *Jedburgh Team Operations in Support of the 12th Army Group*, August 1944 (Combat Studies Institute Press, 1991); and Kiras.

9   Frida Knight, *The French Resistance, 1940 to 1944* (London: Lawrence and Wishart, 1975).

10   John B. Dwyer, *Scouts and Raiders : The Navy's First Special Warfare Commandos* (Westport, CT: Praeger, 1993); and Kevin Dockery, *Navy Seals: The Complete History* (New York: Berkley Publishing Group, 2004).

11   Winston Churchill, *Memoirs of the Second World War : An Abridgement of the Six Volumes of the Second World War with an Epilogue by the Author on the Postwar Years Written for This Volume* (Boston: Houghton Mifflin, 1990).

12   McRaven; and Paul Kemp, *Underwater Warriors : The Fighting History of Midget Submarines*, Cassell Military Paperbacks (London: Cassell, 2000).

13   "National Security Action Memorandum No.57," ed. Department of Defense (1961); and Richard H. Shultz, *The Secret War against Hanoi: Kennedy's and Johnson's Use of Spies, Saboteurs, and Covert Warriors in North Vietnam*, 1st ed. (New York: HarperCollins, 1999).

14   Lieutenant-Commander C. Tortora, "An Analysis of Seal Operations and Effectiveness in the Mekong Delta" (U.S. Naval Postgraduate School, 1970); and D.A. Ablowich, *The Effectiveness of USN SEAL Team Operations in Support of Operation Game Warden* (1967).

15   Austin Long and William Rosenau, *The Phoenix Program and Contemporary Counterinsurgency*, (2009).

16   Ibid.

17   Susan L. Marquis, *Unconventional Warfare : Rebuilding U.S. Special Operations Forces, The Rediscovering Government Series* (Washington, D.C.: Brookings Institution, 1997); Thomas K. Adams, *US Special Operations*

CHAPTER 6

Forces in Action : The Challenge of Unconventional Warfare (London; Portland, OR: Frank Cass, 1998); and Christopher K. Ives, *US Special Forces and Counterinsurgency in Vietnam : Military Innovation and Institutional Failure, 1961-63*, Strategy and History (New York: Routledge, 2007).

18   Lawrence Freedman, *The Official History of the Falklands Campaign*, II vols., vol. II (New York: Routledge, 2007); and Max Hastings and Simon Jenkins, *The Battle for the Falklands,* 1ˢᵗ American ed. (New York: Norton, 1983).

19   Andrew J. Bacevich and Insitute for Foreign Policy Analysis, *American Military Policy in Small Wars : The Case of El Salvador*, Special Report (Washington: Pergamon-Brassey's, 1988).

20   Colonel James H. Kyle with John Robert Eidson, *The Guts to Try: The Untold Story of the Iran Hostage Rescue Mission by the On-Scene Desert Commander*, 1ˢᵗ ed. (New York: Orion Books, 1990).

21   James R. Locher, *Victory on the Potomac: The Goldwater-Nichols Act Unifies the Pentagon*, 1ˢᵗ ed., Texas A & M University Military History Series (College Station: Texas A & M University Press, 2002). See also Marquis and Adams.

22   John B. Dwyer, "SEALs in Desert Storm," *U.S. Naval Institute Proceedings*, 118 (July 1992).

23   Richard Shultz, "Showstoppers: Nine Reasons Why We Never Sent Our Special Operations Forces after Al Qaeda before 9/11," *The Weekly Standard* (2004); and David Tucker and Christopher J. Lamb, *United States Special Operations Forces* (New York: Columbia University Press, 2007).

24   *United States National Security Strategy 2002*, (2002); and Office of Homeland Security, *National Strategy for Homeland Security* (Washington D.C.: Office of Homeland Security, July 2002).

25   David M. Last et al., *Force of Choice: Perspectives on Special Operations* (Montreal: McGill-Queen's University Press, 2004).

26   Tucker and Lamb. Colin Jackson and Austin Long, "The Fifth Service: The Rise of Special Operations Command," in Harvey M. Sapolsky, Benjamin H. Friedman and Brendon Rittenhouse Green, eds., *US Military Innovation since the Cold War: Creation without Destruction*, (London; New York: Routledge, 2009).

27   Jackson and Long.

28   Rich Juergens, Michael Flynn and Thomas Cantrell, "Employing ISR: SOF Best Practices," *Joint Forces Quarterly*, No. 50 (3rd Quarter, 2008); and Thomas R. Searle, "Tribal Engagement in Anbar Province: The Critical Role of Special Operations Forces," *Joint Forces Quarterly*, No. 50 (3rd Quarter, 2008).

29   Christopher J. Lamb and Evan Munsing, *Secret Weapon: High-Value Target Teams as an Organizational Innovation* (Washington D.C.: National Defense University Press, March 2011); Long and Rosenau; and Anonymous, "Inside the 'New' Special Operations," *Proceedings Magazine*, Vol. 135, No. 7 (June 30, 2010). Stanley McCrystal, "It Takes a Network," *Foreign Policy* (March/April 2011), <http://www.foreignpolicy.com/articles/2011/02/22/it_takes_a_network>.

30   Munsing; and McCrystal.

31   Ibid.

32   David P. Fridovich and Fred T. Krawchuk, "Winning in the Pacific: The Special Operations Forces Indirect Approach," *Joint Forces Quarterly*, No. 44 (1st Quarter, 2007); Gregory Wilson, "Anatomy of a Successful COIN Operation," *Military Review* (November-December 2006); Joint Special Operations Task Force – Philippines, "Joint Special Operations Task Force – Philippines Overview," (2008), <http://www2.warwick.ac.uk/.../vigilant/powerpoints/jsotf-p_overview_brief_feb_2008_ver_2.ppt>; and Cherilyn A. Walley, "Civilian Affairs: A Weapon of Peace on Basilan Island," *Special Warfare* 3 (2004). Hy Rothstein, "Less is More: The Problematic Future of Irregular Warfare in an Era of Collapsing States," *Third World Quarterly*, Vol. 28, No. 2 (2007).

33   JSOTF-P Unclassified Command Brief, interview with Special Forces Operational Detachment "B" commander, Basilan, Republic of the Philippines, 2011; and interview with Armed Forces of the Philippines officer at US Naval College, Newport, RI, 2011.

34   Interviews with Commander JSOTF-P, Zamboanga and Manila, RP March 2011.

35   Command Brief, JSOTF-P. Zamboanga RP, March 2011.

36   Eric T. Olson, "U.S. Special Operations Command Strategy 2010," (Tampa, FL: November 1, 2009).

37   Eric T. Olson, "2010 Posture Statement," in *Senate Armed services Committee* (Washington D.C.: 2010).

38   *The North Atlantic Treaty Organization Special Operations Forces Study*; Bernard J. Brister, "Canadian Special Operations Forces: A Blueprint for the Future," *Canadian Military Journal* (Autumn 2004); and James L. Jones, "A Blueprint for Change: Transforming Special Operations," *Joint Forces Quarterly*, No. 45 (2nd Quarter, 2007).

CHAPTER 7

"LETHAL THREE-CARD MONTE": SPECIAL OPERATIONS FORCES AND ECONOMY OF EFFORT OPERATIONS IN SOUTHERN AFGHANISTAN

DR. SEAN M. MALONEY

"I know it's crooked, but it's the only game in town."
WILLIAM "CANADA BILL" JONES

The current military taxonomy regarding SOF mission types categorizes them into direct action, special reconnaissance, and indigenous cooperative/foreign internal defence missions. There is substantial focus on the mechanics of these mission types in the literature and more generalized discussions. For example, the tactical specifics of direct action, including weapons load outs, insertion techniques and the like tend to dominate professional and non-professional discussions. The novelty of working with a particular ethnic indigenous group may be another aspect in the literature. The technical parameters of UAVs and Special Operations Forces Laser Acquisition Markers (SOFLAMs) and how they are employed occupy another sphere. We may also distinguish between "strategic" SOF operations and "operational-level" SOF operations. Strategically, for example, a national command authority may authorize a specific deniable direct action mission to eliminate a terrorist personality or recover a high value individual or item. Those sorts of missions are generally understood to be SOF operations from popular culture (first-person shooter games like "Call of Duty: Black Ops" and the television series "The Unit"), as much as reality. There is relatively little discussion on our understanding of how SOF are used by commanders in the pursuit of their objectives at the operational level, however, and that is one area where SOF have really performed valuable service in the Afghanistan war.[1]

This lack of understanding is not surprising. Operational security considerations, the comparatively mundane nature of some of the activity, the increased complexity of military operations in general and the inability or unwillingness of operators to articulate what they are doing out of cultural norms are some reasons why this aspect of SOF operations is under-examined. In Afghanistan, the centrality of SOF employment has waxed and waned. In 2001, SOF worked alongside the Northern Alliance providing specialist targeting capabilities and liaison/coordination with American air power long before conventional forces were on the ground. In 2002, SOF hunted high value leadership targets and performed special reconnaissance missions at the theatre-level. After 2002, however, this centrality receded as the nature of the war shifted. In 2006, however, US and NATO planning recognized to a greater extent that SOF should play a significant and integrated role in the emergent country-wide strategy. In that strategy, SOF was to play an Economy of Effort role.

Economy of Effort operations are those operations conducted under conditions of scarcity, especially when there are not enough forces to cover a given geographical area. They are conducted in some cases with an eye towards disrupting or deceiving the enemy into believing there are more forces than there are. In conventional operations, reconnaissance organizations generally conduct Economy of Effort operations on the flanks or in areas where no other coverage is possible. Given the nature of the operational environment in Afghanistan, SOF also performed similar tasks.

CHAPTER 7

THE COMBINED FORCES COMMAND – AFGHANISTAN CAMPAIGN PLAN AND SOF IN AFGHANISTAN 2003-2005

Before moving on to the specifics of the 2006 strategy and how it was implemented in 2007-2008, it is essential that we establish how SOF fit into the previous strategy. In 2003, there were serious concerns within the American commands in Afghanistan that there was a lack of synergy between OEF forces and the ISAF. ISAF was about to expand outside of its Kabul enclave. At the same time, Combined Forces Command – Afghanistan (CFC-A) inherited the PRT concept from Canadian Joint Task Force (CJTF)-180, the "division"-level headquarters that ran the show previously. In the OEF PRT concept, PRTs that were located in "front line" provinces along the Durand Line were to have SOF operating from them in a targeting and coordination role. The information that would come in from improved coordination would assist the Tier I and Tier 0 SOF targeting Al-Qaeda, Taliban, HiG and Haqqani Tribal Network leadership targets. At the same time, Tier II SOF would be working with the Afghan Militia Forces in those provinces to improve security and increase the professionalism of those forces. Tier II SOF also targeted local and provincial-level insurgent commanders on an opportunistic basis.[2]

There was no real concept of NATO ISAF SOF employment, nor was there a SOF concept of operations associated with the PRTs that ISAF was scheduled to take over in 2003-2004. These were the "stabilization" PRTs, not the "counter-insurgency" PRTs. The British used their SOF in a counter-narcotics role in northern Afghanistan but on a strictly national basis.[3] Other nations' SOF, including CANSOF, tended to be used in a close protection role in Kabul, or as the Deputy Chief of Defence Staff's "commissars" to keep an eye on Canadian commanders. With the prospects of ISAF expansion and with no prospects of combining ISAF and OEF in Afghanistan, there was initially no real impetus to come up with a country-wide strategy and then situate SOF within it. Ironically, one block to an OEF-ISAF merger revolved around preventing NATO control over Tier I/Tier 0 operations directed against high value targets. This decision was based on a series of poor experiences in Bosnia where the French were suspected of blowing American persons indicted for war crimes (PIFWC or "piff-wick") seizure operations.[4]

When Lieutenant-General David Barno took over as the senior American commander in Afghanistan in late 2003, the American headquarters re-examined their country-wide strategy and came up with a new one in informal consultation with the UN, NATO ISAF, and other interested parties. That strategy, called "Counterinsurgency Strategy for Afghanistan," consisted of five pillars:

- defeat terrorism and deny sanctuary to terrorists;

- enable Afghan security structures;

- sustain area ownership;

- enable reconstruction and good governance; and

- engage regional states.[5]

For the most part, the CFC-A campaign plan was designed to improve interagency and international community coordination and to establish unity of purpose between the various entities seeking to stabilize the country as much as it was to address the security conditions of Afghanistan. The decisive points that the strategy focused on included the 2004 national elections and the 2005 provincial elections, not detailed specifics over how forces in the field should be used to achieve coalition objectives. Barno and his British advisors understood that these elections were critical in establishing the legitimacy of the Afghan government. The role of SOF in this approach was general and identified as continuing the high value enemy leadership hunt with a particular emphasis on Al-Qaeda. It also recognized that Tier II SOF would play an intelligence and targeting role in the "counter-insurgency" PRTs.

That said, the implementation of the CFC-A campaign plan established three command areas: Regional Command (East), Regional Command (South), and the CJTF-76 operating area which corresponded to the other half of the country not adjacent to Pakistan (and overlapping with the expanding ISAF area of operations and their PRTs). The Regional Commands were essentially brigade-level conventional commands. Regional Command (South) for example, consisted of the 173rd Airborne Brigade headquarters, a re-roled artillery battalion, an infantry battalion, an independent recce company, and four PRTs in 2005. At the same time, the Combined Joint Special Operations Task Force Afghanistan (CJSOTF-A) deployed Tier II and allied SOF units to the two Regional Command areas, but under CJSOTF-A command. The Tier I/Tier 0 SOF also had a separate reporting chain. All three units – conventional, Tier II SOF, and Tier I/Tier 0 SOF – were operating in the same area with different mandates and separate control mechanisms.

At some point in late 2004, the situation in Regional Command (South) was rationalized. Nobody could coordinate with Tier I/Tier 0, so they were effectively out of the loop and did their own thing, which apparently was very little given the paucity of high value enemy leadership targets. That left the issue of delineating between conventional and Tier II SOF units.[6] Regional Command (South) had only two manoeuvre units and a sub-unit for all four provinces. At the same time, Oruzgan province was and had been a SOF "playground" going back to 2001. The decision was made to focus the recce sub-unit in Helmand, the re-rolled artillery battalion in Kandahar and the infantry battalion in Zabol province. CJSOTF-A assumed responsibility for Oruzgan province, plus three districts in southern Kandahar.

In effect, this situation constituted an Economy of Effort operation, though it was not formally designated as such. There simply were not enough conventional forces to occupy each and every district in each province in Regional Command (South). Nor was there an apparent need to at the time given the threat level. Tier II SOF, based on TF-71 and then TF-31 (battalion-sized US Special Forces units) worked alongside indigenous Afghan forces mostly drawn from the Afghan Militia Forces (allies from the 2001-2002 period) in areas that the Taliban were known to be operating, (those areas were comparatively limited in the 2003-2005 period compared to after 2006). Dutch and French SOF operated in southern Kandahar province along the border interdicting the then-small Taliban groups passing through their respective districts.

The CFC-A campaign plan was designed for the low-level insurgency that existed in Afghanistan in 2003-2004. SOF's role in that strategy was clearly defined where Tier II SOF occupied their "boxes" and Tier I/Tier 0 hunted leadership targets. The approach was deliberately general and its dispositions were not intended to withstand the calculated assault on Afghanistan that was unleashed in late 2005.

THE CHANGING SITUATION, 2005-2006

In mid-2005, American Tier II SOF commanders noted that the pattern and nature of insurgent activity was changing in southern Afghanistan. The number of direct-fire attacks on SOF-Afghan forces was dramatically up in Oruzgan and Zabol, as well as Paktia and Kowst. Sensitive site exploitation determined that there were increased numbers of Arab and Chechen fighters training Afghan insurgents. Dead foreign fighters were photographed and identified, as were members of the Pakistani government's covert action directorate. "Political" targeting designed to influence the 2005 elections was increasingly sophisticated. The advent of the suicide bombing campaign in Kandahar and the significantly increased use of other improvised explosive devices (IEDs) during September-October were the real harbingers of change. It was becoming a new war.

The situation steadily deteriorated throughout the first half of 2006 as the insurgency took on a more organized, near-conventional turn culminating in the Zharey and Panjwayi district battles in the summer and fall of 2006. TF-31 found itself engaged in a conventional fight near Sperwan Ghar in September and October 2006 during the Op MEDUSA battle. This fight essentially eliminated the equivalent of an insurgent light infantry battalion. Prior to that, Task Force Bushmaster, a CJTSOTF-A controlled organization, cut its way across Oruzgan province and into northern Helmand province. TF Bushmaster was a combination of Tier II SOF from TF-31, a company from the 10th Mountain Division, and indigenous Afghan militia. For the most part, TF Bushmaster acted as a conventional mobile formation. Elements of 2/87 Infantry were inserted by helicopter onto prominent features in northern Helmand. The enemy was drawn to these temporary Forward Operating Bases (FOBs), where they were attacked and attritted. The Tier II SOF, and even Tier I SOF, went after any leadership targets that revealed themselves in the area with a mobile column. The whole process was repeated elsewhere as the force moved west out of Oruzgan and south into Helmand in the summer of 2006.

The TF-31 Sperwan Ghar battle and the activities of TF Bushmaster were conducted by CJSOTF-A and coordinated with Canadian Task Force (CTF) Aegis, the Regional Command (South) brigade. CTF Aegis could not use or task these organizations as part of their larger campaign plan.[7] US Tier II SOF activities were completely separate, as were the strikes conducted by Tier I/Tier 0 forces against Taliban high value leadership targets throughout this time. The opportunistic and reactive nature of SOF operations during this time makes them difficult to classify as planned Economy of Effort missions, though these operations still had the effect of degrading the insurgents' capacity in the areas in which they operated.

TOWARDS THE AFGHAN DEVELOPMENT ZONE STRATEGY

At this time, NATO ISAF was in the process of expanding through-out Afghanistan in a staged plan. The irrational concept of two international coalitions operating in Afghanistan was about to be jettisoned during this process, once Stage III and Stage IV ISAF expansion was completed (Stage III was Regional Command (South) and Stage IV was Regional Command (East)). The incoming ISAF command led by Lieutenant-General David Richards, formulated its country-wide strategy in the spring of 2006 in preparation for the ISAF takeover.

The ISAF planners drew on work conducted by OEF planners back in 2003. One issue with the CFC-A campaign plan was its detailed implementation. An important concept by the CFC-A planners was the Regional Development Zone (RDZ) concept. The idea was to generate a stabilization, development and security synergy in selected provinces, particularly those with large population centres. The RDZ, with prioritized reconstruction monies, would use the PRT in a given province as the main coordination point between the central government of Afghanistan, the provincial leadership, Afghan and coalition security forces, NGOs and other developers. Kandahar was identified as the first RDZ as early as the fall of 2003. The RDZ idea collapsed, however, through a combination of lack of money and little continuity across the stakeholders as they rotated out of the country.

RDZ's were revived under the Richards' strategy and called Afghan Development Zones (ADZs). Unlike the RDZ, in the ADZ concept, it was the approach *in* that was central to the strategy, not just the piecemeal or tentative implementation of a more generalized strategy. ADZs were also linked to the upcoming Afghan National Development Strategy (ANDS), the Canadian-mentored country strategy that essentially replaced the Bonn Agreement and the Barno/Brahimi strategy. There were several ADZs created simultaneously in critical areas. At the core of each zone were the governance structures, the bulk of the population, and development resources provided by a variety of agencies and organizations. The inner security for the zone was to be provided by the Afghan national security forces, police and army. The next outer layer of security for the zones was the ISAF manoeuvre forces. Reconstruction resources were centralized in the zone first, and then pushed out later as the security situation improved. Each ADZ was connected by main service routes, which could become lateral hubs for expansion. The ADZ approach accepted that some districts where reconstruction work was progressing would have to be scaled back or abandoned. Outside of the zone lay the SOF operating areas. These areas were to act as filters and to disrupt enemy activity before it could get into the zone. This organization was pure Economy of Effort – the ISAF planners knew that they did not have enough forces to control the entirety of each province as there were only so many ISAF and OEF manoeuvre units, and the Afghan National Army (ANA) was still a long way from being able to handle even battalion-level activities.[8]

FROM THEORY TO REALITY

The coalition effort in Kandahar province in 2007-2008 was a critical fight during the war and consequently is a good example to explore how SOF were employed within the context of the ADZ strategy. The culmination of two near-conventional operations in the fall of 2006, Op MEDUSA and Op BAAZ TSUKA, presented coalition leaders with a steady-state into the spring of 2007. Working around the province, the Taliban guerilla forces were active in: Shah Wali Kot and the northern districts; Zharey district with some activity in Panjwayi; Maywand district; and in

Ghrak. Registan, Maruf and Arghistan were infiltration areas from Pakistan, while Shorabak and Spin Boldak constituted a special case because of the unique leadership and tribal political situation there. Terrorist cells operated in Kandahar City proper. The pattern of guerilla operations in the rural districts and terrorist operations in the built-up areas were not as supported with religious/political mobilization as they would be by 2009-2010. The insurgents practiced negative governance, that is, they disrupted government of Afghanistan development and reconstruction activities without providing an alternative parallel structure. They specifically targeted the religious authorities in order to shape their information operations.

The implementation of the ADZ strategy in Kandahar province in late 2006 resulted in a re-focus of the coalition effort to contain the enemy in Zharey district and a withdrawal of coalition conventional forces from Shah Wali Kot. The ADZ was defined, for all intents and purposes, as the City and its immediately adjacent districts – Arghandab, which was self-protecting and nearly self-governing under Mullah Naquib; Dand, Daman, and Panjwayi districts. Spin Boldak was almost a mini-ADZ unto itself. At this point the Afghan National Security Force (ANSF) was still limited in capability, especially the "police." For the most part there was one Canadian battle group, the Canadian recce squadron, and one Afghan *kandak* (battalion) available for operations at any one time. Recce Squadron handled Spin Boldak, the 2 RCR Battle Group focused solely on Zharey and Panjwayi with as many Afghans as could be made available from the ANA. "Police" units were essentially untrained militias wearing police uniforms.

The number of available SOF organizations increased in 2007 and became more integrated into ISAF planning in Kandahar. As before, there were not enough conventional coalition or Afghan forces to occupy each and every district in the province. The Polish

SOF unit, Grupa Reagowania Operacyjno-Manewrowego (GROM), deployed around February 2007. GROM was assigned the Maruf and Arghistan districts. GROM's task was to interdict insurgent resupply and reinforcement movement in those districts. GROM operated without the development and reconstruction resources needed to gain the population's support. It lacked a robust integral CIMIC or PSYOPS capability. This was in part due to issues within the Provincial Reconstruction Team and their emphasis on Kandahar provincial governance. PRT priorities were the districts comprising the ADZ; Maruf and Arghistan lay outside the ADZ. GROM was not under the command of Task Force Kandahar (TFK), though it retained close liaison with it. Its reporting chain was through CJSOTF-A. In many ways, GROM's mission was a continuation of the French SOF mission back in 2005, but the force did not bring a coordinated DA-CIMIC-PSYOPS approach to the fight in those districts. There was some coordinated ANSF-SOF approach. At best, GROM was a Tier II unit that performed a disruptive function but it did not set out to shape the district's population to resist insurgent activity in any comprehensive fashion.

Contrast this situation with British SOF operations under TF 42. TF 42 tended to be more of a Tier I "scalpel," but not under TFK or NATO command. It consisted of a combination of elements from the SAS, Special Boat Service (SBS), the Special Reconnaissance Regiment, and integral helicopter support from 7 Squadron, Special Forces Flight.[9] The highly mobile TF 42 tended to work in Helmand province (the SAS component generally) with the SBS working in and around Kandahar City. TF 42 had a close relationship to the police forces, the Canadian PRT, and the Canadian intelligence structures. At times TF 42 and the PRT were the only coalition forces operating in the city as opposed to just transiting it. TF 42 hunted urban terrorists. Later on, TF 42 developed actionable intelligence on cells operating between Kandahar City and in Spin Boldak. The Canadian Recce Squadron, itself already acting in an economy of force role in Spin Boldak alongside local Afghan militia forces, worked with TF 42 to track down IED cells. Like GROM, however, TF 42 lacked a comprehensive approach to the population.

The US SOF generally deployed a battalion-sized SOTF to work in Kandahar, Oruzgan, and Zabol provinces starting in 2006 (before that the task force had responsibilities in Regional Command (East) as well). The American approach was very different from GROM's and TF 42's. SOTFs, TF-31, TF-71, and TF-73, rotated in and out of Kandahar province in 2007-2008 on six-month rotations. The US SOTF, unlike the British and Polish SOF, brought a more comprehensive approach to the fight. Special Forces Operational Detachment Alphas (ODA)'s, generally platoon-sized teams, worked alongside Afghan forces. These Afghans came from different sources. Some were trusted militia forces from the 2001-2002 period who had not been disarmed and demobilized in the various Afghan New Beginnings processes.[10] As the ANA expanded in 2007-2008, the US SOTF leveraged its influence and had regular infantry companies and even a whole *kandak* assigned to it. Later on, when specialized Commando *Kandaks* came on line, they deployed commando companies with the ODAs.

The US SOTF had Civil Affairs and PSYOPS capabilities integrated into their structures and operations. As such, the US SOTF could occupy a district and bring information operations and civil affairs projects to it in order to influence the population. This capability, in theory, could act as a gateway for the larger governmental development projects handled by the PRT, though in practice US SOTF and PRT coordination was not optimal in 2007-2008.

The US SOTF operated in an arc across northern Kandahar province, moving back and forth from Shah Wali Kot into Khakriz and then Ghorak on occasion. Once again, these districts lay outside the ADZ and therefore an integrated development approach was not possible. This left the US SOTF to conduct mobile operations

190

and disrupt insurgent activity (in most cases supported with Canadian M-777 artillery – sometimes a detachment of two guns was cut to the SOTF for operations). Unlike Maruf and Arghistan, Shah Wali Kot and Khakriz hosted comparatively robust and resilient guerilla forces that were supplied through logistic chains running through the mountainous terrain in Oruzgan, Helmand and Zabol provinces.

Once again, the US SOTFs reported to CJSOTF and not Task Force Kandahar. This is a critical point. GROM, TF-42 and the US SOTFs retained different rules of engagement from the NATO ISAF conventional forces operating in the province. This situation had advantages and disadvantages. On the down side, there were problems with effects mitigation when a SOF operation killed the wrong people under looser rules of engagement. It was next to impossible to explain to the media: first, that there were SOF present and operating, because they were special and deniable; and, second, that they did not belong to the Canadian-led command structures in the province. On the plus side, if the coordination measures were acceptable to both parties, non-ISAF SOF could be used by ISAF forces to do things that ISAF was restricted from doing – if the coordination measures were acceptable to both parties.

The CANSOF organizations during this time tended towards a TF-42 model rather than a GROM or US SOTF approach (but without the integral helicopter support). The C-21 organization was direct action oriented and went after vetted enemy leadership targets, IED cells and networks within the ADZ. The C-23 organization sat somewhere between Tier II and Tier III. It did some direct actions within the ADZ. In time, C-23 developed relationships with Afghan Tier III structures. There was no integral CIMIC or PSYOPS capacity to the CANSOF task forces.

As we can see, the Economy of Effort organizations within the ADZ strategy were GROM and the US SOTFs. As in the past, there were not enough conventional forces to go around. SOF were employed to maintain a disruptive influence on the approaches to the ADZ in Kandahar. How well did they perform?

Criteria for success and measures of effectiveness have bedeviled the coalition effort in Afghanistan at the best of times. We can, however, look at this issue broadly. First, to what extent did the SOF organizations attenuate enemy activity? Second, what type of enemy activity was attenuated? Third, how did that attenuation contribute to the situation as it evolved in 2007-2008? To answer these questions, we need to further identify how the enemy was behaving and what tools it was using. In 2007, the situation in Kandahar province had the enemy building up in upper Shah Wali Kot, Nesh, and upper Khakriz and influencing upper Ghorak. It was holed up in Zharey district, and was using Panjwayi and Maywand districts as rest/logistic zones. There were urban terrorism and information operations conducted inside the city. The insurgents had just suffered significant casualties in the fall of 2006 and were shifting gears into the spring and summer of 2007.

Throughout 2007, the enemy eyed Arghandab district. First, Arghandab's tribal/political structure was crucial for the defence of the city proper and, second, any moves on Arghandab would relieve pressure on their allies in Zharey. The death of Mullah Naquib was the kick-off for a campaign versus Arghandab but then it stalled out. It is probable that the SOTF operating in an arc north and forward of Arghandab had a disruptive effect. The enemy mounted a major operation in November, which penetrated to Arghandab but it was routed using conventional forces, police and the US SOTF.

As for GROM over in Arghistan and Maruf, it is difficult to measure how many insurgents were deterred, stopped, or otherwise thwarted from moving through those districts. The rugged terrain was undoubtedly a factor, as was enemy access to other high-speed routes adjacent to those two districts. GROM basically introduced some increased friction into the enemy's plans but it was not seriously coordinated with any other coalition effort.

In both cases, battlefield success was theoretically translatable into local support, but only if there were a permanent security presence coupled with development projects. In neither case could the SOTF and GROM generate a state whereby governance and development could take off. They could set the conditions for it, but without police and ANA there was no way this effect was going to take hold. And, given the ADZ strategy, it was not considered crucial anyway in those districts.

By early 2008, some thought was given to expanding the ADZ into Zharey and then Maywand. For the most part this was a conventional show handled by the Regional Battle Group (South) (RBG (S)) (1 Royal Gurkha Rifles), which conducted economy of force operations in Khakriz and Maywand. The US SOTF generally stuck to Shah Wali Kot and Arghandab, with some forays into Ghorak. The enemy repeated his Arghandab adventure in June 2008 and was handed the same result – conventional forces ejected them from Arghandab. The fact that this was the second time the insurgency was able to penetrate the SOTF screen in Shah Wali Kot-Khakriz indicates that something was not working with the SOTF and its operations, either in concept of operations, target acquisition or response. As for GROM, its effectiveness was questioned by its own leadership and, by August 2008, the organization was withdrawn and sent to Ghazni in Regional Command (East). This left virtually no coalition forces or presence in Maruf or Arghistan.

After the second Arghandab foray, the insurgents altered their approach to the district and emphasized a constant assault on the tribal/political structure using assassination and intimidation. The

US SOTF was not structured to handle this sort of attack; generally, under these circumstances, a policing and governance response is more appropriate. The US SOTF continued with its disruptive operations in Shah Wali Kot and Khakriz. This continuance probably attenuated enemy guerilla forces and kept leadership targets in a state of agitation, but it had no effect on preventing the destabilization of Arghandab. Arguably, the SOTF prevented a guerilla force follow-up and consolidation of the "political" campaign.

Another probable SOTF success was in the upper Shah Wali Kot area, in a zone called "the Jet Stream." This insurgent logistics route running from Zabol into Oruzgan and then to northern Helmand, with branches south into upper Kandahar province, was a serious target of opportunity for the US SOTF. Disruption operations against the Jet Stream would have had a deleterious effect on support for the Shah Wali Kot-Khakriz insurgents who were in turn supporting the Arghandab operations and, to some extent, the insurgents in Zharey district as well. Once again, there are intangibles in play that cannot be measured with existing tools. What amount of money, weapons, leaders, and reinforcements did the enemy put into the system and how much of that made it through the system to its end users, for example? To what extent did the enemy *not* do something or move through an area because they *thought* SOF was working there?

What is clear is that the ADZ strategy, even with its Economy of Effort aspects, was itself under resourced. Of the seven active districts adjacent to the ADZ, only three or four contained SOF in an economy of force role. The RBG (S) operated in two other areas, sharing one with SOF. It was like a game of three-card monte. Recall at the same time there was only one coalition battle group and up to two Afghan kandaks in play, and these were focused solely on Zharey and Panjwayi and then hived off to deal with Arghandab and even to support British operations in Helmand province from time to time. It is highly likely that the SOTF and

GROM played a role in interfering with the enemy's designs on Kandahar province.

Ultimately, the ADZ strategy was subsumed by subsequent headquarters and commanders who had, in their view, better ideas. Richards' replacement spent the bulk of his time attempting to establish a replacement strategy in 2008, yet to no avail. During that time, the SOF involved with economy of force missions continued with their tasks in the province, but operated in a strategic vacuum as the province-level concept of operations supposedly governing the behaviour of its adjacent units changed repeatedly. Having two coalitions occupy the same battle-space but having different concepts was not a useful proposition and reduced the ability for the SOF to be fully effective. At the same time, the lack of progression in the governance and development arenas meant that SOF in the Economy of Effort role were buying time, but for something that was not to emerge in Kandahar province.

NOTES

1   This study is based on the author's observations during several deployments to Afghanistan from 2003 to 2010 in a military historical capacity and on interviews with TF-31 personnel. It does not pretend to be a comprehensive overview of coalition SOF in Afghanistan.

2   The categorization of SOF into "tiers" means different things to different people. For the purposes of this chapter, Tier I refers to units that exclusively conduct direct action missions, while Tier 0 conduct operations in a deniable fashion. Tier II SOF conducts indigenous training as well as direct action, while Tier III SOF tend to be light infantry that protect Tier I-type operations from outside interference or assist with their extraction.

3   Mark Nichol, *Ultimate Risk: SAS Contact Al Qaeda* (London: Macmillan, 2004).

4   See Richard Newman, "Hunting War Criminals," <http://www.
specialoperations.com/Army/Delta_Force/bosnia.html>.

5   David W. Barno, "Fighting the Other War: Counterinsurgency
Strategy in Afghanistan 2003-2005," *Military Review* (September-October
2007), <http://usacac.army.mil/CAC2/MilitaryReview/Archives/English/
MilitaryReview_20071031_art006.pdf>.

6   Anonymous, *Hunting Al Qaeda* (Zenith Press, 2005).

7   CTF AEGIS established a relationship with TF-42 the UK SOF task
force which was at this time largely based around the Special Boat Service
(SBS) and the Special Reconnaissance Regiment. TF-42 had its own national reporting chain and tended to focus on SR operations in Helmand
and direct action in Kandahar City.

8   Briefing to the author, Kandahar, June 2006.

9   See   <http://www.eliteukforces.info/uk-military-news/200810-
task-force-42.php> for TF-42 structure.

10   These included the Demobilization, Disarmament and Reintegra-
tion (DDR) and Disbandment of Illegal Armed Groups (DIAG) programs.
See Barbara Stapleton, "Disarming the Militias: DDR and DIAG and the
Implications for Peace Building," <http://www.sak.se/arkiv/artiklar/
artiklar/2009/peace/stapleton.pdf>.

CHAPTER 8

REFLECTIONS OF A JOURNALIST

DAVID PUGLIESE

This chapter will cover the past, present and future of the relations between CANSOF and the news media from the perspective of a journalist who has reported on CANSOF since their inception.

First, let us look at the past. In 1992-1993 when JTF 2 took over the counter-terrorism responsibilities from the RCMP's SERT, the Canadian Forces made the decision that all aspects about the new unit, except for its name and mandate, would be secret. Although journalists such as myself had toured the Dwyer Hill Training Centre and photographed RCMP SERT in action, the military unit doing exactly the same job, based at the same location, using similar equipment and techniques, was now off limits to the news media.

In those days the CANSOF public affairs policy – if it could be called that – bordered on the ridiculous. DND, acting on JTF 2's advice, claimed that it could not discuss the type of weapons the unit used for reasons of national security, yet then sent media outlets photographs of JTF 2 operators using MP-5 submachine guns. At first DND declined to name the location of where the unit was based, even though it was obvious JTF 2 took over the Dwyer Hill Training Centre from the RCMP. The Canadian Forces would claim that the names of JTF 2's commanding officers were secret, yet would then go and post those same names on the DND internet site.

In my view, the low-point of this so-called media relations policy occurred when in response to one of my Access to Information requests someone at JTF 2 decided to invoke the national security clause to censor details about particular items of equipment. I have been told that there was much amusement at the Dwyer Hill Training Centre when those Access Documents, all blank pages, were released to me. I have also been told the laughter stopped after I found out that one of the pieces of equipment – its existence concealed for reasons of national security – was a coffee maker. My article about JTF 2's "secret coffee maker" ran in eight newspapers, and those in the Counter-Terrorism/Special Operations organization spent more than a few days trying to explain to representatives of the Privy Council Office just why the release of information about a coffee maker could undermine the security of Canada.

With the development of CANSOFCOM and the stand-up of the CSOR in 2006, there was what I would describe as a positive shift in attitude towards the news media. I believe this change can be traced to the realization by the senior Canadian Forces leadership that there had to be some level of openness, some information released to the public and parliamentarians, in part, to justify the expense and the expansion of SOF. The previous levels of intense secrecy that had surrounded JTF 2 would not have gone down well at House of Commons committee meetings when members of parliament (MPs) started asking for explanations about how and why hundreds of millions of dollars were being spent on expanding SOF.

As part of this initial shift in attitudes towards the media, journalists from *Legion Magazine*, the *National Post*, the *Ottawa Citizen*, CBC TV and other news outlets were invited to watch initial CSOR training and selection. I, along with other journalists, also spent time with 427 Special Operations Aviation Squadron and the

CJIRU. JTF 2 was, as it is now, off limits. Former CSOR Commander Colonel Jamie Hammond was a leader in opening up his unit to interact with the news media. Former CANSOFCOM Commander Colonel Dave Barr gave interviews to those journalists who asked about the command. Present CANSOFCOM Commander Brigadier-General D. Michael Day, originally reluctant about interacting with the media, took this policy even further. He made significant improvements in CANSOFCOM media relations, providing numerous interviews to journalists, encouraging visits by reporters to some of the Command's units, and in the case of the 2010 Special Operations Forces Symposium in Kingston, Ontario, invited journalists to speak to operators and command staff on military-media relations. This type of interaction would have been unheard of just a few years ago.

It is important to also examine the context in which these changes were taking place to understand the full significance of these efforts by the SOF leadership. This level of openness on CANSOFCOM's part started in the spring of 2006. Ironically, it coincided with the exact opposite situation that was unfolding in the rest of DND and the Canadian Forces. From 1999 to 2006 DND and the Canadian Forces had what many in media and within the military saw as one of the most professional and effective public affairs operations in the federal government. There were some problems of course, but for the most part, questions from journalists were answered promptly. Journalists were able to interview subject matter experts, gaining knowledge and insight on a particular issue, which, in turn, was reflected in the coverage.

This situation no longer exists. Outside of the Afghanistan mission, it is rare for DND and Canadian Forces to allow a journalist to talk to a subject matter expert within these organizations. Often there is no voice communication at all. A civilian or military public affairs specialist simply presses a button and emails to a journalist a series of talking points approved by the Prime Minister's Office. Media deadlines are ignored. It can take one to three weeks for these emails to be provided to journalists, sometimes months. Sometimes a reporter's request is simply ignored. The result is that the viewpoint of the Canadian Forces and DND is often missing from broadcasts and articles these days. Except for the coverage of the Afghanistan mission, media reporting on Air Force and Army activities has significantly dwindled. News coverage of the Navy is almost non-existent.

Ironically, some in the military's public affairs world seem to think Brigadier-General Day and his one public affairs officer have somehow stumbled on to PR gold since media coverage of CANSOFCOM since 2006 – from a DND point of view – is largely viewed as being generally fair and balanced. Have these two CANSOFCOM individuals somehow stumbled on a magical formula that has eluded the 575 employees of DND's public affairs branch? No, they are simply following the same professional public affairs system that existed at DND before 2006. That is, if you are asked a question, respond to the best of your ability. Respond promptly. Explain to the best of your ability the issue at hand. And do not lie because that only destroys your credibility. These are key attributes that some in the DND public affairs' organization have unfortunately forgotten.

So does this mean that there are no issues with media relations and CANSOFCOM? Not at all. There have been and will continue to be problems. For instance, *Legion Magazine*'s Adam Day and myself were invited by Brigadier-General Day to travel to Camp Pendleton, California in 2008 to watch CSOR training. We did see about sixty minutes of training before a former JTF 2 operator, assigned to CSOR, objected to the presence of journalists on this approved trip and was able to convince a major on the scene to have us removed from the exercise area. We had not violated OPSEC; the individual in question simply did not like journalists. With nothing further to do we flew back to Canada, a largely wasted trip. The highlight for me was watching this JTF 2 operator, with his hands on his hips, circle Adam Day and myself, glaring at us and trying to stare us down. If it had not been for the money I had spent on my airline tickets, hotel and rental car, the scene would have been amusing. Faced with this operator's behaviour, it was difficult for me at the time to reconcile the often-repeated claim that JTF 2 members were mature and quiet professionals. Now, one individual does not represent an entire command or unit. However, this incident should be a reminder to CANSOF personnel, and other members of the Canadian Forces, that the actions of a few can influence the public perception of an organization.

As a journalist I will always push for more openness and, although I understand the limits of operational security, I do not always agree with how that is applied by the military. There are going to be times where CANSOFCOM will not agree with the news media's reporting on a particular subject. I also fully understand not all in CANSOFCOM are happy with the senior leadership's decision to interact with the media. There are those who want a blanket of total secrecy. In this day and age I do not think that is even possible anymore.

So why should CANSOF interact with the media? Whether they like it or not, the news media is a presence on the battle-space, whether that is in on an international operation or in a domestic situation, such as a hostage rescue. You do not have to look any further for evidence of that than the photographs taken by journalists of JTF 2 operators in Haiti in 2004 or of the JTF 2 operator standing beside Prime Minister Stephen Harper as he is buying a Tim Horton's coffee at Kandahar Airfield. The media will not go away and will gather information on CANSOF, with or without their help. In my view, it makes more sense for SOF to make an effort to interact with journalists. The results will not be to the Command's liking at all times but, at least, such interaction allows the CANSOFCOM viewpoint to be presented in broadcasts and articles.

Secondly, educating the media and public about CANSOFCOM accomplishes a longer-term communications role that is important in a democracy. CANSOFCOM personnel see themselves as quiet, mature professionals doing an important service for Canadians. But not everyone shares that view. Many times, I have received a different view from serving military personnel about CANSOF. That is, one of arrogance and cliquishness. JTF, I've been told on more than one occasion, is short for "Just the Friends." Some parliamentarians have a similar perspective. I have had both Members of Parliament and Senators explain to me their viewpoint of CANSOF; they see CANSOFCOM and its units, particularly JTF 2, as lacking accountability and oversight, organizations that, at times, seem to be above the law. These types of concerns are now being voiced in the House of Commons and in media articles in regard to the Sand Trap investigations. Openness and transparency, within the rules of OPSEC, is one way to educate and reassure the public, media and members of the Canadian Forces about the roles performed by CANSOFCOM and its units.

So what about the future of CANSOFCOM-media relations? Much of CANSOFCOM's current attitude towards the media is personality-based. In other words, specific commanders, from Colonel Hammond to Brigadier-General Day, have decided that interacting with the media has advantages, as well as risks, for special operations. This viewpoint, of course, can change as new individuals come in to command. Because of this situation I believe it is important for a more extensive debate to take place in CANSOFCOM about its interactions with the news media.

Is there value in examining how other SOF organizations conduct media relations? The British SAS, for instance, supposedly has an official policy of not discussing SOF operations, yet obviously deals with journalists using back channels to get information out into the public domain. The Australian SAS has what appears to be quite an open policy, although it is my understanding that this was somewhat forced upon it by the Australian government and is not keenly embraced by all of its operators. USSOCOM has an interesting media policy, with openness to an extent that some journalists have accompanied Green Berets and Navy SEALs into combat operations.

CANSOFCOM will have to figure out its own way. It will have to balance transparency and openness with its OPSEC concerns. Consistency in this policy will be important. There is little point in having a Canadian Forces spokesperson claim that the military does not discuss JTF 2 operations in Afghanistan when a day later journalists are approached by government sources with details of some of those same operations, simply because the government wants a particular message out into the public domain. I have spent hours using Photoshop to blur the faces of CSOR operators in the photos I have taken because of OPSEC concerns of the unit, only to find similar pictures on the Canadian Forces Combat Camera website with the faces of the same individuals readily recognizable.

Brigadier-General Day will obviously move on and a new commander will take his place. That individual will face enormous pressures from those bureaucrats in National Defence Headquarters who believe that secrecy is paramount, not for any OPSEC concerns, but because they are risk-averse and do not want any potential media coverage that could impact on the government or Defence Minister of the day. The new commander will also face pressure from inside the Command from those who would want to turn back the clock and return to the days when secrecy, for secrecy's sake, was the rule. It will be a strong person indeed who can weather these pressures and continue on with the current commitment of providing some information about CANSOFCOM to the media and public.

CHAPTER 9

STEPPING OUT OF THE SHADOWS: CANADIAN SPECIAL OPERATIONS FORCES AND MEDIA RELATIONS

DR. EMILY SPENCER

Communication is a vital enabler in today's security environment. ...it is a lever that when properly used can empower organizations and influence decision-makers. Conversely, managed poorly it can erode credibility and support. The time has now come for the Command to take the necessary steps to educate and inform its key stakeholders and Canadians at large on the identity, capability and contribution of their special operations forces.

Strategic Communications Plan
Canadian Special Operations Forces Command

Globalization and the proliferation of communications technologies have underscored the power of the media with regard to the COE. Moreover, not only is the media omnipresent in the COE, the rapid dissemination of information via global networks assures that each message will be judged simultaneously by a plurality of audiences. As such, scholar Philip Hammond remarks that for contemporary belligerents "producing the right image appears to be at least as important as any tangible result achieved on the ground."[1]

American SOF seem to understand this connection. For example, on 23 March 2003, US Private (Retired) Jessica Lynch was captured by Iraqi forces. Just over a week later, on 1 April, she was rescued by Navy SEALs and Army Rangers. Her dramatic rescue became a media sensation, aided in part by the film footage that American forces produced with helmet mounted video cameras. Importantly, the event occurred at an opportune moment for the US government as Americans were questioning the invasion. Following the news coverage, US citizens were much more optimistic and supportive of the war in Iraq.

Nonetheless, two weeks later, the heroism of American SOF on this mission was discredited when the truth was revealed. First, the only reason that Private Lynch needed to be rescued was because the ambulance that had secretly been arranged by a doctor at the Iraqi hospital was fired on as it attempted to approach a US checkpoint. Second, at the time of the "rescue," there were no enemy present, only medical practitioners and patients.[2]

Regardless of the reality, however, the image of fearless, highly trained US SOF rescuing an American service person proved enduring. This effect has not been lost on American decision-makers. In addition to media coverage of SOF "in action," General David Petraeus has continuously highlighted how US SOF have assisted operations in Iraq and Afghanistan in order to boost public confidence in the war effort.[3] More recently, the *Wall Street Journal* chronicled that "Once in disrepute, secret warfare," by which they mean CIA and SOF driven operations, "is now embraced even by the Obama administration to fight terrorism and weapons of proliferation."[4]

Whereas US SOF have been accused of orchestrating their image on the scale of a blockbuster Hollywood movie,[5] the CF and political decision-makers have let the pendulum swing in the opposite direction preferring to remain out of the media limelight when it comes to CANSOF. This is perhaps a natural course for a group of people who prefer to be quiet professionals. This silence, however, can have negative consequences. "For instance," as Colonel Bernd Horn notes, "few realize Canadian SOF personnel have removed an entire generation of Taliban leadership in Kandahar, many of whom were responsible for the deaths of Canadian service personnel."[6] Brigadier-General D. Michael Day, Commander, CANSOFCOM also lamented this silence noting, "Clearly this guarded approach has not allowed us to fully exploit our success, capability and relationships."[7]

In an era where information is power and where technology has enabled the media to gain a disproportionate share of the distribution of information, to avoid participating in the information battle-space can have adverse consequences. In fact, the silence vacuum created by CANSOF has more often than not been filled with "misconceptions and misunderstandings"[8] that cause some to question the validity of having a SOF capability. Journalist Peter Worthington comments, "The trouble with our secretive commando force that proponents like to hint is as good as — or better than — Britain's SAS, or the U.S. Delta Force, Rangers, Green Berets, etc., is there's no way the public can ever know." He continues, "Maybe they are as good as their quiet publicity implies. Maybe not."[9] Worthington surmises the view likely held by many Canadians: "One can applaud the idea of an elite commando force, but a secret army within the army is anathema to democracy. And ultra-secrecy seems a formula for potential corruption and abuse."[10]

Fellow journalist Allan Woods also comments on the difficulty of having a secret force noting that if JTF 2, the pointy end of CANSOF capabilities, appears in the media, "it often means something has gone wrong."[11] Mercedes Stephenson, also a journalist, notes that "In the media and popular culture, speculation has been substituted in the place of fact to fill the information vacuum created by the secrecy surrounding Canada's elite commandos." "At best," she suggests, "the lack of information and answers generates a legend out of touch with reality."[12]

This disconnect is the crux of the problem that CANSOFCOM faces in the information battle-space. In an information vacuum, the CF allows others to fill the void, often, if not almost always, with erroneous information. Certainly in the Canadian context, equally as challenging as an information vacuum to winning public opinion would be an abhorrent intentional misrepresentation of CANSOF roles in the COE. As such, the controlled and accurate release of SOF information, while adhering to OPSEC, is critical to the successful employment and survival of SOF in Canada.

Before devolving further into the importance of media relations to SOF, it is first important to clearly define what is meant by popular terms such as "mass media," "propaganda" and "information operations." This discussion in turn necessitates the need to explore what is meant by "truth," particularly as it pertains to the COE. Finally, it follows that an explanation of the importance of winning the media war in the COE is examined, as well as the benefits and challenges to SOF in general, and CANSOFCOM in particular, for releasing information to the media.

UNDERSTANDING NUANCED TERMINOLOGY AND ITS IMPORTANCE TO THE COE:

Mass Media

Mass media is an overarching concept. Arguably, in this day and age, it is probably easier to define what is not considered mass media rather than what is. Put simply, "media are means of reaching others."[13] As such, media include all forms of communication. Mass media generally refers to the means of communication that reach and influence large numbers of people. These forms of communication are broadcasted through media technologies which include the internet, television, newspapers, magazines, movies and the radio, just to mention a few. As such, as information and communication technologies advance so too does the potential influence of mass media.

The advancement and maturation of media technologies impact the COE because they allow diverse groups and individuals the ability to communicate and influence large numbers of people through various readily available and relatively inexpensive means.[14] The mass media in this sense is used to influence public opinion regarding conflict. Speaking on the subject of contemporary combatants, Professor Cori E. Dauber explains that "they fight a battle to shape the perceptions and attitudes of the public – a battle over the public's very will to continue fighting, whether that is the indigenous public insurgents they seek to intimidate or the domestic American public they seek to influence so as to force counterinsurgents to withdraw from the battlefield prematurely." Dauber surmises, "in the modern world, this will, of necessity, be a battle to shape media coverage."[15] One way to do so is through the use of propaganda and censorship.

Propaganda and Censorship

A common tool used to influence public opinion via the use of mass media is to spread propaganda that supports your point of view while simultaneously censoring opposing views. While perhaps seemingly simplistic, "To attempt to define propaganda," cautions author Nicholas Jackson O'Shaughnessy, "is to tread lightly on a conceptual minefield."[16] Nonetheless, for the purposes of this chapter, propaganda will be defined as a means of communication that attempts to influence a group of people towards a cause. The term "official propaganda" will refer to those crafted messages that are put out by the government or government institutions to achieve a desired effect. Censorship, or the intentional withholding of information that challenges your position, will be considered a component of propaganda.

The discussion of propaganda is germane to the COE as information is often manipulated during periods of belligerence in an attempt to sway public opinion. O'Shaughnessy explains, "...propaganda is not just a branch of military activity. Military activity itself is inherently propagandist, in part, or entirely."[17]

Moreover, as Walter Lipmann, advisor to former US President Woodrow Wilson, noted, "We must remember that in times of war what is said on the enemy's side of the front is always propaganda, and what is said on our side of the front is truth and righteousness, the cause of humanity and a crusade for peace."[18] Today's omnipresent media has simply magnified these effects while simultaneously making it more difficult to control the flow of information. As such, the importance of, and challenges to, information operations are underscored in the COE.

Information Operations

With the present rate of globalization and the growth of new information technologies during a period that has aptly been dubbed "the Information Age," the control of information is of critical importance in the COE. Professor Keith D. Dickson explains that "The onrushing global economy and its accompanying technological and social transformations that have given rise to an electronic, computer-regulated, media-saturated, and mass consumer society mark modernism giving way to postmodernism." He continues, "In the postmodern era, knowledge and information are new principles of social organization." Consequently, in describing the COE, Dickson states that "Power is defined by how much information is controlled to define and shape what is known."[19]

While there is still no clear consensus on the definition of information operations within the NATO community,[20] essentially IO are "coordinated military activities within the information domain to affect information and information systems to achieve desired

effects on will and capabilities of adversaries and others in support of mission objectives while sustaining own information and
information systems."[21] The US military dissects this concept and
describes IO as the "integrated employment of electronic warfare
(EW), computer network operations (CNO), PSYOP, military deception (MILDEC), and OPSEC, in concert with specified supporting
and related capabilities, to influence, disrupt, corrupt, or usurp
adversarial human and automated decision making while protecting our own."[22] Essentially, IO use a variety of means to control the
flow of information in order to influence a target audience toward
a desired end state. Through this control of information, IO can
help to establish new "truths" about the state of global affairs that
support a specific point of view.

Truth

In 1917, US Senator Hiram Johnson remarked, "The first casualty
when war comes is truth."[23] Nearly a century later, there is no
denying the validity of his comment.

Truth is a difficult concept to define, especially as it pertains to
the COE. Something is said to be true when it is consistent with
"fact" or "reality" but these relatively simple terms can also be
quite difficult to define. Fact, or knowledge or information based
on real occurrences, is itself subjective and couched in relative
terms. While simple facts may exist in war, such as shots were
fired, complex issues involving intent and, more importantly, effects are considerably more nuanced and subject to debate and
relativism. As such, Dickson argues that "the possibility of objective knowledge and truth as goals of inquiry" in the COE must
be rejected. Rather, he suggests, "reason or truth are products of
dominating ideological or political interests."[24]

Importantly, the proliferation of the media and new information
technologies facilitate the rapid dissemination of constructed

"truths" – or propaganda – to a wide audience in little time, with potentially lasting effects. For example, it was recently reported that Taliban detainees were locked in "dog pens." Subsequently, there was a large public outcry about the treatment of these detainees, particularly since in the Muslim faith dogs are considered impure. In the end, it did not really matter that the story was fabricated and that the detainees had never been treated in any such manner. Propagandists had already taken advantage of the situation and once that image had been formed, it was impossible to separate perception from reality.[25] As Colonel Horn chronicles, "Repeated often enough or pervasively enough, perception becomes reality."[26] Consequently, since the media is a common tool used to influence public opinion and create "perceptions" about "reality," making effective use of the media as well as other means of communication is "mission critical" in the COE.[27]

THE IMPORTANCE OF WINNING THE MEDIA WAR IN THE COE

Global security or, perhaps more accurately, global insecurity, in the 21st century is not simply a linear continuation of the problems that plagued the world during the proceeding hundred year period. While individual aspects of the COE, such as the use of terror as a tactic and the reliance on alliances and coalitions to achieve common goals, are not unprecedented, the COE is markedly different from conflict during much of the 20th century.

Enabled by globalization and the proliferation of the media, and fuelled by the global power vacuum that the end of the Cold War created, the 21st century brought with it the "perfect storm" of conditions that has now created substantive global instability. Scholars, military and security analysts, and practitioners in particular, tend to agree that the COE is extremely complex, ambiguous, volatile, dynamic, and exponentially more dangerous than previous periods.

Arguably, the concurrent end to the Cold War and the rise of globalization in the 1990s created the conditions that were ripe for the ambiguous, complex, volatile, and ever-changing operating environment in which we now find ourselves. An economic and political power vacuum was created as the superpowers disengaged from many areas around the world. Very quickly, failed and failing states mushroomed around the globe. Exacerbating the situation were other significant problems such as ethnic violence, narco-trafficking, transnational crime, and competition for resources. At the same time, the world was becoming more interconnected or "globalized," as demonstrated by an increase in international traffic, both economic and cultural, linking peoples of dispersed geographic regions and thereby redefining power relationships and enabling the proliferation of non-state actors on the world stage.[28]

As such, the enemy is no longer limited to symmetrical, uniformed rivals aligned to one of two superpowers. Rather, our adversaries run the gamut of rogue states, regional rivals or power blocks, warlords, globally networked transnational criminals, narco-traffickers, as well as radical extremists. Modern insurgents are fuelled by ideology and/or religion and empowered by readily available information technologies, which, thanks to the rapid pace of globalization, provide a fast and inexpensive means of spreading messages.

Moreover, the proliferation of information technologies has given new credence to the old saying, "information is power," especially as it pertains to the COE. Notably, at least in part because of high levels of information availability, the distribution of power in the 21st century has shifted from a focus on nation-states to the individual. As Dickson explains, "The interplay of the people, the army, and the government that has been the guiding light of the nation-state in the conduct of modern war now operates far more disproportionately in favor of the people." He continues,

"Unlike the modernist approach that views a political endstate as preeminent in determining the outcome of conflict, control of the population may be more important than gaining political control in the postmodern context." Dickson suggests, "How much is known about what, and through what means, are the two basic questions that must absorb military planners facing war in a postmodern context."[29]

Mass media has been, without doubt, one of the main venues for shaping the modern discourse on conflict and war. In fact, media have been significant players in every post-Cold War conflict.[30] "Mass media," note researchers Stig A. Nohrstedt and Rune Ottosen, are "essential in framing and creating an understanding of global issues like terrorism and war."[31] Media have the latitude to choose from a large pool of potential stories and are empowered by the freedom of the press – and the proliferation of media technologies with little or no governance – to have much leeway in their interpretation of events.[32] As such, researcher Juan LaLlave debunks the myth that "journalists must be objective and refrain from taking sides in a conflict because they must not influence the political event." Rather, LaLlave notes that the simultaneous "utility construct" of journalism, "that violence sells news … represents an implicit bias that serves to influence political events in favor of conflict escalation."[33] The conclusion that can be drawn is that no form of media is unbiased.

Consequently, not only do militaries have to win the kinetic battles on the ground, they must also win the battle for media, and thereby public, support. Certainly winning the public's trust and support is of vital importance to Western democracies whose governments depend on votes to remain in power.[34] As President Barack Obama stated, "Our strength abroad is anchored in our strength at home."[35] The omnipresent media of the 21st century paradoxically both facilitates the spread of propaganda and challenges the controlled release of messages. More importantly, its pervasiveness and ability to shape the "truth" about events and thereby shape public opinion make winning the media war paramount to success in the COE. Professor Joseph J. Collins explains, "Today, the ugly realities of low-intensity conflict continuously stream into the living rooms of the Western public. The sense of gain or loss, or the effectiveness or ineffectiveness of operations is magnified greatly by the work of dedicated, relentless journalists, whose editors and producers freely admit that 'if it bleeds, it leads'." Collins goes on to thus lament the valuable contributions to peacekeeping and humanitarian assistance/reconstruction that remain in the shadows of the media glare and which consequently deny the public the "truth" about the COE in favour of "media coverage [that] wears down the public and tests the patience of Western audiences."[36]

In fact, no amount of victory in combat will make up for the loss of public support that is so easily influenced via the channels of mass media. As Professor Cori E. Dauber argues, "the military force fighting today against a terrorist organization in defense of a democratic state is really fighting a two-front war." She explains, "There is on the one hand the *ground war*, meaning the war that has to actually be won on the ground, the state of play on the ground as it exists in reality." In contrast, she continues, "But there is also the *air war*, meaning the war as it exists on the nation's front pages and television screens." She concludes, "For a democracy, winning one and not the other will always mean losing, and losing in a very real sense, because the loss of public support means that the war will come to an end, period."[37]

Additionally, the media assures that actions in any cultural milieu may, and likely will, be judged in other domains where people may have different sets of beliefs and values. While this might simply be construed as a harsh fact for some, many are keenly aware of the advantages that this type of media environment can provide. As Dauber explains, "sophisticated propagandists ... are not only constructing sophisticated texts meant to simultaneously reach multiple audiences, they are also constructing multiple texts targeted to reach a variety of different categories of audience."[38]

Thus, to avoid participating in the information battle-space is akin to withdrawing from the race and accepting defeat. As US Major Jim Gregory notes of American SOF, "The days of 100% secrecy are long past. We must embrace the new environment or lose credibility in the eyes of those we serve."[39] He elaborates, "more often than not, we within special operations must make it a point to engage with the media to be successful in today's 21st century battle of ideas. In fact, we must do it often and long before crises emerge, not just occasionally or WHEN crises arise. Doing so develops a rapport with individual media members, and more importantly, with the public as a whole."[40]

CANSOFCOM is also heeding this new reality. Brigadier-General Day stated after a recent SOF symposium, "We find the myths and speculations that the public is exposed to, either on purpose or inadvertently, need to be addressed." He explained, "It's a little bolder, but we want to be a little more open to having a discussion with those people [the media] so that some of the factual inaccuracies that they tend to rely upon, that we have not corrected, get corrected and, secondly, that we better understand their issues and concerns and either explain them away or explain why we're not interested in explaining them away." Brigadier-General Day surmised, "There's a realization that I want people to have that CANSOFCOM does understand that, as part of the institution of the Canadian Forces, we have a responsibility to educate and expose ... we are now sophisticated enough to talk about ourselves and what we do in an open forum without jeopardizing operational security."[41]

THE BENEFITS OF SOF INFORMATION RELEASE

There are many positive benefits that SOF can accrue with increased information release, not least of which is the active participation in the all important information battle-space. After all, few military theorists or practitioners would argue that awareness and public opinion do not matter. As the CANSOFCOM *Strategic Communications Plan* correctly identifies, "In today's environment information is a weapon."[42] Quite simply, more open release of CANSOF information via the mass media, including liaisons with journalists, hosting conferences and symposiums, and via websites, will help to further educate government decision-makers, military members and the public, not to mention journalists, in order to dispel myths, gain support and prove SOF utility. Importantly, when others are more aware of the reality of SOF — for example, its roles, capabilities, reporting framework and successes — they will be less likely to jump to false conclusions or believe non-factual, sensational reporting. For instance, such myths as SOF are a law unto themselves, SOF do not adhere to CF regulations or procedures, SOF are prohibitively expensive and SOF have no discipline will be understood to be baseless allegations. However, without a level of trust, credibility or familiarity, people will be more likely to believe assertions, particularly since Canadians tend to be suspicious of secret and/or elite organizations.[43]

In addition, information release can showcase CANSOF capabilities which can readily be used as a deterrent to potential belligerents. Put simply, those who would do harm to Canadians would have to think hard whether to choose Canada as a target since a robust SOF capability ensures that the nation is not a soft target. Greater awareness also acts to strengthen bonds with allied SOF through an increased awareness of its capability and record of excellence. In the end, educating the greater public will only strengthen CANSOFCOM. As Stephenson notes, "Like most issues surrounding the secretive Canadian special operations community, the truth is more nuanced and complex than the myth."[44] It is time this "truth" is exposed.

First, it is important to remember that communication is a two-way street in which a message is both delivered *and* received. With the potential blurring of the message via the means of communication – often the mass media – and potentially different beliefs and values held by the sender and the receiver, in order to minimize miscommunications and obtain the desired effect, it is necessary to make sure that the intended message is clearly and precisely delivered.

Additionally, it is important to keep in mind that while the media might help to project a specific view, the content and emphasis placed on the message by the media are determined in part by what they believe the public wants to hear or, in more pragmatic terms, what they think will sell. As such, as many scholars are beginning to argue the media, presumably inadvertently, supports war over peace as blood and carnage is more apt to sell in comparison to peaceful resolutions.[45] As researcher Cheryl DesRoche notes, "as a means of getting their story heard, journalists must compete for space – in papers, on the radio and television. Sensationalism becomes a loathsome technique but often a necessity in a competitive media market."[46]

Therefore, the inherent "truth" of the message is shaped not only by the person crafting the message but also by the person receiving the message, as well as the means through which it is delivered. As such, it becomes important to ensure the message, as well as the overall debate, is crafted as accurately as possible.

Even though "the truth," if there ever was such a singular concept, may indeed be the first casualty of conflict, research suggests that the contemporary Canadian mass media, while still following the mantra, "if it bleeds, it leads," nonetheless does attempt to provide as little bias as possible. Moreover, research suggests that it does not simply report government propaganda in its coverage of war and conflict.[47] Taking the additional premises that news media is readily believed[48] and its content is at least partially influenced by what producers believe the public wants to hear, one can conclude that the Canadian public does have a desire to be "truthfully" informed about war and conflict.

The CF appear to have recognized this reality and the power of the media in the mid-1990s. Following the negative news coverage of the Canadian military after an unarmed Somali teenager was killed by a CF military member in Somalia in 1993, the CF experienced a sharp decline in public support. Public support did not swing back in favour of the CF until the late 1990s. This reversal was quite arguably due, at least in part, to the modernization of the CF's public affair's approach introduced by Larry Gordon following his appointment in 1996 as chief of public affairs for DND. Gordon instigated a more "open door" policy in which all members of the CF, irrespective of rank or position, were allowed to speak openly to the public and media. Moreover, he helped to establish web pages that further mitigated the distance between the public and the military and helped to inform the Canadian public about the important roles and functions that the CF performed.[49]

In fact, evidence suggests that there is a direct relationship between how informed the Canadian public feels about defence issues and their support for the CF. As former Minister of National Defence, David Pratt remarked, "It is apparent to me that the more informed Canadians are about defence issues, the more supportive they are about the needs of the Canadian Forces."[50] Arguing for increased public awareness of the CF, Major Jeff Dooling concludes "that if the Canadian Forces hopes to receive the budgetary increases required for it to remain relevant in the 21st century, then its public affairs efforts should focus on increasing the Canadian public's sense of the importance of the Canadian Forces to them."

This goal, as Major Dooling notes, was at least partially fulfilled by reporters embedded with the CF in the early part of the Afghan war but its potency has arguably faded as "other stories have taken over the media's attention and thus the public's interest."[51]

The central lesson that should be taken away from this discussion is that an informed public matters in terms of garnering support for the CF. Given the relationships between the media, the public and the military in Canada, information operations by the CF need to be as complete, transparent and truthful as OPSEC allows, and need to be readily available and up to date so that the media and public do not forget the importance of the CF to national security nor fill an information vacuum with negative images.

The CF as a whole are learning the power of an informed public and CANSOFCOM is also starting to appreciate this reality. In fact, the CANSOFCOM *Strategic Communications Plan* acknowledges that they "have a moral obligation to ensure our fellow Canadians understand what CANSOF is and how their special operations forces are dedicated to preserving the Canadian way of life and the national commitment to a safe and stable world."[52]

Undeniably, educating the public about their roles and functions will empower CANSOF. Being more proactive with information release will help CANSOFCOM to educate government decision-makers, conventional force members and the public, including journalists. In an age where information is power, it is important to participate within the information battle-space that characterizes the COE. CANSOFCOM knows that "failure to adapt to the new communications reality may result in catastrophic failure at the strategic level." For CANSOFCOM, the force of choice and the force of last resort, this shortcoming "is not an option."[53] Quite simply, if the first time Canadians learn about CANSOF is during a negative event, then the consequences will more than likely be more severe than the situation warrants. Indeed, fear and suspicion often fuel over-reactions.

Moreover, particularly for CANSOFCOM, for which there is a dearth of academic publications, media attention provides one of few ways to inform Canadians (and others) about the organization and its capabilities. In fact, several academic papers regarding CANSOF rely on media accounts for "factual" information.[54] In general, however, there is simply a lack of information. As scholar Simon Anglim notes of SOF in general, "Despite their potential significance for policy makers, Special Forces are largely overlooked by academia." This lack of information is a shame for, as Anglim continues, "their utility to policy makers and their general effectiveness ensures that by any description, Special Forces are *special*."[55] Certainly, as it is the public domain that drives public perception and debate with regard to SOF, government decision-makers who are properly educated about CANSOF capabilities through various, open and accurate venues are empowered to make more accurate decisions about the defence of the country than they would be without such information.

For example, more open communication of SOF can help provide accounts of the utility that SOF provide the Government of Canada. Journalist David Pugliese remarks that "Details of special forces missions are considered secret, but both JTF 2 and CSOR have been in operations in Afghanistan, hunting down insurgents involved in the production of improvised explosive devices." He is quick to add, "The majority of the 150 Canadian soldiers killed in Afghanistan have died because of IEDs."[56]

In a recent newspaper article, Woods is also eager to point out the accomplishments of CANSOF in Afghanistan since 2001. He writes of their first mission, "The inside story of that mission [Task Force K-Bar] can now be told for the first time following a *Toronto*

Star investigation into the top-secret operations that would ce-
ment Canada's reputation as one of the top special forces teams
in the world."[57] Interestingly, JTF 2's accolades were only widely
recounted because of a journalistic investigation and thereby, as
Woods notes, obscured from the general public for almost nine
years.[58] This type of silence can hinder support for the service.

Furthermore, an educated public is more likely to support decisions to employ SOF abroad if they understand – or, at least, are
exposed to – the issues and have a base upon which to judge SOF
actions. As US Major Jim Gregory explains, "By communicating
often with others, special operations forces build trust amongst
the public ... so that when something goes wrong – and something will inevitably always go wrong at some point – the public
maintains their faith in the special operations community. But if
there are no assets in the 'trust bank,' the public will turn on the
community."[59]

Certainly, engaging with external audiences can help build trust
and ensure that the "true" story is presented rather than one that
is overtly propagandistic, overly harsh, wantonly false, or simply
void of information. This trust can also be built with reporters
by establishing open lines of communication in hopes that they
will publish accurate and informed stories about SOF and perhaps avoid publishing wildly sensationalist accounts like CTV
recently reported of JTF 2 soldiers: "Secret commandos accidentally detained at Tim Hortons. Drop the donut and show me your
hands."[60] Stories such as this one do not serve to accurately portray
CANSOF but they can be used to fill a void if no better information
or stories are provided. Furthermore, if the public does not already have an understanding of SOF, negative images derived from
comments such as these can prove enduring and be detrimental to
the growth and sustainability of CANSOF.

Indeed, CANSOFCOM recognizes this reality. Its communications strategy notes, "...it is vital that decision-makers and the Canadian public understand the importance and contributions of CANSOFCOM." The document explains, "That way, when 'threats' materialize such as economic downturns that will force budgetary pressures; individual indiscretions that may reflect poorly on SOF; anti-militaristic attitudes that may impact on the CF overall, or any other factor that may threaten the existence, funding, autonomy or capability of CANSOFCOM, action taken by political and military decision-makers, particularly when influenced by public reaction, is considered based on a full understanding of the capability at risk."[61]

Filling the information vacuum can also help to dispel some of the many myths that exist about SOF and, instead, provide accurate information upon which the public can more appropriately assess the value of CANSOF. Thankfully this type of relationship is starting to develop between CANSOFCOM and external audiences such as scholars and the media. For example, recently CBC News pointed out that "While the Canadian government and military are still highly secretive about JTF 2's numbers and deployments, the veil of secrecy has slipped somewhat." CBC noted that "The group has a website, for example, complete with recruitment posters, FAQs [frequently asked questions] and a section debunking myths about JTF 2."[62] Not only does JTF 2 have a website, CANSOFCOM's other three units CSOR, CJIRU and 427 SOAS also have sites that help dispel myths and provide information about their functions.[63]

Myths about SOF — their Rambo-like appearance, deference to discipline, authority and order, and high cost, just to mention a few — will likely continue despite evidence to the contrary, but their potency might be diluted as SOF realities emerge. For instance, as Stephenson noted in a recent newspaper article, "This column isn't long enough to smash every special operations myth, but there's one more worth mentioning: SOF are expensive. The entire budget for Canadian special operations this year [2010] is $205 million." She continues by educating her readers that $205 million is "peanuts in the defence budget."[64] When one considers the flexibility, rapid reaction capability and long list of capabilities that CANSOF provide the government of Canada, it is easy to understand her point.

Open lines of communication should also be fostered directly and via the media with conventional CF members, otherwise myths of SOF being apart from the CF and a law unto themselves will continue to be propagated both within the military and the general public. For instance, Worthington reported that "Canadian regimental soldiers in Afghanistan have mixed feelings about JTF2. For soldiers (and they are soldiers, despite not mixing with the regimental units), they play the secrecy role, but hardly blend unnoticed into the surroundings. JTF2 ... members are distinguished in camp, often by beards, wearing dark non-uniform clothes, sunglasses and ear pieces. Sort of Men in Black without the humour."[65] This imagery is not necessarily accurate, does not flatter the CF or CANSOF and discounts the often forgotten fifth "SOF truth" that SOF rely on conventional forces to assist in most of their mission sets.[66]

Importantly, accounts of SOF accomplishments can also contribute to CANSOF being used as a deterrent and can be used to strengthen bonds with allied SOF. For instance, when CANSOF first deployed to Afghanistan their US counterparts were hesitant to utilize them in a SOF role, wondering rather who JTF 2 were. Once having proven themselves as part of Task Force K-Bar – one mission resulting in an intelligence coup that earned accolades from the American National Security Agency – JTF 2 members soon won the praise of their American brethren, even being awarded the Presidential Unit Citation in 2004 by the US Government for service in Afghanistan.

Clearly, increased interaction with external audiences, particularly the media, can serve CANSOF well. Not only will it help to educate government decision-makers, military members and the public in order to dispel myths, gain support and prove SOF utility, but it could also help to strengthen bonds with allied SOF and mean that CANSOF could act as a deterrent to potential aggressors. As Brigadier-General Day remarks, "…it is in the best interest of CANSOFCOM to ensure that we provide the necessary transparency and education so that key decision-makers, the CF at large and the Canadian public have the required understanding of who we are, the importance of our mission and how we serve the country and specifically the needs of Canadians. After all, we are their special operations forces." He concludes, "In the end, it is important for us to remember that transparency builds credibility and trust, which in turn, allows for freedom of action."[67] Nonetheless, while the benefits to increased media co-operation are undeniable, there are also some challenges to releasing information that need to be explored.

THE CHALLENGES TO SOF INFORMATION RELEASE

Despite the clear benefits to SOF information release, there are some factors that limit the amount of information that can or should be released. These factors include OPSEC breaches that can endanger the well-being of CANSOF personnel and the success of the mission, as well as be detrimental to allied SOF relationships. Whether unintentional or otherwise, OPSEC breaches represent the biggest challenge to SOF information release. In addition, the release of too much "positive" information may be interpreted by others as propaganda and/or can provide a false sense of security that in the end erodes actual measures to improve security if decision-makers place undue reliance on one capability. Furthermore, too much "positive" information can also increase inter-service rivalries, particularly during resource restrained periods as other services perceive CANSOFCOM is trying to gain an unfair advantage with decision-makers at their expense. Therefore, the controlled and accurate release of SOF information, while adhering to OPSEC, is critical to the effective and efficient employment of SOF in Canada.

According to CANSOFCOM's *Strategic Communications Plan*, OPSEC is defined as "an analytical process that helps maintain CANSOFCOM's security and freedom of action by denying adversaries information on the dispositions, capabilities and intentions of CF and friendly forces." The document continues, "OPSEC analysis is a risk mitigation strategy that balances a multitude of requirements. For example, the need to safeguard lives and ensure mission success is balanced against the need for transparency to the Canadian public." It explains, "OPSEC does not recommend the safeguarding of information for trivial issues, such as embarrassment, nor does it limit the distribution of information concerning unlawful actions."[68] In fact, CANSOFCOM recognizes that approximately 80 percent of intelligence is derived from open source information.[69] Rather, "OPSEC analysis is intended to safeguard information or activities that if exploited, would result in unacceptable levels of risk to CANSOFCOM personnel and operations."[70]

Clearly, OPSEC is a fundamental requirement for SOF and is rooted in two basic principles: first, is the moral imperative to do everything possible to assure the safety and protection of personnel; and second is to guarantee mission success.[71] As such, OPSEC underscores all SOF activities, especially given the types of operations SOF conduct, the volatile environments in which they are conducted and the nature of the enemy who generally does not operate on the same moral plane or adhere to the same ethical principles as Canadians. Moreover, for the same reasons, OPSEC is also important for safeguarding allies and allied relationships. As a result, CANSOFCOM is enabled with "the freedom to provide the Government of Canada with agile, high-readiness Special Operations Forces capable of conducting special operations across the spectrum of conflict at home and abroad."[72] Importantly, this freedom is coupled with a responsibility to protect Canadian citizens and interests as directed by the Government of Canada.

While seemingly simple enough on one level, it is actually quite a complex art to achieve a balance between OPSEC and providing the proper information to key stakeholders and desired audiences, often resulting in issues of over-classification. There are clear guidelines for classification levels which reside on the principle that "information must be classified to the minimum level for the least amount of time in accordance with legitimate guidelines [as] anything else is an attack on democracy and restricts the rights of Canadians."[73] Nonetheless, issues of over-classification do occur, often with detrimental results.[74] When over-classification does transpire it means that information may not get disseminated as required, increased costs may result, and delays in procuring services and/or equipment might be present. Additionally, refusing information to public access because of misclassification is a breach of the law.[75] Importantly, over-classification can also erode trust and credibility, which can cast a shadow on everything else that is done.

Another factor to consider with regard to the release of information is the political level of comfort. Often western governments are loath to admit that they employ forces that delve into "the shadows." Actions such as "capture/kill," although critically important to the war effort and exercised totally within the approved Rules of Engagement (ROE), often have a sinister air to them and are consequently not usually broadcasted by democratic governments. Importantly, SOF missions, which may include "capture/kill" options are conducted with surgical precision and normally end successfully with no shots fired. The mental or physical image of black-garbed operators conducting raids in the dead of night, however, does not always resonate well with civilians or politicians.

Further adding to this potential of "political" hesitancy with respect to releasing information on SOF is the often-negative image that exists in the media with regard to SOF in general. For example, the criticism of excessive night raids and a perceived disproportionate use of force by some SOF in both Iraq and Afghanistan have caused a degree of bad press for SOF in general. Unfortunately, "truth" is not generally the issue when it comes to reports on SOF and the overall benefits of SOF – whether intentionally or not – are often ignored by the press. Rather SOF writ large are tarred in the press. While arguably not the best course of action, it appears that some decision-makers have found it easier to limit the public exposure of SOF rather than attempt to dispel myths by communicating more widely with the public and the press about the roles and contributions of SOF. The result is usually the proliferation of negative imagery rather than an expression of the "truth."

While it is clear that OPSEC may legitimately limit the release of certain information and SOF do not want to be accused of over emphasizing their prowess, it is simultaneously true that withholding information can have negative consequences, not least of which is the loss of trust and credibility in the public eye. As such, while it is important to adhere to OPSEC and not endanger the safety of personnel or the success of the mission, as well as protect allied SOF relationships, it is time for CANSOFCOM to step out of the shadows.

CONCLUSION

While SOF have historically maintained a very low profile, there is now more than ever a recognition of the need to inform and educate the public, the wider military and especially decision-makers with regard to the importance and contributions of SOF. Nonetheless, despite the importance and need for transparency and understanding, OPSEC considerations must always come first. Importantly, at the end of the day, SOF have increasingly been accepted as a vital capability in any military arsenal. In fact, SOF generally achieve what can be colloquially termed, "a big bang for their buck."

In the end, there are tremendous benefits to the increased release of SOF information. In today's world, it is undeniable that information is power. When faced with an information vacuum, it is easy to fill it with misconceptions and falsehoods. Historically, with respect to SOF, these myths tend to be negative. By being more forthright with the release of information, SOF roles, capabilities, accountability frameworks and the large number of successes will be able to be judged more accurately by an informed Canadian public. Additionally, this information will help to build trust and provide context in which to judge a negative incident should one occur. Moreover, increased release of SOF information can help strengthen bonds with allied SOF and not only provide the Government of Canada with a highly capable force at its disposable but also the ability to use this tool as a deterrent.

As such, transparency and the controlled release of SOF information, while adhering to OPSEC, are critical to the continuing success of SOF in Canada. This path will only strengthen the trust and credibility between the Canadian public, the wider military and decision-makers, and CANSOFCOM. The first step to achieving this goal is to educate others with regard to the roles, capabilities, responsibilities and contributions of SOF through more open and transparent communications.

NOTES

1   Philip Hammond, "The Media War on Terrorism," *Journal for Crime, Conflict and the Media* 1 (2003), 23.

2   Hammond, "The Media War on Terrorism," 27; Keith D. Dickson, "War in (Another) New Context: Postmodernism," (Winter 2004), 84; and

CHAPTER 9

John Kampfner, "The Truth About Jessica," *The Guardian*, 15 May 2003, <http://www.guardian.co.uk/world/2003/may/15/iraq.usa2>, accessed 26 January 2011.

3   Sean D. Naylor, "Beyond Bin laden Petraeus: Success in Afghanistan," *Army Times*, 27 October 2008, 28.

4   Max Boot, "Covert Action Makes A Comeback," *Wall Street Journal*, 5 January 2011, 15.

5   See Hammond, "The Media War on Terrorism."

6   Bernd Horn, "Love 'Em or Hate 'Em: Learning to Live with Elites," *Canadian Military Journal*, (Winter 2007-2008), 40.

7   D. Michael Day, "Commander's Introduction," *Strategic Communications Plan*, Canadian Special Operations Forces Command, 3.

8   Horn, "Love 'Em or Hate 'Em," 40.

9   Peter Worthington, "JTF2 – Canada's Secret Weapon or a Place where Trouble Hides," *Toronto Sun*, 14 September 2010, <http://www.torontosun.com/comment/columnists/peter_worthington/2010/09/14/15351521.html>, accessed 15 September 2010.

10   Worthington, "JTF2 – Canada's Secret Weapon or a Place where Trouble Hides."

11   Allan Woods, "Elite Force Operates in Kandahar Shadows," *The Star.com*, 26 February 2010. <http://www.thestar.com/news/canada/article/771774--elite-force-operates-in-kandahar-shadows>, accessed 15 February 2011.

12   Mercedes Stephenson, "Canada's Elite Commandos aim to Capture, not Kill," 13 December 2010, <http://www.torontosun.com/comment/columnists/mercedes_stephenson/2010/12/10/16509801.html>, accessed on 13 January 2011.

13   Arjen Mulder, "Media," *Theory, Culture and Society*, Vol. 23 (2006), 289.

14   Scholar Cori E. Dauber notes that information or communication technology becomes mature when it is available "off the shelf," is "relatively affordable," is "small enough to be portable," and fourth, "is available in most of the world." Cori E. Dauber, *Youtube War: Fighting in a World of Cameras in Every Cell Phone and Photoshop on Every Computer* (Carlisle: Strategic Studies Institute, 2009), 5-6.

15   Dauber, *Youtube War*, 2.

16   Nicholas Jackson O'Shaughnessy, *Politics and Propaganda: Weapons of Mass Seduction* (Glasgow: Bell & Bain Limited, 2004), 14.

17   O'Shaughnessy, *Politics and Propaganda*, 36.

18   Walter Lippmann, Advisor to US President Woodrow Wilson.

19   Keith D. Dickson, "War in (Another) New Context: Postmodernism," *The Journal of Conflict Studies*, (Winter 2004), 80-81.

20   For a discussion on different definitions of information operations see Neil Chuka, "Note to File: A Comparison of the Information Operations Doctrine of Canada, the United States, the United Kingdom and NATO," *Canadian Army Journal*, Vol. 12 (2009), 91-99.

21   Based on the definition given in the Multinational Information Operations Experiment Whitepaper Version 1.0, 4 October 2004, RTG SAS-057 "Information Operations in Smaller-Scale Contingencies – Analysis Support and Capability Requirements," NATO Working Group, 2, 34. <http://www.sse.gr/NATO/EreunaKaiTexnologiaNATO/9. Information_operations_analysis_support_and_capability_requirements/ RTO-TR-SAS-057/$TR-SAS-057-Report.pdf>, accessed 9 February 2011.

22   Joint Publication 3-13, *Information Operations*, US Chiefs of Staff, 13 February 2006, ix. <http://www.fas.org/irp/doddir/dod/jp3_13. pdf>, accessed 9 February 2011.

23   US Senator Hiram Johnson, 1917.

24   Dickson, "War in (Another) New Context: Postmodernism," 81.

25   Jason Hayes, "Preparing Our Soldiers for Operations within Complex Human Terrain Environments," *Australian Army Journal*, (Winter 2009), 106.

26   Bernd Horn (ed.), *From the Outside Looking In: Media and the Defence Analyst Perspectives on Canadian Military Leadership* (Kingston: CDA Press, 2005), 1.

27   Dauber, *Youtube War*, ix.

28   This definition of globalization is paraphrased from Professors David Held and Anthony McGrew, who argue that globalization denotes "the expanding scale, growing magnitude, speeding up and deepening impact of transcontinental flows and patterns of social interaction.... It refers to a shift or transformation in the scale of human organization that links distant communities and expands the reach of power relations across the world's regions and continents." David Held and Anthony McGrew, *Globalization/Anti Globalization: Beyond the Great Divide* (Cambridge: Polity Press, 2002), 1. Notably, there is no real consensus as to the actual definition of globalization or if it is unique to the late 20th/early 21st century. See: Jan Aart Scholte, *Globalization: A Critical Introduction, Second Edition* (Houndmills, U.K.: MacMillan, 2000), and Lui Hebron, and John F. Stack, Jr., *Globalization: Debunking the Myths* (Upper Saddle River, NJ: Pearson/Prentice Hall: 2008).

29   Dickson, "War in (Another) New Context: Postmodernism," 82, 85, 88.

30   Vladimir Bratic, "Media Effects during Violent Conflict: Evaluating Media Contributions to Peace Building," *Conflict & Communication Online*, Vol. 5, No. 1 (2006), 2.

31   Stig A. Nohrstedt and Rune Ottosen, "War Journalism in the Threat Society: Peace Journalism as a Strategy for Challenging the Mediated Culture of Fear," *Conflict & Communication Online*, Vol. 7, No. 2 (2008), 2.

DR. EMILY SPENCER

32   Christoph Schaefer, "The Effects of Escalation- vs. De-escalation-oriented Coverage of the Evaluation of Military Measures," *Conflict & Communication Online*, Vol. 5, No. 1 (2006), 2.

33   Juan LaLlave, "The Acceptability of Arguments in Favour of an Against the Iraq War," *Conflict & Communication Online*, Vol. 4, No. 2 (2005), 2.

34   In fact, when examining the future security environment, the Chief of Force Development, Department of National Defence, takes into account the Canada's changing demographics. Chief of Force Development Department of National Defence, *The Future Security Environment 2008-2030. Part 1: Current and Emerging Trends* (Ottawa: Government of Canada, 2010), 105.

35   President Barack Obama, "Presidential Address on Libya," CNN Live, 28 March 2011.

36   Joseph J. Collins, "Afghanistan: Winning a Three Block War," *The Journal of Conflict Studies*, (Winter 2004), 63-64.

37   Dauber, *Youtube War*, 3.

38   Ibid., 13.

39   Jim Gregory, "Special Operations Media Engagement ... the Future of Investing," *Official Blog of United States European Command*, <http://useucom.wordpress.com/2010/10/06/3403/>, accessed 24 January 2011.

40   Gregory, "Special Operations Media Engagement ... the Future of Investing."

41   D. Michael Day cited in Lesley Craig, "Symposium Shines Light on CANSOFCOM," *The Maple Leaf*, 12 January 2011, 4.

42   *Strategic Communications Plan*, Canadian Special Operations Forces Command, 16.

43   Horn, "Love 'Em or Hate 'Em: Learning to Live with Elites," 32.

44   Mercedes Stephenson, "Canada's Elite Commandos aim to Capture, not Kill."

45   For example see: Bratic, "Media Effects during Violent Conflict,"; Nohrstedt and Ottosen, "War Journalism in the Threat Society,"; Schaefer, "The Effects of Escalation- vs. De-escalation-oriented Coverage of the Evaluation of Military Measures," and Cheryl DesRoches, "Appendix A: An Assessment of the Influence of the Media on the Public's Perception," in Horn (ed.), *From the Outside Looking In*, 155-210.

46   DesRoches, "Appendix A," 159.

47   Interestingly, this finding contradicts that found about the American mass media. Ibid., 173, 177. Additionally, it should be noted that this relationship is debated, especially in the historical context. For some of the historical debates see Jeffrey A. Keshen and Serge Marc Durflinger, (eds), *War and Society in Post-Confederation Canada* (Toronto: Thomson-Nelson, 2007), 61-92.

48   For example, the hoax put on by Orson Welles in the 1930s warning via the radio of an imminent invasion from Mars was readily believed as was the 1971 April Fool's joke, published as a letter to the editor that advocated for the abolishment of golf courses. See DesRoches, "Appendix A," 156-157.

49   Ibid., 194.

50   David Pratt cited in Jeff Dooling, "New Horizons: Increasing Public Awareness of the Canadian Forces," *Canadian Forces College CSC 31 Paper*. <http://www.cfc.forces.gc.ca/papers/csc/csc31/exnh/dooling.pdf>, accessed 22 February 2011.

51   Dooling, "New Horizons," abstract, 11.

52   *Strategic Communications Plan*, Canadian Special Operations Forces Command, 20.

53   Ibid., 9.

54   For example see: Jamie Hammond, "Special Operations Forces: Relevant, Ready and Precise," *Canadian Military Journal*, (Autumn 2004), 17-28; and J. Paul de B. Taillon, "Canadian Special Operations Forces: Transforming Paradigms," *Canadian Military Journal*, (Winter 2006), 67-76. The same type of situation also occurs in the US. See for example: Andrew Feickert and Thomas K. Livingston, "U.S. Special Operations Forces (SOF): Background and Issues for Congress," 3 December 2010. *Congressional Research Service* 7-5700 <www.crs.gov> RS21048.

55   Simon Anglim, *Special Forces, Strategic Asset*, Article 4, Issue 2.

56   David Pugliese, "Military Forms a Quick Reaction Task Force," *The Ottawa Citizen*, 17 July 2010. <http://www.ottawacitizen.com/news/Mil itary+forms+quick+reaction+task+force/3290244/story.html>, accessed 18 July 2010.

57   Woods, "Elite Force Operates in Kandahar Shadows."

58   Ibid.

59   Gregory, "Special Operations Media Engagement ... the Future of Investing."

60   The Canadian Press, "Secret commandos accidentally detained at Tim Hortons," *CTV News*, 15 February 2011. <http://www.ctv.ca/CTV News/TopStories/20110215/jtf-tim-hortons-110215/>, accessed 16 February 2011

61   *Strategic Communications Plan*, Canadian Special Operations Forces Command, 9.

62   CBC News, "Joint Task Force 2: Canada's Elite Fighters,"

63   Each unit's website can be accessed from the CANSOFCOM home page at: <http://www.cansofcom.forces.gc.ca/gi-ig/cct-tbc-eng.asp>.

64   Stephenson, "Canada's Elite Commandos aim to Capture, not Kill."

65   Worthington, "JTF2 – Canada's Secret Weapon or a Place where Trouble Hides."

66   The four other SOF Truths are that: humans are more important than hardware; quality is better than quatity; SOF cannot be massed produced; and competent SOF cannot be created after an emergency occurs.

67   Day, "Commander's Introduction," 3.

68   *Strategic Communications Plan*, 10.

69   Ibid.

70   Ibid., 10.

71   Ibid., 7.

72   *Security Classification*, 4.

73   See for example, CANSOFCOM, *Security Classification*, quote, 4.

74   See for example David Pugliese's chapter in this volume.

75   CANSOFCOM, *Security Classification*, 3-4.

CONTRIBUTORS

Dr. David Charters is Professor of Military History and Senior Fellow of the Gregg Centre for the Study of War and Society at the University of New Brunswick. He has taught, researched, published and lectured widely in the field of low intensity conflict, including terrorism, insurgency and counter-insurgency, special operations, and intelligence. His most recent major work is *Kandahar Tour* (2008), of which he is co-author.

Colonel Bernd Horn, OMM, MSM, CD, PhD, is an experienced infantry officer who has commanded at the unit and sub-unit level. He has filled key command appointments such as the Deputy Commander Canadian Special Operations Forces Command, Commanding Officer of the 1st Battalion, The Royal Canadian Regiment and Officer Commanding 3 Commando, the Canadian Airborne Regiment. Dr. Horn has a PhD from the Royal Military College of Canada where he is also an Adjunct Professor of History. He has authored, co-authored, edited and co-edited 32 books and over 100 chapters and articles on military history and military affairs.

Colonel Bob Kelly is currently the Chief of Staff for Force Development at CANSOFCOM and has been in the position since the Command's stand-up in 2006. His background includes Army experience based mostly in Western Canada and Europe. It also includes Project Management time involving several large projects for DND. With almost 34 years experience in the CF, he finds his current post both challenging and rewarding. The SOF Mission dictates that capabilities be constantly evolving and this makes for plenty of room for imagination and ingenuity.

Dr. Sean M. Maloney is a history professor at Royal Military College of Canada and taught in the War Studies Program for ten tears. He is currently the historical advisor to the Chief of the Land

Staff for the war in Afghanistan. He previously served as the historian for 4 Canadian Mechanized Brigade, the Canadian Army's primary Cold War NATO commitment, right after the re-unification of Germany and at the start of Canada's long involvement in the Balkans. Maloney has extensive field experience in that region, particularly in Croatia, Bosnia, Kosovo and Macedonia from 1995 to 2001. His work on the Balkans was interrupted by the 9/11 attacks and from 2001 Maloney has focused nearly exclusively on the war against the Al-Qaeda movement and particularly on the Afghanistan component of that war. He has traveled regularly to Afghanistan since 2003 to observe coalition operations in that country and is the author of a number of books dealing with the conflict there.

US Colonel (Retired) James F. Powers, Jr. served 30 years as a career U.S. Army Special Forces officer. Following his retirement, from October 2001 through mid 2006, Colonel Powers served as a Special Operations consultant with KWG Consulting of Waterford, Virginia; an adjunct Faculty Instructor with the U.S. Army War College, Carlisle Barracks, Pennsylvania; and a Senior Fellow with the Joint Special Operations University, U.S. Special Operations Command, MacDill Air Force Base, Florida. On 5 June 2006, Powers was appointed as Pennsylvania's Director of Homeland Security, retiring in 2010. As Director, Powers served as the Commonwealth's primary point-of-contact on homeland security issues and the Governor's senior advisor on homeland security issues.

David Pugliese, an award-winning journalist, covers military issues for the *Ottawa Citizen*. He is the author of two best-selling books on special operations forces: *Canada's Secret Commandos: the Unauthorized Story of Joint Task Force Two* and *Shadow Wars: Special Forces in the New Battle Against Terrorism*.

Lieutenant-Colonel Mike Rouleau, MSC, CD joined the CF in 1985 and served in 5 and 4 Brigade Groups in Quebec and Germany respectively. He also partook of a brief interlude as an Ottawa Police Service Emergency Response Officer 1999-2002. Additionally, Rouleau has a decade of service at JTF 2 commanding at the Assault Troop, Sabre Squadron and Chief Instructor levels culminating as Commanding Officer from 2007-2009. Additionally, he commanded a Special Operations Task Force in Afghanistan from 2006-2007. Moreover, Rouleau has other operational service in the Balkans and Africa. He is a Graduate of Command and Staff College (2006) and the National Security Program (2010) and holds a BA from the University of Manitoba and MA from the Royal Military College of Canada. Rouleau currently serves as the Executive Assistant to the Chief of the Land Staff

US Captain (Navy) Thomas C. Sass, USN (SEAL) holds the Major General "Wild Bill" Donovan Special Operations Chair at the US Naval War College. He also serves as a military professor in the Joint Military Operations Department and as the Deputy Direc-tor of the US Naval War College's Center on Irregular Warfare and Armed Groups. A career Naval Special Warfare Officer, he gradu-ated in Basic Underwater Demolition/Seals class 151 and began his operational career at SEAL Team Three and concluded his operational career as Commanding Officer, SEAL Delivery Vehicle Team ONE. His academic credentials include a BA from Yale Col-lege, a Master's of Public Administration from Harvard University, a Master's of Arts in Law and Diplomacy and a PhD (ABD) from the Fletcher School at Tufts University, as well as Professional Military Education Phase II from the Armed Services Staff College.

Dr. Emily Spencer is the Professor-in-Charge of the Canadian Special Operations Forces Command Professional Development Centre. She is also an Adjunct Assistant Professor at the Royal Military College of Canada. Her research focuses on the importance of cultural knowledge to success in the contemporary operating environment, as well as the role the media plays in shaping understandings of world events.

GLOSSARY OF ABBREVIATIONS

2IC	Second-in-Command
9/11	Terrorist Attacks on the World Trade Center on 11 September 2001
ADZ	Afghan Development Zone
ANA	Afghan National Army
ANDS	Afghan National Development Strategy
ANSF	Afghan National Security Force
AO	Area of operations
APC	Armored personnel carrier
ASG	Abu Sayaf Group
Assn	Association
BATT	British Army Training Teams
BGS	Brigadier-General (Staff)
BSP	Basic Security Plan
C2	Command and control
CANSOF	Canadian Special Operations Forces
CANSOFCOM	Canadian Special Operations Forces Command
CBRN	Chemical, Biological, Radiological, Nuclear
CBRNE TF	Chemical, Biological, Radiological, Nuclear and Explosives Task Force
CDS	Chief of the Defence Staff
CENTCOM	Central Command
CF	Canadian Forces
CFC-A	Combined Forces Command – Afghanistan
CFDS	Canada First Defence Strategy
CFOO	Canadian Forces Organizational Order
CGS	Chief of the General Staff
CIA	Central Intelligence Agency
CIDG	Civilian Irregular Defense Group
CIMIC	Civil-Military Cooperation
CJATC	Canadian Joint Air Training Centre

CJIRU	Canadian Joint Incident Response Unit
CJSOTF	Combined Joint Special Operations Task Force
CJSOTF-A	Combined Joint Special Operations Task Force Afghanistan
CJSOTF-S	Combined Joint Special Operations Task Force – South
CJTF	Canadian Joint Task Force
CMBG	Canadian Mechanized Brigade Group
Cnd AB Regt	Canadian Airborne Regiment
Cnd Para Bn	Canadian Parachute Battalion
Cnd SAS Coy	Canadian Special Air Service Company
CNO	Computer Network Operations
CO	Commanding Officer
COE	Contemporary Operating Environment
COHQ	Combined Operations Headquarters
COIN	Counter-insurgency
CONPLANS	Concept Plans
CORDS	Civil Operations and Revolutionary Development Support
CP	Counter Profileration
CPAT	Canadian Physical Ability Test
CSOR	Canadian Special Operations Regiment
CSSBN	Canadian Special Service Battalion
CT	Counter-terrorist
CTF	Canadian Task Force
DA	Direct Action
DDC	Dhofar Development Committee
DDMA	Defence, Diplomacy and Military Assistance
DHH	Directorate of History and Heritage
DND	Department of National Defence
DoD	Department of Defense
DZ	Drop zone
EOE	Economy of Effort
EOF	Economy of Force
ERT	Emergency Response Team
EW	Electronic Warfare

F3EA	Find, Fix, Finish, Exploit and Analyze
FAQs	Frequently asked questions
FBI	Federal Bureau of Investigation
FID	Foreign Internal Defence
FLQ	Front de la Libération du Québec
FMC	Force Mobile Command
FOB	Forward Operating Base
FOE	Future operating environment
FSE	Future Security Environment
FSSF	First Special Service Force
GIGN	Groupe d'Intervention de la Gendarmerie Nationale
GoC	Government of Canada
GROM	Grupa Reagowania Operacyjno-Manewrowego
GSG9	Grenzshutzgruppe 9
GWoT	Global War on Terrorism
HALO	High Altitude Low Opening
HARP	Hostage Assault and Rescue Program
HR	Hostage Rescue
HRO	High reliability organizational
HVT	High Value Tasks
ICEX	Intelligence Coordination and Exploitation Program
IED	Improvised Explosive Device
IO	Information Operation
IRA	Irish Republican Army
IRTF	Immediate Response Task Force
ISAF	International Security Assistance Force
ISR	Intelligence, surveillance and reconnaissance
JAS	Joint Air School
JCS	Joint Chiefs of Staff
JI	Jamai Islamia
JNBCD	Joint Nuclear, Biological, Chemical Defence (Company)
JSOTF	Joint Special Operations Task Force

JSOTF-P	Joint Special Operations Task Force – Philippines
JTF	Joint Task Force
JTF 2	Joint Task Force Two
LAVs	Light armoured vehicles
LRDG	Long Range Desert Group
LZ	Landing zone
MACV-SOG	Military and Assistance Command Vietnam-Studies and Observation Group
MAD	Mutually Assured Destruction
MiD	Mention in Dispatches
MILDEC	Military Deception
MND	Minister of National Defence
MP	Member of Parliament
MSC	Meritorious Service Cross
MSF	Mobile Striking Force
MSM	Meritorious Service Medal
MTAP	Military Training Assistance Program
NATO	North Atlantic Treaty Organization
NCO	Non-commissioned officer
NDHQ	National Defence Headquarters
NEO	Non-Combatant Evacuation Operations
NGO	Non-governmental organizations
NJM	New Jewel Movement
ODA	Operational Detachment Alphas
OEF	Operation ENDURING FREEDOM
OIF	Operation IRAQI FREEDOM
OODA	Observation, orientation, decision, and action
Op	Operation
OPEC	Organization of the Petroleum Exporting Countries
OPSEC	Operational Security
OSS	Office of Strategic Services

PA	Public Affairs
PDRY	People's Democratic Republic of Yemen
PIFWC	Persons indicted for war crimes
PMO	Prime Minister's Office
POW	Prisoner of war
PPCLI	Princess Patricia's Canadian Light Infantry
PR	Pubic Relations
PRAF	People's Revolutionary Armed Forces
PRT	Provincial Reconstruction Team
PSYOP	Psychological Operation
R22eR	Royal 22nd Regiment
RAF	Royal Air Force
RBG (S)	Regional Battle Group (South)
RCAF	Royal Canadian Air Force
RCMP	Royal Canadian Mounted Police
RCN	Royal Canadian Navy
RCR	Royal Canadian Regiment
RDZ	Regional Development Zone
RIB	Rubber Inflatable Boats
RN	Royal Naval
ROE	Rules of Engagement
RT	Response Team
SAB	Student Assessment Board
SAS	Special Air Service
SBS	Special Boat Service
SDTF	Standing Deployed Task Force
SEAL	Sea Air Land
SERT	Special Emergency Response Team
SHAEF	Supreme Headquarters Allied Expeditionary Force
SO	Special Operations
SOAS	427 Special Operations Aviation Squadron
SOCEUR	Special Operations Command – Europe
SOE	Special Operations Executive
SOF	Special Operations Forces
SOFLAMs	Special Operations Forces Laser Acquisition Markers

SOTF	Special Operations Task Force
SR	Strategic Reconnaissance or Special Reconnaissance
SRR	Special Reconnaissance Regiment
SS	Special Service
SSE	Sensitive Sight Exploitation
SSF	Special Service Force
STS	Special Training School
TELS	Transporter Erector Launchers
TF	Task Force
TFK	Task Force Kandahar
TTPs	Tactics, techniques and procedures
UAV	Unmanned aerial vehicle
UN	United Nations
US	United States
USAF	United States Air Force
USMC	United States Marine Corps
USAID	United States Agency for International Development
USSF	US Special Forces
USSOCOM	United States Special Operations Command
UW	Unconventional warfare
VCI	Viet Cong infrastructure
VIP	Very important person
WME	Weapons of mass effect
WTC	World Trade Center

INDEX

INDEX

INDEX